The Nightmare Raid

Meeks still could not quite reconcile in his mind what had happened after they had entered the clearing, though some of it was vividly clear: the cluster of tumbledown shacks, the old truck jacked up on logs, wheelless, the broken still, disused, empty bottle crates, and packing straw torn up to make firewood. The bootleggers—or what were they?—all standing around the bonfire they'd made in a perfect circle, close enough to the flame to scorch, not moving, not one of them, utterly still, unaware of their approach.

Then they saw the bodies, strapped and pitted to the dead trees around the clearing, with fencing nails and loops of rusted barbed wire all facing inward, all mutilated. Meeks remembered shouting, then chaos, gunplay, the shotgun bucking in his hands as he fired. Then it all became tangled, incomplete. Running, shooting, screaming, and through it all a strange piping noise, thin and horrible, like ice being forced into your ears. Something running in the dark, snarling—dogs? Somebody had shouted that: "Dogs!" But they weren't dogs—one of Sykes's men, open-mouthed, screaming, being snatched…upward?

An

ARKHAM HORROR®

Novel

The Hungering God

Book Three of the Lord of Nightmares Trilogy

by Alan Bligh and John French

Fantasy Flight Publishing, Inc.

To Howard Philips Lovecraft, Robert W. Chambers, Clark Ashton Smith, and Robert E. Howard, et al, with thanks.

Paperback edition published in 2014.
Printed in the United States of America.

Cover illustration by Jim Pavelec.

ISBN: 978-1-61661-804-9

Fantasy Flight Publishing, Inc.
1995 West County Road B2
Roseville, MN 55113
USA

Find out more about Fantasy Flight Games and our many exciting worlds at

www.FantasyFlightGames.com

The Hungering God

Prologue

The Dunwich Road

September 10, 1929

The murderers waited for night to cover the road before they approached the house. There were four of them huddled down in the Packard, silence settled on them like a shroud. Wrapped up like invalids in mismatched greatcoats and ragged scarves, the brims of their hats drawn down, they were scarecrow-shapes rather than men, and just as still. Waiting beneath the cover of a gnarled willow tree, they sat without sound or movement, the Packard's engine having ticked into cold slumber hours before.

The house was set back a ways from the Dunwich road on the other side of a rolling incline. From the dirt road, only the second-story gables of the house with their blind windows were visible, that and the tumbling roofs of the few remaining outbuildings, not that many passersby cared to look.

It had been the Gardner place once, just as the bleak, abandoned fields on either side of the road up to the tangle of the woods had been theirs; that was until the Gardners had come to a bad end a couple of years back. Since then the spread hadn't been much of anybody's save maybe on paper to some banker over in Arkham—or at least so the murderer who did the talking for the rest had found out in the nearby towns, once clean folding bills freely offered in hard times had done their work and overcome the locals' reticence with strangers. They'd said, "Good luck finding anybody to buy it, anybody in their right mind at least." What went unsaid was the why; the Gardner place backed up on one side to the Devil's Hopyard and beyond that, to what was left of the old Whateley farm, and that was only part of it.

It had been the boy in the Aylesbury dry goods store that had broken ranks and told them the rest. He'd ran out after them as soon as he was out from under his father's eyes and found them idling on the edge of town, waiting if not for him exactly, then for somebody like him. The roll of crisp bank notes casually held in the talker's hand had been more money than the boy had seen gathered in one place in his whole life, and its memory drew him like moth to a flame.

"*The woman*," the boy had said in hushed tones, he'd heard tell of the woman that was staying there now, though he'd not seen her—couldn't say that anybody had for sure, but he'd heard of her all the same. He'd been warned; taken aside one night with his father's steely fingers dug into his arm and warned; had that warning shaken in to him. "Stay off, stay away from the old Gardner place; and if you see her, run on home."

After the boy had been paid in full for his troubles, the murders had been sure, and so now here they waited by the lonely road as the pale sun turned weakly in the overcast and troubled sky, the shadows lengthening across the dirt road until darkness descended and the whippoorwills started to call.

The night had fully conquered the day, abyssal black and moonless, when by unspoken agreement the murderers broke their vigil. Unfolding from the Packard, they passed into the ditch beside the road; low and quiet they went, cleaving to the darkness. Once beyond the ditch, they spread wide in a curving line and as silent and relentless as time they crested the rise before the house, unimpeded by night or the rough ground. Here they went dropped forward, stooping, seeming sometimes to craw on all fours with sure but cautious speed, like jackals advancing on a herd of prey.

They paused as one in the shadow of the broken-down picket fence that surrounded the inner farmstead. Motionlessly they watched the house for a time, took in the dark bulk of it, the sagging, corroded outline of the derelict building. A single lamp light burned in a window to the right of the front door, and that was the only sign of its inhabitation. The talker was the first to draw his weapon, a butcher-knife with wet soot smeared over it to dull the blade's gleam, and then as one the others followed suit: a trench dagger, a slender skinning knife, a long straight razor—each had brought a gift of their own for the tenant of the house.

As one they came over the fence silently, like tattered rags carried on the wind, and surged across the clear ground toward the house without sound.

Within, the woman waited. She sat alone in a broken-down arm chair before a meager fire in the open grate in what had once been the Gardners' front parlor; mildew-blighted pictures of the dead family looked down on it still. The hurricane lantern on the mantlepiece cast long shadows over the table beside her, showing it strewn with papers and documents, discarded ribbons and moldering books. Like the woman, the yellowed pages were invaders, uninvited guests in this house of the dead.

Her fingernail tapped a silent tune against the carved armrest of the chair as she waited for them to enter the house. Feeling but not hearing the window sashes of the room across the hall slipped up and the shadows of the murderers slithering within in unnatural quiet, she absently flicked a long-legged spider from the knee of her skirt and waited.

The parlor door opened slowly, the blanket of silence the murderers carried with them swallowing the protesting groans the warped wood of the door should have made.

The woman smiled a humorless, mocking smile, her eyes never leaving the dim embers in the grate.

"Why come in, dontcha," the woman said.

The murderers paused, caught off guard entirely by the pronouncement, wavered, then surged into the room, surrounding the tableau of the woman and the fireplace, their blades bared, paused to strike like fangs in a serpent's mouth.

The talker leaned in, his neck craning low, head turning almost to the horizontal as he stared at the woman.

"You…you are not…," he hissed.

"Not her?" the woman cut in sharply. "No, I ain't the girl you're after. Comin' here was the worst mistake you ever made, you misbegotten worms."

The light died.

Moments later, the parlor window exploded in glittering splinters as one of the murderers barreled through it. Landing roughly, he bounded up with boneless agility and made to run, the only one of his brothers to make it out of the room. He was not quick enough; the black talons that fastened around his chest were each as long as a man's arm and pale as smoke. Remorselessly he was dragged inside the darkness of the house, his fingers frantically digging helpless rents in the soft earth.

After it was done and all was still, the woman felt a slender hand placed on her shoulder, a gesture as if in solidarity.

"What will be, will be," she whispered softly.

Chapter One

Arkham

November 9, 1929

Professor Harvey Walters laid his hand heavily on the brass stair rail and paused to catch his breath. *You're an old man, Harvey, slow down*, he admonished himself quietly. *Just one more flight and then you can have a breather at the picture window for a spell.*

He juggled the package under his arm into a slightly more comfortable position and started out again, absently humming a few bars of Gilbert & Sullivan between somewhat labored breaths.

Four flights of admittedly somewhat steep stairs was nearly enough to defeat him these days it seemed, but as his birthday the proceeding spring had seen him closer to seventy than sixty he supposed he couldn't argue the case too much for it being otherwise. Besides, he'd readily concede if asked if a life in academia hadn't exactly outfitted him for extended periods of exercise, even when a young man. Still, how old age crept up and blindsided you time and again often managed to surprise him, particularly on days like today when his mind was fully preoccupied on other matters.

The service staircase in question was drafty, dim, and more than a little forlorn in an impersonal white-washed walls sort of way, occupying a tower annex at the back of the Miskatonic University's Administration building accessing no more or less than a series of storerooms, the backs of office floors, spare rooms, and general dead space. The idea, he supposed, was to provide discreet access for the custodial staff and a way out in case of fire for the more public-facing parts of the building, but in practice, the elevators they had installed twenty years back had rather left the rear stairs in disuse, which had been all to the good in this case. After all, a secret people passed by on a daily basis without even seeing was more likely to remain hidden than something concealed by pure artifice and contrivance, in his experience.

What he referred to as "the picture window" in his mind was, of course, simply a larger-than-average window on the final landing before the roof access, but it did afford a surprisingly pleasant view of the grounds to the rear of the university, the playing fields, and the boating pond leading down to the river and the thickets. Shrouded now by mist as it seemed it so often was these days, the scene was still striking if somewhat unwholesome in aspect, like the memory of a dream if not entirely a welcome one. The muted shadows of the few figures moving across the playing fields were suggestive and strangely lifeless thanks to the mist and failing light. One seeming no more than a child in aspect seemed to pause for a moment and look back up at him, but just as soon faded, a ghost in the fog.

He wasn't just getting his breath back—he was honest enough to admit to himself—he was stalling, putting off what he was about to do, the meeting he was about to have. "Get a grip, old boy," he muttered under his breath, and turned to walk toward the second of a trio of otherwise identical numbered doors which led to the only rooms on this uppermost landing.

He knocked, a key turned, and the door swung open as the sole inhabitant of room 402 let him in.

"Good afternoon, Professor Walters, do come in," she said warmly, and seeing the package under his arm continued, "Oh, you shouldn't have brought it yourself. I'm sure Mulligan would have brought it up for me later on."

Harvey Walters's heart caught in his chest and skipped a beat when his eyes laid on her, just as it always did now, but he could not say why. She was the same, the same as she always had been in every particular save one, and that single oddly dull grey streak that ran through her blond hair now could hardly be the cause of his reaction, could it? Nor was it the guilt.

"It's no trouble, no trouble at all, after all, I found the blessed thing for you, didn't I? May as well see the whole job through. Not to mention our esteemed head custodian can be somewhat hard to find at times," Harvey said as jovially as he could manage. "Besides, I wanted to have a talk with you, before you...you know...see how you were."

"Before I went away, you mean? That's very kind of you Professor Walters, and thank you. I really can't thank you enough for what you have done for me, the dean as well."

"It's been nothing, really, no more than we were bound to do, given the circumstances."

Daisy fixed him with a probing look. "You're a good man, Harvey Walters; you know that?"

Harvey found himself demurring uncomfortably at the compliment.

"The dean, however, I'm not so sure about," she said with a smile, and Harvey assayed one of his own in return, but the jest was a little hollow to him as it wasn't perhaps that far from the truth.

Harvey had genuinely sought to help Daisy both because he liked her, and because he felt it was his moral duty; for much that had happened he shared part of the responsibility, not by malice or ineptness, but perhaps by ignorance and omission of care—responsibility all the same. The dean and certain others of the faculty that knew of Daisy's covert presence took their part for reasons of their own; not least of all a fear of dreadful scandal and perhaps criminal prosecution should the past be exposed.

Harvey's own sense of responsibility was to the bright young woman Daisy had once been, and also to the altogether more troubling and mysterious woman she had since become; that was also why he had agreed in part to help her current course of action, even if he didn't understand the full ramifications of what she planned. He did, however, begin to grasp the possible dire consequences should she fail, and that was more than enough for him.

"You're sure then, quite sure?" he asked.

"Yes," she said firmly. "The die is cast. Tea?" she asked, closing the subject firmly.

"Thank you," he replied absently as she swept some loose papers off a chair by the high classroom-style window and sat him down, before moving behind a poorly painted Chinese screen to set a kettle boiling on a camper's Primus stove.

Harvey was left looking at the room for what he supposed might well be the last time with sudden melancholy. The screen was like much in the improvised study-cum-living space, looted from various abandoned university stores; in the screen's case no doubt, he thought, a relic from some forgotten drama society play or other. Tacked to one side was a lopsided map of the Miskatonic Valley: Arkham, Deans Corners, Aylesbury, Dunwich, right out to Kingsport on the coast, with fragments of closer detail maps tacked to strategic locations, along with three pin-marked points connected in red thread. It's actual meaning, like much in the room, was lost on him. What wasn't bric-a-brac was paper, old manuscripts and older books, laid around in great profusion, but to his eye it all seemed—finished—somehow used up and discarded, forlorn.

"If you put it on the desk, I'll open it up in a minute." Daisy Walker's voice floated from behind the screen, making him jump.

Harvey looked down, surprised to see he was still holding the brown paper-wrapped package almost defensively in his lap. He read its smudged shipping stamps and carriage label for what must have been the twentieth time since receiving it from the courier agent.

M. Mason—Antiquities & Curios—London—Prague—Shanghai.

With deliberation and curious reluctance to let the package go, he set it on the table just so, and went back to his chair. As he did so, he noticed a battered notebook that was darkly familiar to him, now half-stuffed with extra papers and bound shut with a small greenish-black strap that looked to him like alligator hide. He had no urge to confirm his suspicions, very little in fact would have convinced him to pick up that notebook again, even though once he had kept it himself for many months in trust for its owner. *No*, he realized with a cold feeling in his bones, he would rather have put his hand in hot coals and pluck one out of a fire than open up that notebook and read its contents.

All his life Harvey Walters had been around books. He loved them and would gladly confess it to anybody that asked. He loved the history and the wisdom that could be found within them, the stories, the knowledge; they were to him like gateways to other worlds. Now, there was an irony to be sure. Quite late in his career as an academic of some middling repute, Harvey Walters had learned to his cost—he and the others, old Armitage (somewhere in Switzerland now for his health and well out of it), Angell, and the rest—had learned that some knowledge carried a heavy price and some books were perilous. Such books were often ancient things: a legend passed down and often adulterated, copies of copies passed like bad pennies down the ages, the *Necronomicon*, *De Vermis Mysteries*, *The Song of Khorazin*—all of them. He had never considered before now the particular fact of the genesis of such a book—its birth—but was he not seeing one now? The notebook of Daisy Walker; a prosaic enough name, but just as dangerous as the rest of that litany of names, perhaps more so. And here he was, aiding and abetting…what exactly?

Again his mind turned to the past and he turned it over in his thoughts again. He had felt responsible—they all had—for what had happened to Daisy. She had just been a promising young librarian then, clever, always that, but not driven, nor overly ambitious, just, well, kindly. Her brush with death, the amnesia that had followed, it had been their fault collectively, remiss in tidying up after the mess with Dunwich, putting things right. Perilous books indeed. Then something else came, something he still did not understand, and swept her up in something far worse, and he'd returned that notebook to her, he had hoped…somehow it would help her, armor her… Had that been it, was that his worst sin? Or had the matter somehow been out of his hands; had it simply been meant to be? Was he truly so noble as she had suggested? Or was such thinking just his own way of assuaging his guilt for what was to come after; the Kingsport massacre and the rest.

She walked back around the screen carrying a tray loaded with a mismatched tea service and smiled warmly, and Professor Harvey Walters wondered in a moment of razor-edged clarity, *When was it, I wonder, that I stopped being afraid* for *you, Daisy Walker, and started being afraid* of *you?*

Chapter Two

Arkham

November 20, 1929

Arkham was slowly dying under the late autumn sun, or so it seemed to him. There had always been something wrong about the town, something moldering and rank under the skin, but now its true face grinned from beneath its cracking mask. Raker could taste its slow death in the river mist running through the streets, lingering now long after dawn. He could see it in the paint flaking from signs above boarded windows. He could feel it in the eyes that followed him and then vanished when he turned to look back. There was no one else on the lonely street, just scraps of yellow newspaper scuttling over the sidewalks with the dry leaves. He had stopped several times on his way to the old Merchant District, each time certain that he was being watched, and each time he had seen nothing. Of course, that didn't mean anything.

I should not have come back, he thought as he ducked down a narrow alley between neglected buildings. The wet reek of the river was thick in his nose, and the chill that reached under his jacket had a clammy caress. He stopped after ten paces and looked back at the alley mouth, reassured by the weight of the hammerless automatic tucked into his belt in the small of his back, its steel cold against his spine.

It had been four months since he had left Arkham, hanging onto the bottom of a train in the night, four months of looking over his shoulder. They would come, he knew, and not just the musclemen out of Boston, but someone worse. He did not know who, or what, but he was certain they would come. You did not live through the things he had without consequences. Perhaps if he had run far enough and fast enough he would have been able to disappear, but he would not have been able to forget. His dreams would have never allowed him that peace.

He had nothing now of his old life. All that was left to him was Arkham, and the secrets it cradled to its chest as it rotted and died.

He waited, eyes fixed on the slice of grey light at the alley's end, his heart a steady beat in his ears.

Nothing.

Just a feeling dancing across his nerves like the wind—just like before.

Raker let out a long breath, which he did not realize he had been holding, and turned to move down the alley.

"Spare some change?"

Raker leapt back, his hand moving to the butt of his gun as he whirled. The figure sat curled at the base of the brick wall, his legs and hands folded into a frayed coat. The wind had gathered a drift of trash and dry leaves around him, and it was only when he had moved that he became anything but another shape blurring at the edge of sight. Eyes glinted at Raker from a bearded face under a shapeless cap. He looked at the grime-stained hand extended toward him, palm open. After a second Raker shook himself and his hand drift away from the small of his back.

"Sure," he mumbled, and dug in the pocket of his jacket. In truth, different times would have seen people assume he was a beggar himself; his suit was mismatched, its edges frayed and its fabric leeched of color by washes that had not removed the patina of deep stains. Grime and sleepless night had stolen the handsomeness he'd once traded on from his face, leaving lines and a hard edge to his rare smiles. He was one of a growing breed; the children of a world which wore the soiled finery of the past while shuffling blank-eyed to an unknown end. It was a world in which Charles Raker had yet to touch the bottom. "Take care of yourself," said Raker, and dropped a few coins into the man's hand.

"Bless you, friend," said the beggar as his fingers closed over the copper and nickel coins. Raker nodded and glanced back down the alley.

"You never saw me," said Raker. "Got it?"

"You bought my blindness, friend," said the beggar, and Raker saw teeth flash from amongst the matted beard. For a second he paused, caught by something he could not grasp. Then he shook himself, and moved down the alley. Behind him the beggar rolled the coins through his fingers and watched Raker with bright eyes.

Raker stopped when he reached the lower end of the alley. The building he wanted was on the opposite side of the street. It had been a warehouse, but the sign above its loading doors told of a different purpose: "House of Solace" it proclaimed in black letters which were flaking away from the sagging white board. A small door with a brass handle sat closed next to the loading bay. Raker glanced up and down the street and checked his watch. The street was empty, and it was time. His eyes flicked back to the House of Solace, and caught the line of yellow chalk on the brickwork beside the green side door. The line ran diagonally down from left to right; just as agreed. Raker did not move.

A full minute past the agreed meeting time slid around the face of his watch, then five, then ten, and still he watched.

After fifteen minutes he unfolded from the alley's shadows and moved across the street. The gun was in his hand, held loose at his side. He was just into the narrow passage beside the House of Solace when the side door opened. Raker went still and watched as a thin man in a badly fitting suit looked up and down the street and then muttered something under his breath.

The man was thin and his skin looked clammy, as if the day was ten degrees hotter. To Raker's eyes he looked like the kind who began the day with too much coffee and ended it with too much liquor.

The man was turning back to pull the door shut when Raker slid out of the shadows. He was beside the man before he could turn around.

"Very still!" hissed Raker into the man's ear, and nudged the barrel of the pistol into the man's ribs, "Understand?" The man nodded quickly, his tongue flicking over his lips before he spoke.

"It's you, isn't it?" said the man.

"Back inside. Once we are through the door stay a pace in front of me."

The man nodded again and pushed the door into the House of Solace. Gloom filled the space beyond, broken by grimy streams of light from sky lights in the high roof. Dust rose in thick clouds from their steps and the air smelled as if it had not moved for a long time. The room had been a loading bay, and it rose to the full height of the building and ran back to a series of brick arches covered in chipped blue plaster. Banners hung from its walls, all showing variations of an emblem of two hands clasped together.

Raker's eyes fastened on the symbol and cold memories rose through him. He remembered Stonegroves House glittering in the soft dark of a summer night, he remembered the dead piled on the rich carpets, and figures in grey robes. He thought of silvered broaches and rings carrying that symbol on the hands of murderers who had killed hundreds for a lie masquerading as hope. He blinked and shivered as he forced the memories out of his mind.

The thin-faced man had taken five steps into the room in front of him.

"That's far enough," said Raker. The man turned, and went still when he noticed the gun still pointing at him.

"You Raker?" the man asked.

Raker nodded, his gun never wavering from a dead line with the man's heart. "Tucker?" He replied.

The man nodded vigorously, saying, "You said you wanted help, Mr. Raker, that we could help each other, that we could do each other a favor." He gave a nervous smile that showed broken teeth cheaply replaced. "But you don't seem like a man who wants help to me. You look like a man out for blood." Tucker grinned again, and ran the cuff of his sleeve across his forehead. Raker could see a fresh sheen of sweat form on the man's pale skin. "Not sure I want a story that much as I'm willing to get shot for it," Tucker ran on nervously, eyeing the pistol poised to end his life.

"You don't know what the story is yet, Tucker," said Raker.

"So what have you got?" said Tucker. "Ball's in your court it looks like." Tucker's eyes were still on the gun in Raker's hand as he lowered the pistol to his side but remained wrapped in his fingers—a threat deferred, but not removed.

"Have you ever heard of Stonegroves?" asked Raker. Tucker frowned.

"Stone—"

"Helena Bradbury?" Raker said the name before Tucker could finish his question. Tucker shook his head, still frowning as Raker carried right on. "Heard about a party that a lot of important people went to and never came back?"

"What? …No." Tucker flicked a glance up at Raker's face, studying him, and Raker could see the doubt behind the man's eyes, the nervousness warring with an increasing sense that he had made a bad decision coming there. Raker wasn't surprised; he'd stopped expecting others to look at you like a sane human when you told them the truth.

"Look I don't know about—," Tucker began.

"Over a hundred people go to a party." Raker's voice rose harshly, and Tucker went quiet. Raker stared at him, his eyes bright and hard in the half-light. "Not a small party, and not small people—glittering the way only real money can make something glitter. The house they go to is old and huge, and people know about it for miles around. You see, it's a bad place, built on the wrong ground; that's what some say if the conversation turns that way and the person talking happens to be from Arkham, where things like that don't get laughed at, and for good reason."

Raker looked away from Tucker, his eyes going up to the shaft of dust-filled light falling from the skylights above. "But the people who buy the house don't care about that, money you see, but not local, not Arkham.

"Oh, people talk about the owners as well; their name runs good all the way to high places, spoken of well in drawing rooms and country clubs, so when they invite people to a party, people come. They come in masks and jewels, trying to outdo one another, but in truth it is no party, no party at all. The guests have been invited to their own murder. Every last one bleeds out, and the fine people who own the house hold the knives. And then…"

Raker paused, and for a second he just watched the dust motes stirring in the weak light. Tucker was watching Raker, still frowning but eyes unmoving, waiting, like a mouse might watch a cat to see whether it will attack. After a long minute Raker spoke again. "Then something happens, and it's gone: the people, the house, everything. All forgotten; like they were never there."

Silence filled the seconds after Raker finished speaking and Tucker licked his lips carefully before he thought of replying.

To Tucker it sounded insane, of course, like the ravings of a fantasist. A while ago he might have filed it to the pulps as a "true-life ghost story," the type of bunk that everyone read but no one believed. He might still do that, just as news of Raker himself might well be a commodity worth selling to certain interested parties in Boston's underworld who he owed big, but he had bigger fish to fry for the moment. Besides, his time in Arkham, short as it had been, had tested the boundaries of his own sense of the impossible. Now he just needed to get the rest from Raker without seeming too eager for the story. He had his own payday to think of, after all.

"Except you remember it all?" Tucker asked at last, trying to put just enough incredulity in his voice to sound convincing, but not so much as to shut Raker down.

Raker nodded, still not looking at Tucker, the gun still in his hand at his side.

"The house was called Stonegroves, and the people who owned it were called Bradbury."

"Never heard of it or them," said Tucker, in a voice which was stronger than he felt. Tucker hissed out a breath from his nose and shook his head again. Raker was still looking off into space.

Something has snapped in this man, Tucker realized. He'd seen the look on men that had come through the trenches. *Something inside him is just not there anymore.*

"They were real," said Raker, and looked straight at him. Tucker saw it now, a dead look to the eyes behind their hardness, like metal coins covering empty sockets.

He shivered despite himself, but kept talking. "And why

would someone do that?" Tucker gestured to the air. "Kill so many people, like that?"

Raker did not move. "You heard of the Hand of Solace?

"Sure, you mentioned them," Tucker shot back, "so I did my homework when you said to meet here.

"Charitable fellowship started here in Arkham a year or two back, but kinda gone quiet of late. They are supposed to help people who have lost everything. These days there's a lot that are that way, a lot buying what they're selling, I suppose. This building was their place, where they started, but they don't use it anymore."

"Lyman Fields?"

Tucker ignored the question and tried to keep his face neutral. He licked his lips and gave a weak chuckle to cover his nerves. "You saying they were mixed up in this…party?"

"I am giving you a thread, Tucker; you want the rest, I have to know if you are going to live up to your side of the deal. Murder, mayhem, scandal, and wealth—you can sell that coast to coast and you know it."

Tucker raised his hands. "Slow down. So far all you have given me is a story that no one but you will think is true, no proof—cold print, paper trail, some nice black and whites even. Can you give me any of that?" Tucker felt his heart racing inside his chest and sweat prickling the skin of his forehead.

Raker said nothing and Tucker forced himself to talk as if Raker's stillness was not making him think of running while he had the chance. "So now I am going to ask you something, and then we will see if I even want to start to believe you." His tongue flicked across his lips before he could stop it. He took a breath and played the first of his cards. "I looked you up, Raker, took some time and a little money, but I got there. I got some connections." He shook his head as if in apology. "Those debts of yours in Boston don't just go away, and those kinds of people don't forget."

The gun came up in Raker's hand, the muzzle an empty echo of Raker's eyes. Tucker took a step back. "Easy, they don't know where you are, and I didn't give you up. Like I said on the wire, I think we can be useful to each other and I don't like making enemies."

"Useful?" said Raker carefully, and did not lower the gun.

"You have skills I don't, Raker. You can go places I can't."

"Can't or won't."

Tucker shrugged. "What's the difference?" He had to turn all the cards face up—well, almost all the cards.

"Now here's where you could maybe help me. There's this girl, Daisy Walker, and a hard case, a man called Morgan, Tony Morgan." Tucker paused, but there was no hint of recognition on Raker's face. "You see, there's a man with a lot of money that's after them, a lot of dough and a lot of clout. They're somewhere here in Arkham, and he needs them found."

"So find them," Raker retorted, and pulled the gun up level with Tucker's face and held it there unwavering. "What's it to do with me?"

"Hey!" Tucker raised his hands again, this time as if in surrender. "Look, I ain't cut out for the rough stuff, not like you; hell, I'm having a hard time not pissing myself right now with that heater pointed at me. But you, you got a reputation, Raker, a reputation that says you can handle yourself and I don't doubt it. You could find them; me, I just want a finder's fee, cut of the take."

Tucker bit his lip and waited. For the first time Raker smiled; it was not a kind smile, but a slow crack spreading up the cheeks under cold steel eyes.

"Why would I want to do that?"

"Because of some of the other people who are after them, after the girl in particular, so my information tells me. They got feelers out all over New England, only because of my guy's interest, the one with the money, nobody's buying, even if they did know."

"Who? Who's looking for her?"

It was Tucker's turn to smile as he raised his fingers to the enfolding gloom of the House of Solace in an expansive gesture. "Oh, I think you know already. You see, that's why you got me interested."

"Tell me!" Raker demanded, and Tucker laid it all out for him.

* * *

The sun was a low arc of hot-iron orange in the sky as Raker and Tucker finally left the House of Solace. Thin mist rose afresh from the river and snaked through the town, coiling through streets and stroking the grimy windows.

Tucker left first, slipping from the small green door into the streets growing shadows. Hurrying away, he did not look back.

Raker emerged several minutes later. He stood in the gloom, pulling up the collar of his jacket and pulling it close. He turned, watching the street for a lengthening moment. Only the leaves moved, stirring slowly in the mist-thickened breeze. Finally he stepped into the street and began to walk toward the light of the dim sun. After he had taken four steps, he stopped and turned sharply, eyes scanning the fronts and blind windows of the buildings.

His head twitched as if straining to catch a faint sound. For a second his mouth opened as if he was going to call out. Then he shook himself and walked on.

Above the street, something slid across the moss-covered roof tiles. Frost formed in its wake, glittering in the faltering light.

* * *

The blue door opened before the silver-topped cane could knock a third time. The footman looked down at the man who stood on the doorstep in the chill air.

"Good morning," said the man, smiling up at the footman. He wore a black coat of fine fabric over charcoal black. His face was narrow, lined by age and framed by a neat, white beard. A pair of clasped silver hands capped the black cane which the caller returned to his side. The man looked as if he was in mourning. The footman's eyes met the caller's cold blue gaze. "My name is Dr. Lyman Fields. I expect they are waiting for me."

The footman frowned. There was something familiar about the old man, but he did not recognize him, and the Silver Twilight Lodge did not expect visits from those they did not know.

"I am afraid…," began the footman.

"Let him pass," came a voice from beyond the open door.

The footman did not look around, but just nodded once and stood to one side. Dr. Fields's mouth twitched as if at a subtle joke it would have been ill-mannered to laugh at, then he nodded to the footman and stepped across the threshold. His eyes glided around the hallway, taking in the varied marble busts staring down at him from niches in the white walls, and the brass five-pointed star inlaid into the marble floor. He nodded to himself as if he had made a satisfactory comparison against a clear memory.

"Lyman."

The voice came from behind Dr. Fields, and he could hear the ring of falsity to its welcome. He turned to face the speaker with unhurried slowness. He did not want to be here, but like so much else, it was necessary. The man that faced him was smiling, his open hand stretched out in greeting. He was almost the same age as Dr. Fields, but a taut energy flowed from him, and at a glance most people would have said he was the younger by at least a decade. Dr. Fields looked at the man's proffered hand, and folded his own fingers on the top of his cane.

"You always were too familiar, Mortimore."

Mortimore's eyes flickered, their green irises contracting around hard pupils. His hand dropped to his side and the smile dropped from his lips. His mouth matched his eyes now.

"You should not have come here," Mortimore's voice was low.

"One must always pay debts. That is the honorable thing to do. Would you not agree?"

Mortimore's lip curled into a sneer and his face hardened. He came forward suddenly, his hands rising as if he meant to seize Dr. Fields by his collar.

"*Ul'gnthar'hsh'al'lk.*" The syllables came from Dr. Fields's mouth like the cracking of a whip. Mortimore froze, and then stumbled to his knees, hands still raised. The light had dimmed in the hallway, and a thick burnt cinnamon stench rolled through the charged air.

Unable to hold himself upright, Mortimore curled into a ball on the floor whimpering, his arms wrapped around his torso and his legs drawn up beneath him.

Dr. Fields looked down at the figure shuddering at his feet, shadows seeming to pool in the creases of his face. Fields dabbed blood away from his lips with a white handkerchief. There was sorrow in his eyes.

Mortimore moaned, sucking heavy breaths of air. When he looked up, his eyes were bloodshot and his skin was the grey of cold ashes.

"You dare such a thing here?" Mortimore hissed through clenched teeth. "In our house? You will—"

Dr. Fields laughed. It was a soft laugh, the laugh of a kind man not wanting to hurt the feelings of the teller of a particularly poor joke.

"Daniel," he said with mocking familiarity, "your arrogance and self-righteousness is equaled only by your ignorance." Dr. Fields stepped away, the tip of his cane clicking on the floor as he glanced over to where the footman was also crumpled in the corner, a pool of vomit spreading from his downturned face. "Do you remember saying that when I last was here, when I came as a friend?" he continued.

"You will never leave here," gasped Mortimore as he tried to rise, only to collapse as his body twitched and pain twisted his face.

Dr. Fields stopped, a frown creasing his face as he shook his head. "It is all right, I am not here for revenge, or to settle some imagined challenge." He frowned, and sorrow seemed to crease his face. When he spoke again his voice was low. "You are a weak thing, Daniel. Your concern for yourself blinds you. You do not see clearly, you do not see your place in things. You are limited in ways you don't even suspect." Mortimore looked up into the cold blue eyes in the kind old face. "I pity you, Daniel."

Mortimore snarled futilely in reply, and tried to lunge to his feet. Dr. Fields's cane pushed him back to the floor with ease.

"Please allow him to stand, Dr. Fields." The voice was deep and resonant and seemed to fill the hallway though it was no louder than someone speaking to a friend across a table. Fields looked up to see the figure standing by an open door, the speaker's hand resting on the handle. The man's face was round, and the grey eyes set under the smooth scalp were like the dead eyes of a statue. Silver buttons gleamed down the front of his deep blue waistcoat, and jewels gleamed from every finger of his hand.

The man's name was Carl Sanford and the house of secrets in which they stood was his. Fields met the gaze of the master of the Silver Twilight Lodge, and for a second, everything in the hallway became still as if time itself waited to see on which face the coin of fate would land.

After a long moment, Carl Sanford gestured with an open palm at the figure of Mortimore curled on the floor. "This is not how I wish to proceed."

"I mean you no harm," said Dr. Fields, and this time it was Sanford's mouth which twitched in amusement.

"That you do not wish it will not stop you from using it if it serves your ends." Sanford cocked his head. "That is right, isn't it?"

Fields said nothing, but removed the tip of his cane from Mortimore's chest. Sanford nodded as Mortimore got to his feet and limped to Sanford's side.

"You are a man of unforgiving conviction, Dr. Fields." Sanford smiled again, eyes and teeth glinting as insincere humor creased the soft flesh of his face. "I am pleased you have found yourself since we last met."

"You know why I have come," said Fields as if Sanford had said nothing.

"For the same reason you came to us before; you wish for our help."

Fields nodded once, his eyes never leaving Sanford's, as if the man was a tiger waiting only for a glance away to pounce.

"The fragments…the Kingsport fragments, I must have them," said Fields, and let the words hang in the air. Sanford shook his head slowly.

"You have come a long way, Dr. Lyman Fields, son of Bartholomew, but I say to that even with the truth you have found, you do not understand the path you tread." Fields opened his mouth, but Sanford spoke again. "The fragments are beyond my reach and I will not help you to find them. It is a madness in which we will have no part." He glanced at Mortimore who was leaning against the door frame by his side, breathing hard. "You are a dangerous man—perhaps even to us. But understand that I do not misunderstand what you intend, nor what you are. You are alone in this, you and the broken souls that you keep at your heels. But not alone in your search."

Fields closed his mouth and looked down at the single ring on the forefinger of his right hand, a loop of silver fashioned into a chain of clasped hands. For a second something raw and angry drifted under the skin of his expression. Controlling himself with visible effort, he looked up and nodded to Sanford before stepping toward the door.

"Dr. Fields." Sanford's voice stopped him with his hand on the door. Dr. Fields looked back. "Do not come back here and do not bring your troubles to my door again." Fields held his gaze for a second and then pulled the door open and stepped out into the pale light of day.

When the door clicked shut, Sanford looked at Mortimore. "I look for you to see the future security of this house," said Sanford.

Mortimore shivered where he stood and tried to straighten up more under his master's gaze, failing miserably.

"You will see to it that no other unwarranted intrusions occur, from now on our doors are barred, do you understand?"

Mortimore nodded shakily.

"You have questions," Sanford pronounced. "Ask them."

"Why did you allow him to go?" Mortimore asked hoarsely.

Sanford smiled coldly. "He is right, you know, Daniel. Your vision is limited." Sanford turned his wide head to look at the closed door through which Dr. Fields had left. "Despite that little display of stolen power, Fields is no true threat to us; and if he was, we could simply expend the force needed to crush him and his followers, and then scrape the remains from our boots, be certain of that. He is still only human after all." Sanford paused and the pupils in his eyes seem to have grown so that his eyes were wholly black. "But what he seeks, what is coming because of it, is a force that we cannot face and survive." Sanford paused and ran a ringed hand over the bare skin of his scalp as if suddenly exhausted. "It cannot be avoided now. The signs cannot be doubted, the future circles a vortex of oblivion, and its coming stirs that which should not be disturbed in this place we have come to call home. We, the Silver Twilight Lodge, must endure no matter what comes to pass."

Daniel Mortimore nodded his assent, and on seeing this, Sanford continued, "I will watch Fields and his ilk while you and the rest of the inner circle seek to secure our defenses further. There are others coming, both willing and ignorant, and some perhaps are already here. They are circling, drawn in like buzzards to a banquet of carrion.

"Our Dr. Fields will draw them out; he cannot help it. He is strong now, but he is as naive as he always was. Let him be our lightning rod so we can see where the storm will strike, our Judas goat for the beasts to smell blood on. Let those from outside feast on his entrails, not on ours."

"And what then?"

"Stay outside of the fray, Daniel; we must not call attention to ourselves. We stand aside, let them destroy each other, and ensure that we remain when all is done—or at least may escape the worst of the carnage, if we can."

Mortimore slumped off, swaying almost drunkenly from his ordeal and Sanford watched him go impassively. Alone again in the corridor Sanford began to retreat again to the inner sanctum of the Lodge when he caught himself in the mirror and paused. His eyes swept back and forth, reassuring himself that he was unwatched, and confirming that he was so, he studied himself in the mirror, turning this way and that as a man might in a set of new clothes in a tailor's fitting room. Satisfied, it seemed, by what he saw, a strange, twisted grin transformed his face for an instant and was gone, like a cloud skidding across the sun. Carl Sanford crossed his be-ringed hands in the small of his back, as aloof and imperious as ever, and walked on.

Chapter Three

Arkham

November 22, 1929

"Wyatt Meeks?" the young man asked, offering a hand in greeting.

"That's Mr. Meeks to you, or Marshal will do. You're Sykes, I take it?" he replied, looking down at the young prohibition agent, who nodded diffidently at the great slab of a man who loomed up over him, glowering.

To Sykes the older man looked as if he'd been roughly carved from a great block of wood, all six and a half feet of him. *Like somebody dressed a tobacco store Indian chief in a funeral suit and it came to life!* Sykes thought suddenly.

Meeks for his part had an even less favorable impression of the younger man as he folded Sykes's hand in his, covering it as he might a child's. The prohibition agent to him seemed altogether too narrow shouldered and too vainly well-dressed for a government employee at the sharp end of law enforcement, and his grey-blue eyes were as watery as his grip.

Graft was the word that went through Meeks's mind, *graft and petty corruption*, but then again it was what he'd come to expect from the agents of the Bureau of Prohibition over the years, particularly out in the sticks.

"Any word on Banks?" he demanded without prelude.

"What?" Sykes stammered in reply, his prepared speech already faltering into a disorganized mess in his mind now he was in the presence of the U.S. Marshal whose grim and bloody reputation had preceded him.

"Federal Agent Roland Banks, the man who was originally supposed to be in charge here," Meeks replied grinding his teeth audibly.

"Oh, no, nobody's seen him for days. I left another message with his office in Boston this morning, but they were none the wiser. According to them, he's still in Arkham somewhere, I just don't know where." Sykes shrugged and gave a hollow smile that Meeks assumed was meant to seem charming in a *don't blame the messenger* sort of way.

Meeks grunted in reply. Finding and debriefing Banks on the frankly insane reports he'd handed in about recent events in the Miskatonic Valley was just one part of the hangman's noose of an assignment Meeks had been given by the Department of Justice; one of the parts that Sykes didn't need to know too much about.

"I need to eat," Meeks said. "Then you can tell me about tomorrow night's raid." It wasn't a request.

"There's Velma's Diner, that's still open and the grub's pretty good. It's just around the block," Sykes offered, happy with a question he could answer, and some fifteen minutes later they were both seated in a booth table that had clearly seen better days. It was quiet for an early evening crowd, and the few other patrons were determinedly not looking in their direction while Sykes chatted with amiable familiarity with a freckle-cheeked waitress as he ordered two of the specials and coffee.

Meeks ate in silence, having made it clear without actually

having said as much out loud that he didn't want a word out of his companion until he was finished.

As he mechanically worked his way through some sparse but admittedly well-cooked pork chops and green beans, he took in Sykes and what he'd seen of Arkham so far since he'd arrived that morning—well in advance of the time he'd told Sykes to meet him—and didn't particularly like any of it.

Meeks had been a U.S. Marshal for getting on to fourteen years, and for six years before that he'd cut his teeth as a town deputy in a dead-end coal-dust Missouri burg where life was cheaper than fresh-baked bread. He'd long ago learned to let the way he looked make people's minds up about him—big, mean, and stupid, he liked it better that way, particularly as the first two were true, and the third most definitely wasn't.

He'd seen towns strangled by fear more than once before, from Texas border stops caught up in bloody wars for smuggling routes, to Alaskan mining camps turned tyrant's kingdoms, but none of them had anything on the feel of this place, this Arkham.

Taking aside the whole derelict, mist-shrouded unpleasantness of the place itself, the freshly boarded-up shop fronts, the shuttered windows, the absence of children playing in the street, he'd seen it all before. The people too—the hopeless, hunted looks on the faces of the men and the bleak resignation on the faces of women. The watchfulness, the eyes that wouldn't meet yours, but bored into your back from across empty streets, these Meeks knew as well, but there was something else at work here, something worse—the way people jumped at the slightest odd noise, the way they kept looking over their shoulders, just like the forced laughter and strained flirting of the waitress that was so much at odds with the barely restrained and strangely directionless panic in her eyes. Somebody had put the fear into these people like he'd never seen, and it had eaten right into them.

Meeks pushed his empty plate away and pulled the coffee cup close.

"Tonight, tell me about it."

"Everything's in place. We're a dozen strong and mounted up in two trucks; we've got two locals leading us in."

"Locals? Isn't that a risk?"

"I don't think so. The Dunwich folk and the Sheldon Gang, well they don't get along, shall we say. I think the Dunwich lot will be as glad to see the back of the Sheldons as anybody else around here."

"You don't sound too sure, Sykes."

"Agent Banks, it was his plan, eh...originally. He found a source prepared to name the location of the Sheldon Gang's main still—outside of Arkham in a backwoods place the locals call Cold Spring Glen, not far from Dunwich—and it was he got the help from the Dunwich people on the quiet. Tomorrow night was...*is* the night. The rumor is that the gang's going to pick up a big shipment...or so the tip-off goes. Agent Banks's plan was to bust them when it was being loaded, get everyone at once: the bootleggers, paymaster, the money, the hooch, the drivers and wagons, all of it, scoop it all up. But Agent Banks, well..."

"Disappeared," Meeks finished for him.

"Yes, about a week and a half ago."

"So you telegraphed Boston and called the raid off?"

"Well, yes, when it looked like Banks wasn't coming back. But then they wired back that you were coming to conduct the raid...and take charge."

Meeks's nodded, his expression unreadable. "Tell me about the Sheldon Gang."

"A bad lot, a worse bunch of 'shiners you couldn't hope to meet," Sykes began, lowering his voice. "They're backwoods types mostly, but not stupid. Vicious within, killers every one, hooked in with gangs and bootleggers in Boston, Maine, and New Hampshire as well, from what we've been able to find out. We've taken down a few of their stills before, busted a few of their customers, put a few of them in jail, but we've never been able to touch the family itself. People are too afraid of them to testify in court and if you ask me, they're too well-connected hereabouts for the local law to do more than look the other way unless they have to; too scared, all of them."

"So that's Arkham's big problem, eh, the Sheldon Gang? That's what's been layin' this town low?"

Sykes fidgeted nervously in his seat. "I don't know what you mean, Marshal."

Meeks fixed him with his dark eyes and spoke quietly but with force enough to all but pin the younger man in his seat. "Arkham, Sykes, Arkham. You've been here how long?"

"I don't know, a year and some, in the area," Sykes said, a lump in his throat.

"One year, three months, and six days, barring leave, you have been attached to the Miskatonic Valley task force of the Bureau of Prohibition. During that time you have personally made exactly sixteen arrests and participated in three raids in the Arkham vicinity, and as far as I can tell never fired a shot in anger. I've read your file."

"But, sir, you don't—"

"*Sixteen*, Sykes! In more than a year! And yet somehow you're still on the payroll."

The color had drained from Sykes's face. "I perform a lot of duties, sir," he mumbled, "processing paperwork, visiting important people in the area on behalf of the Bureau, coordinating with local—"

"Oh, I don't doubt it, Sykes, not least of all covering up for the inadequacies of your colleagues being principle among them.

Oh, and I know how you've gotten away with it, too; your entire task force here is like some bad joke. You have the worst record for arrests, sickness, and outright desertion and dereliction of duty I have ever seen, and yet the Bureau, the Department of Justice, the district attorney's office, all of it, looks the other way and says exactly…nothing. Now that, I don't know why."

Sykes had nothing to say. He just sat and stared at the hulking marshal sitting in judgment over him with a look on his face like a man who already knows he's being measured for a pine box.

Meeks waited and flagged the waitress back over to clear the plates and refill his coffee cup.

"Say something, Sykes. You look like a man seldom lost for words."

"There are other, local issues as well. It's not…healthy here, there's sickness…" Sykes struggled to say what he meant. "And the people in the surrounding countryside are very…superstitious… There are stories, they just don't talk to outsiders much. It's hard for anybody to…"

"Stories? Stories you tell me, 'not healthy'—that's an understatement. This town has had more murders, assaults, and tragedies in the last few years than a place twice the size and drowning in poverty could expect to see in a decade or more. On top of that, there are an unknown number of disappearances that have been brushed under the carpet, and then people going crazy like it's contagious in batches. Now these are hard times, and people have it bad all over, but this here stinks of something a lot worse. But you talk to the people that should know just what's going on here—people like you—and all you get is 'stories' and hints and rumors and pointed silence.

"Now on the rational side of things, from what I was told in Boston, is that on top of that, the university here is shedding students like leaves in autumn, and any resident not deadlocked in a mortgage is selling up and moving away. The only ones staying are those without a choice in the matter and the old town families gone to ground.

"The town is dying on its feet, Sykes—and you're telling me that's all down to a few moonshiners throwing their weight around and superstitious New Englander gossip getting out of hand? Truly? This place is too big, too old, too established, and too damn close to the rest of civilization to fold up that easy. This is New England, damn it, not the God damned jungles of Brazil."

"Do you have a point, sir?" Sykes said looking cowed, but grim.

"The point is, Sykes: not on my watch. I am here to do a job, and you are going to help me do it, ghosts and goblins and fear of things going bump in the night notwithstanding, because I will have none of it, and the Department of Justice will have none of it, understand?"

"Look, Mr. Meeks," Sykes offered weakly, placing his hands palms up on the table in a gesture of supplication, "I don't want any trouble, and I'm not your enemy, okay? I'll do whatever you ask."

"Order, Sykes, whatever I order," Meeks corrected coldly, and the younger man, looking distinctly sicker and less cocksure than he had when they'd sat down together only a few minutes before, nodded in reply.

"Good, well the raid will be a start," Meeks continued in a more level tone, "and there's this you will be assisting me with as well while I'm here in Arkham." Meeks opened the battered leather briefcase he had brought with him and dumped a manila file on the table top between them, the contents spilling out. Arrest reports, newspaper clippings, and fingerprint swatches filled the space between Sykes's hands. Principle among them were an Immigration-stamped photograph of a rugged man that looked dangerous even in a black and white mugshot, and what looked like a college yearbook picture of a conservatively dressed but far from unattractive-looking blond.

"What is it?"

Meeks pulled an eagle-headed paper out of the file and put it on top of the other documentation. "This," he said, "is a federal arrest warrant for one Anthony Morgan and one Daisy Walker on multiple charges of murder, conspiracy, and grand larceny."

Chapter Four

Arkham & Cold Spring Glen

November 23, 1929

Nate Fellows had been a cook once; nothing special, but he'd been second man to the chief of a big hotel in Providence, he'd had staff of his own, his own specialties, a family, his own house, and his self-respect. That was before everything had been stripped from him like an onion, one layer at a time. His wife had been first, the influenza taking her back in '18, and in his darkest moments he called that a blessing, as it spared her from what was to come. The Crash had broken the back of the hotel's owner in a lightning flash, and his job with it. Then it had all came rotting down so damn fast—the house he couldn't afford the payments on, the bottle, the pawn shop, the roach-infested dive he and his son had been forced to move into. The rat bites on his boy's ankle that got infected and turned bad. One look at his son on plywood crutches, the stump where once a whole leg had been, the tired, broken look in his boy's eyes…that had been enough for him to climb into the bottle and stay there. They'd taken the boy from him while he was in jail, given him away, changed his name.

He was skin and bones then and nothing more, but even ragged as he was, he couldn't bring himself to die. He'd been waiting for something, he realized now, waiting for the truth, waiting for the Hand of Solace.

Their promise had filled the void inside him; he could have it back, he could have it all back, better than before, perfect. In faith of that promise he lived for them, breathed for them, lied, stole, and killed. Now, now he watched. He'd watched the two men enter the old House of Solace separately, talk together and then part ways. The one he had seen before, the newspaperman he had followed, followed and learned much, eavesdropping on his frantic, almost excited phone call from the bus station kiosk.

He had broken his vigil then, such had been the importance of what the man had said, and now was hurrying back along the backstreets of Arkham's Merchant District in the gathering darkness, toward the new place of Solace. To Dr. Fields, who he was sure would reward him further with ecstatic visions of all he had lost. He craved those blessed moments to come with the fervor of the most debased addict, and it blinded him, half-starved as he was, from the things that were closing in on him until it was too late.

Fellows collided squarely with a man who a mere second before had simply not been there. The impact poleaxed him as if he had slammed into a brick wall and he dropped backward onto his rump, his feet skidding from under him.

He was about to snarl his anger when the man's urbane voice cut across him, mocking and superior. "In quite the hurry, isn't he, Mr. Fetch?"

Fellows jerked his head backward and saw a huge shape looming behind him.

"But I'm afraid we can't have that can we, Mr. Fetch? Tattling tales, not yet. Spoil the game so early on. Tut-tut."

Fellows went for the pistol underneath his raincoat, but no sooner than he had the Colt in his hand, a vice-grip caught round his elbow from behind and jerked him clean off the ground and into the air. As helpless as a fish on a hook, his legs kicked frantically but found nothing, and the handgun fell from his grasp as the bones in his elbow ground together like broken glass. He would have screamed but another massive hand had fastened around his face, cutting off his vision and stifling his screams. All he was aware of now boiled down to a morass of raw pain and the dead-fish reek of the tainted flesh ensnaring him.

"And goodnight," the urbane voice mocked and laughed.

Fellows's world blossomed in agony and his last clear thought was the chill terror that he could not remember the faces of his dead wife or his lost boy.

When the task was done and Fellows's body was bent treble and stuffed in a trashcan, the pair walked at an easy pace back to the street side by side, just as two heavy trucks piled with armed men growled by.

"It's going to be a fine night, Mr. Fetch, a fine old night," the one said to the other.

* * *

Meeks raised the .38 and fired three times in rapid succession into the night, the shots echoing crazily through the tangled woodland. On the fourth and fifth trigger-pulls, the hammer snapped empty and Meeks swore violently and fumbled at his belt for fresh shells.

He had no idea if he had hit it or not, but the figure that had danced in the darkness on the edge of sight was gone.

"Murtry, Murtry, stay with me!" he barked at the man slumped against the tree beside him, and let the smoking empties fall from the revolver's cylinder.

"Still here, sir," Murtry replied faintly, his hands folded over his stomach and shivering as if he were terribly cold.

"Good man," Meeks said vehemently. *Only two bullets left. How many times did I reload? I can't remember!*

Meeks slammed shut the revolver and pulled back the hammer, his head swinging back and forth, searching the strangely angled nightmare of the dark wood on all sides of them for attack, for movement, but there was nothing.

The world was painted silver and black by the high moon, silent and still. In a flash of sudden apprehension, Meeks conceived of the total blackness that would fall if the clouds were to cover that moon, and made an involuntary whining sound in his throat. He caught himself and swore again angrily, rage and shame forcing back the fear that threatened to eat him from within with cold pincers.

"Do you still have your sidearm, Murtry?" Meeks asked in a cracked voice.

"No, I'm sorry, sir…I lost it; I dropped it when you were carrying me."

Meeks nodded furiously, his brain working again at breakneck speed, replaying his retreat through from the clearing, Murtry over his shoulder in a fireman's lift, the kaleidoscope of shadows…he'd crashed through the woods, away from the bonfire, shooting blind behind him.

Murtry had carried a .45; the ammo was useless even if he still had it with him, and Meeks's shotgun was gone. *Just the .38 then, two bullets, just two bullets, and I have no idea where I am, no idea how to get us back to the trucks—they could be a stone's throw away but they might as well be on the other side of the world…* The knowledge settled on him like a funeral shroud.

"Sir, what happened, was…where…," Murtry said in a faraway voice, failing to form what he wanted to say properly.

"Stay easy, son," Meeks managed to say with a false confidence that sank hollowly in his belly for the lie it was, "I'll get us out of here."

Meeks wiped the cold sweat from his brow and realized he'd lost his hat somewhere, and almost laughed that that should startle him. *How had it gone so wrong so fast?* Meeks just couldn't put it together in his mind; it was a flickering, jumbled mess, like a movie reel that had slipped its sprockets and jammed fast, burning and bubbling away to white.

"Boss!" A whisper hissed through the trees to his left. Meeks's heart leapt in his chest, but he still spun smoothly to face the sound, arm straight, revolver braced to fire.

"Boss!" the voice hissed again with startled impetus. "It's me, Corey, and Fry's with me. We came to find you."

The pale faces resolved themselves in the moonlight and Meeks almost collapsed with relief. It was the Dunwich men, the damned Dunwich men. Meeks sagged against a tree. "You find anybody else?"

Earl Corey shook his head slowly. "Only you. Heard your pistol and we circled back around; thought it had to be one of our lot involved, one way or 'tother."

Regaining his composure somewhat, Meeks looked the Dunwich men up and down; Corey looked haggard but unharmed, and still had the ancient repeating rifle he'd brought with him cradled in his hands. The older of the two, the grey-bearded Fry, was the worse for wear, though. He had taken a good blow to the head by the looks of him, one eye now swollen shut. Fry had lost his own rifle along the way, but held a jackknife steady in his hand.

"You hurt, boss?" Corey said, nodding at him.

Meeks looked down to see his shirt and coat glittering wet and black in the moonlight and it took him a second to realize he was half covered in blood. "No," he replied simply, and nodded to where Murtry lay slumped, his expression unreadable in the moonlight, his meaning plain to the Dunwich men.

"We have to get him out of here," Meeks said challengingly, as if he expected the newcomers to disagree. "No sense blundering around here looking for the others in the dark. They either made it out or they didn't," he added bitterly when neither of the Dunwich men gave comment.

The rest Meeks left unspoken; the fear, what might be waiting for them in the darkness, what they had all seen at the clearing in the madly flickering light of the bonfire. *Bootleggers? The Sheldon Gang? Dear God.* The only Sheldon they'd seen had been strapped to a blasted tree on the edge of the clearing. Sykes had recognized him, what was left of him—even with the top of his head missing and the insides scooped out. *Sykes, you coward, if you made it out of this mess alive then heaven help you when I catch up with you.*

"I'll carry him," Fry grunted and put away his knife.

"We'll both carry him," Meeks countered. "We'll go faster that way." He nodded to Corey. "Can you get us back to the trucks?"

Corey simply spat into the underbrush in reply as if moderately insulted despite their situation, and led on.

The tramp through the broken, half-dead woods that bounded Cold Spring Glen would echo in Meeks's nightmares, and although it took them no more than a quarter of an hour before the sure-footed Earl Corey with the barrel of his rifle going before him led them to where they had left their trucks at the edge of the dirt path that led from the Dunwich road into the glen, it seemed a lifetime of pent-up fear had passed to Meeks. Every broken branch underfoot, every rustle of dead leaves was like the footfall of death; every labored breath sounded as loud as a hurricane and sure to bring terror down on them. *Terror of what?*

Meeks still could not quite reconcile what had happened after they had entered the clearing in his mind, though some of it was vividly clear: the cluster of tumbledown shacks, the old truck jacked up on logs, wheelless, the broken still, disused, empty bottle crates, and packing straw torn up to make firewood. The bootleggers—or what were they?—all standing around the bonfire they'd made in a perfect circle, close enough to the flame to scorch, not moving, not one of them, utterly still, unaware of their approach.

Then they saw the bodies, strapped and pitted to the dead trees around the clearing, with fencing nails and loops of rusted barbed wire all facing inward, all mutilated. Meeks remembered shouting, then chaos, gunplay, the shotgun bucking in his hands as he fired. Then it all became tangled, incomplete. Running, shooting, screaming and through it all a strange piping noise, thin and horrible, like ice being forced into your ears. Something running in the dark, snarling—dogs? Somebody had shouted that: "Dogs!" But they weren't dogs—one of Sykes's men, open-mouthed, screaming, being snatched…upward?

"Boss, boss we've gotta go." Corey had laid a calloused hand on his shoulder, shocking him back to his senses. He was in the back of one of their two flatbed trucks, looking down into Murtry's ashen face, a rough bandage made from the lining of Meeks's overcoat strapped round the gapping, ugly tear that had laid open the man's chest.

The other truck had already gone. *Sykes.*

"He'll never make it to Arkham," Meeks pronounced bleakly.

"Dunwich is closer," Corey replied.

"You got a doctor there?"

Even as exhausted and disturbed as Meeks was he didn't fail to catch the strange look that passed between the two Dunwich men.

"No, but somebody about as good, I reckon," Corey answered after the pause.

"Some chance is better than no chance," Meeks conceded, and leapt down off the flatbed to start up the engine.

* * *

Grace Zabriski was woken from a formless dream halfway to grey nightmare by the charge nurse's pinched hand worrying at her shoulder. She jerked up violently in the chair and the startled nurse stepped back sharply. "Yes…yes," she asked, rubbing the heels of her hands into her eyes. "What is it?"

"There's an emergency, Doctor," the older nurse responded primly, clearly put out to find her sleeping, but utterly powerless to do anything about it but pointedly disprove. "A sheriff's deputy injured downstairs, and another man, a federal agent, I think; they need help."

"What…but…," she began, but then it came back to her. Arkham Asylum was handling the overflow emergency cases now, along with the university medical school, and as the junior doctor on call it was her responsibility to help where she could. Ordinarily they would have gone to St. Mary's Hospital, of course, but these weren't ordinary times, and after the terrible ward fire, the venerable old hospital was all but shut down after hours. "What time is it?"

The nurse peered at her lapel watch. "A little before midnight."

"Oh joy," she replied with no joy at all. "Come on then."

As expected, the evening chorus was already beginning, and as the young psychiatrist walked from the secluded office where she had sought sanctuary for a while, the sounds from the wards and private rooms (as the administration preferred to call the padded cells so far as the general public was concerned) rose up to greet her. To the accompaniment of moans and whispers, sighs and exultations, she walked quickly down the dim corridors, taking time to nod to the sparse crew of harrowed-looking orderlies and nurses she encountered at checked doors and stations along her way as she hurried past; it was camaraderie of shared trouble and burden.

She tried not to think about how bad it had gotten and how quickly. Arkham Asylum had been one of the most respected psychiatric institutions in New England; it still was, she supposed, really, at least on paper. She had counted herself very lucky to get a placement here when one of its previous psychiatrists had left unexpectedly. There were still many obstacles to a woman in her field, and she'd encountered a great deal of prejudice on her less than untroubled pursuit of a medical career, but she was still a Bowery girl at heart, and had flint to cope with adversity that many didn't. Still, that resilience was being sorely tested now. She'd been with the institution for nearly a year now, and if she let herself dwell on matters, the signs had been there all along, the portents; but it had been in the last four or five months a tipping point had been reached.

The rise in those from the surrounding area committed for a host of serious conditions ranging from emotional breakdowns and sleep disorders at one extreme to catatonia and full-blown delusional mania at the other, was both extraordinary and unprecedented. It was as if an epidemic of madness were taking hold of the Miskatonic Valley, and Arkham in particular.

Those affected came from all walks of life—they were university students, clerks, grandmothers, farmers, bank officers, there seemed no rhyme or reason save geography and a strange resistance to conventional treatments in all cases. But it was the strange consistencies in the visions, an undercurrent of the monstrous and the repeated imagery of nightmares between the subjects that they all noticed first. It had been the subject of much theorizing, just before the trouble really started and a trickle of cases became a deluge. Soon the "outbreak"—for what else was there to call it—started to show itself in members of the staff. The patients grew more disturbed and more violent, and sedation and restraint started to be used in an almost cavalier fashion just so they could cope, but it barely helped. A wave of suicides followed, and one incident that they'd branded a suicide because they had no other explanation how a man in a straightjacket tore himself to pieces in a locked room without first removing it. It was inexplicable, it was horrible, and it defied every rational explanation—so they simply ignored it and carried on. What else was there? Arkham itself and what dark malady that allied it needed them sorely.

Soon fellow institutions across the state and beyond began to shun them, politely but unmistakably. First Danvers, then even Sefton Sanitarium, whose very close ties had cut off assistance and consultation. They "regretfully" could no longer take on overflow cases, citing their own increase in workload and diminishing resources in troubled times—but the truth was Arkham Asylum was a "troubled house" to them.

When the Asylum's clinical director simply resigned and disappeared a month ago, they were left a rudderless ship and an exodus of the medical staff had followed, leaving only a few remaining, her included, either unable or unwilling to terminate their contracts, or like her too bloody-minded to give in. In terms of psychiatrists left at the institution, there was only herself, a few other juniors, and the senior resident Dr. Mintz now. Between them they struggled to keep the place going despite everything, although more and more she feared they were all just going down with the ship.

"But evil things, in robes of sorrow,
Assailed the monarch's high estate…"

She muttered the lines to herself as she waited impatiently for a reinforced inner door to the ground floor infirmary to be opened. Hearing her, the orderly looked up in alarm.

"Don't worry, Thomas," she said with a lopsided smile. "Just a little Poe, *The Haunted Palace*."

He nodded in agreement despite clearly having no ken of what she was speaking, and she hurried passed him with a sigh, her face a mask now of professional calm, her exhaustion dispelled by force of will. She smelled the blood immediately.

A pair of nurses tended to a writhing man in a blood-spattered police uniform on the examination table, attempting to keep him still, but by the hesitancy of their movements clearly worried about doing more harm than good. The night porter stood vulture-watchful by the pharmaceutical cabinet, bundle of keys held in his hand like a talisman, while lurking in a corner of the room was another stranger, a young, narrow-shouldered man in what had been an expensive suit, but now looked like he'd been rolling in a ditch in it. The young man held his right hand pressed to his left upper arm, and she could see a trickle of blood between his fingers.

Taking charge swiftly, she set about examining the man on the table first, reasoning that the walking wounded could wait till later. The man had an ugly open gash on his thigh through which she could make out bone beneath the welter of blood as she removed the improvised wadding that had been thrust into it. The wounded man was ashen-faced, his eyes rolled white in his head like marbles.

"What is this, some kind of animal bite? He needs a qualified surgeon immediately," she barked at the porter. "Take the van and fetch Dr. Lee at once. Tell him I need him now."

The man blinked slowly and drew back, "Now?"

"Yes now!" she barked back, jamming an ampoule of morphine into the wounded man's other thigh. "Take Thomas with you if you're frightened to go alone!" she snapped more angrily than she meant.

The man nodded in relief and vanished.

She repeated her question about the wound to the man in the muddy suit, and he merely nodded and said, "Sure, dogs, big ones, we were on a raid, bootleggers, it all went to hell and the deputy got bit, so I—"

But the facts established for treatment, she had already tuned him out. The desperate work of long minutes passed and when it was done, she leaned back and stretched her suddenly stiff back.

"He going to live, Doc?" the other man asked casually from the shadowed corner of the room.

She started, having forgotten for a moment that he was there, so intent had she been on her bloody work. "Yes. Yes I think so, at least if he doesn't have another crisis in the night. He's lost a lot of blood, but I've transfused him, and it wasn't quite as bad as it first looked—no major vessels were ruptured but a good deal of tissue is missing. That and he's young and strong means his heart will hopefully have coped with the strain. Whether or not he keeps the leg will be the surgeon's call rather than mine when he gets here." *And if he's sober*, she added silently to herself. "We shouldn't move him tonight, but we'll get him an ambulance and transfer him to Boston General in the morning. He'll get the best care there."

"You're not a surgeon?" he asked quizzically, tapping out a cigarette from a pack and lighting it. As he did so, she saw the shallow wound on his upper arm had already stopped bleeding, the sleeve of his shirt and jacket were torn around it and blackened. *Powder burns*, she thought.

"No, this is an asylum," she said with a snap of sarcasm she couldn't quite keep out of her voice. "As I imagine you know, St. Mary's is closed to emergency patients at the moment," she said, walking over to him. "Psychiatry is my chosen specialty, but before I chose that path, I cut my teeth in hospitals in New York during my residency. I'm a fully qualified M.D. and I know my way around a scalpel and suture, I can assure you. Now let's take a look at that arm."

"It's just a scratch," he said with a smile she was sure was intended to be charming, but she had already taken a dislike to the man. "My name's Sykes," he continued. "I'm with the Bureau of Prohibition."

She merely nodded and led him over to the light to wash and disinfect the bullet graze. Afterward, she busied herself with the stricken deputy and ignored the young man as he attempted to flirt with her, until, equipped with an entirely needless sling, he departed to find the sheriff and inform him what had happened once the blurry-eyed surgeon at last arrived to pronounce his judgment that the leg was still viable, at least for now.

She was thankful to see the back of Sykes at the finish. She had no time for liars; a bear perhaps she might have believed, but she had seen enough dog bites to know this wasn't one of them, no matter how large the hound in question.

As for why the prohibition agent had clearly shot himself in the arm, and been delicate enough about it so as not to do any real damage, she neither knew nor wanted to know. She had problems enough of her own.

Chapter Five

Arkham

November 26, 1929

There was no reason for the fight.

Raker was leaning over a plate of grey meat at a diner counter. There was no one else in the diner except the soft-dough-faced girl behind the counter and an old guy taking his time over a mug of coffee and a copy of the *Arkham Advertiser*. Raker liked it this way: quiet and a clear view of the door and the street outside. He looked up at the sound of a shout, his hand moving to the gun in his pocket. He hadn't heard back from Tucker yet and he was killing time while chasing down a few leads of his own.

Out beyond the grime-misted glass a man in a crumpled cap and sea-faded clothes was turning to face a thick-shouldered man in a badly fitting suit. The deckhand in the cap was shouting something in another language, spit flying from his lips, flushed red spreading up his neck and face. The bigger man gestured, half in dismissal, half in insult. The street was not busy, but the few passing figures stopped at the sound, drawn to watch the argument in jittery silence as it raged on.

The deckhand hawked and spat at the big man's feet. The

big man looked down and then stepped forward, hand rising to jab at the deckhand's chest. The deckhand sneered, yellow teeth flashing in his weathered face. Raker realized what was going to happen a second before he saw the knife in the deckhand's fist. One of the onlookers must have realized it too, because a shout rose in warning, but the big man stepped forward, heedless, his eyes intent on the deckhand's face. The knife edge flashed eye-blink fast, and suddenly the big man was stumbling, falling, a dark stain spreading over his chest like a blooming rose.

For a second the world seemed to freeze. Raker could hear the girl behind the counter gasp, and the old guy look up. The faces of the onlookers were a wall of wide eyes and open mouths. The deckhand was bouncing backward, the knife bright in his hand, face snarling. Someone bellowed with rage, and Raker saw shock and relish flash across the watching faces. Raker had seen a lot of fights in his life, from the clumsy violence of drunks, to the slow beatings handed out to bad debtors and finks that left men begging and broken. But this was different, as if in a second the flash of the knife and the wet gasp of the falling man had become a focus for something that had been floating in the nervous looks and hurried steps of the people out on the street. As if it had released something.

The big man finally hit the ground. At least half of the onlookers surged forward. Someone lunged at the deckhand, and the knife flashed out, fast and bright, and there was more blood on the cobblestones; bodies clashed, jostled, fell and the street was screaming and roaring in a confusion of violence. Argument had become a fight involving a dozen men and the sound of fists swinging, cries of anger and pain, of feet stamping on those that were already on the ground all came through the glass, dulled as if under water.

A man reeled out of the crowd and hit the diner's window, and a spider web of cracks spread from the point of impact. The girl behind the counter was already making frantically for the door, hands reaching for the bolts as the man who had hit the window slumped to the ground, blood smearing down the cracked glass. The old guy at the other end of the counter was just staring, his paper forgotten on the counter beside his cooling coffee.

Raker stood up and began to turn away from the scene of the riot, but after one step he dodged back and picked up the newspaper from under the old guy's unresisting hand. The man's eyes did not move from the violence rolling through the street outside. Raker nodded thanks to the man's blank face and hurried through the doors that led to the restrooms. He did not run, running just made you a part of the chaos, part of whatever was going on; walk while the world spun and people had a habit of ignoring you, as if you were part of the backdrop rather than the action. That was another lesson he had learned to take to heart long ago.

He had checked the stalls as soon as he had entered the diner and broken the catch of the window in the second cubicle; it always paid to be careful, particularly in Arkham, particularly now, and paranoia kept a man alive.

He pushed the window wide and dropped clumsily into the alley behind the building.

The alley was quiet and smelt of blocked drains and autumn rain. Raker glanced down it and began to jog to its far end. He could hear the distant cries from the other side of the row of buildings, and the bell of a police wagon drawing closer. From somewhere he heard the sharp crack of a gunshot. It was not the first of these types of incidents he had seen since he'd come back to Arkham. Two days before he had seen an elderly man pull a gun on another who jostled him in the labor line down by the rail works, but that at least had not ended in bloodshed. The night before he had heard painful cries from the yard beside a boarded-up store and found a young man in a good suit beaten so badly he could not open his eyes. The boot marks of at least five people had churned the muddy ground around the man. He'd dropped a dime in a phone booth and watched from a distance as the ambulance picked up the victim without ceremony, and stayed in the shadows for nearly twenty minutes more waiting for the police to show up, but they hadn't. It was as if Arkham was teetering on the edge of hysteria, that it felt but could not see or understand, and nobody was doing anything about it.

Raker kept moving at a fast walk once he reached the main streets. He reached into his coat pocket and pulled out the paper he had taken from the man in the diner. He had been going to ask the man for it before the fight had started outside, ever since he had caught the headline on the front page.

DERANGED MANIACS DRIVEN MAD BY POISONOUS LIQUOR

His eyes flicked down the story, taking in the details between the overly sensational language. There had been a still raid gone bad out near Dunwich, but within the purple prose and wild assertions, there were surprisingly few solid facts—just how many had been killed or injured for a start, including the lawmen involved. What was plain was the claim that the still was supposed to be producing raw liquor cut with all manner of poisons that polluted the booze, from mercury to weed killer. The reporter on the story said that the tainted moonshine was linked to instances of civil unrest, sickness, and hysterical delusions across the county. Raker discounted the inference, sneering a smile to himself; Arkham and its sibling towns were choking under a growing malaise, but it was nothing so simple as a bad case of the demon drink. Such a rational cause would have been reassuring.

Most of the story was irrelevant, just the line put out by the local law offices repeated with some suggestive trappings to make it seem like a revelation. But folded amongst the banalities a few lines stood out like bright coins in churned mud. The writer made a passing reference to the bootleggers being drawn from "the destitute and the desperate" and having "seemed possessed of an irrational fury." The writer inferred that this ferocity was because they had been poisoned by their own work and driven mad, but Raker remembered the grey-robed members of the Hand of Solace, their sleeves red with blood to the shoulder, their eyes hard with conviction.

For a second he stopped and took a slow breath of chill air. The distant sounds of the riot and police bells had faded, and around him Arkham moved in furtive, hurried steps.

It might not be them, he thought. *It might be nothing to do with the reborn Hand of Solace…it might be nothing. But it might be them.*

He glanced back down at the paper. In the final paragraph it said that some of the survivors had been taken to Arkham Asylum for treatment and their own protection. Raker felt coldness lick his spine; he thought of the chained gates of the asylum grounds, and the clang of metal doors closing on small rooms.

He had almost never left the last time he had gone asking questions at the asylum, and Vivian had died there because of the secrets she had uncovered.

After a second he pulled out a pouch of tobacco and rolled a cigarette. He realized that his hand was trembling when he put it in his mouth. He lit it and took a deep draw before breathing smoke into the mist-touched air.

There was no choice, of course. He had to do this; its end was all that was left to him, and he would see it through. The bootleggers might be members of the Hand of Solace, or they might know something of them, and what they planned next.

That or the lawmen involved might have seen something important to him if not to them. Either way, they were a place to start. The light was fading and he could smell the charge of a storm building in the air; it would be dark by the time he got across town. He began to walk, his feet hurrying but his head filled with memories of pain and screams hidden behind sealed doors.

* * *

His dead daughter's face came to Dr. Fields in a dream. Her blond hair fell around her face, and her eyes glittered with the possibility of tears. She was neither as old as she had been when she met her end nor as young as she had been when he last remembered her being happy. Her mouth was a blurred smile, and behind her the dream was a smeared fog, rolling with impressions of places and people that had been part of her when she lived. There were glimpses of the small, serious child, of the laughing girl in bridal white, of the widow crying in a room that stank of spoiled food and rot.

"Amelia," he said, and heard his voice echo in the fog of memory. His daughter's face grew, filling his sight, its lines solidifying out of the grey. She had been crying, he saw. Wet runnels lined her cheeks. She was always crying in his dreams, as if his mind could only draw on memories of her pain. "Amelia, I am sorry," he said. "I am so sorry." His voice sounded flat, but he knew somehow that on the narrow bed where he lay there would be tears forming in his eyes. "I will put it right, all of it. This will never have happened; it will not even be a dream."

His daughter's mouth moved, as if she was about to smile or speak. In the dream he tried to smile back.

Her mouth opened, and darkness poured from it. Two pits opened where her eyes had been. Cracks spread across her face as if it was shattering porcelain. Her hair rose, blond burning to ashen grey and cinder black. He felt the scream rolling over him like an endless peal of thunder.

He tried to speak, to say that he was sorry, that he would set it all right, that they were close, so close to what they needed, but her face was vanishing, sinking into a boiling night.

For a second as he fell he thought he saw the darkness harden into sharp-edged fragments which glittered like polished obsidian and flowed with symbols and figures that moved like the flicker of reflected starlight. Recognition shivered though him. Here they were again, before his sight, as if they were real, as if they were already in his hands. He reached out, dream eyes straining to read the symbols on the spinning fragments. An image of his hand touched a fragment which loomed above him to the height of a cliff.

He felt pain, bright, clear pain, as if he had dipped his arm in burning oil. He screamed, and knew that somewhere beyond the dream he was screaming in truth. He held his hand, trying to grasp the fragment which was suddenly smaller than the span of his palm. Its edges cut his skin as cold as a razor. Blood fell like dust from his dream hand as the fragment fell and spun and fell without ending. He dove after it, scattering the dream of blood in his wake, but the darkness folded over him, and he felt himself fall through his own thoughts, spinning end over end, as his memory of his daughter's last scream chased him down into the abyss.

He woke in the dark to the sound of thunder rolling overhead. A second after he opened his eyes, lightning blinked in through the window. The glass rattled in the frame, and the narrow room flooded with white light and hard shadows. Then darkness snapped back into place and the room returned to vague outlines of cupboards and a sagging desk. Rain rang on the tin roof above, almost overwhelming the loud beat of his heart in his ears. He sat up and felt the mattress shift underneath him. For a second he stared around, straining to see anything. Pain throbbed behind his eyes.

The dream had been different in small details, but in every other way it was the same as the one that had woken him the night before, and had been drifting through his sleep for the last few months. Always he would see Amelia's face, always the darkness would come, and always the fragments of stone would rise through the depths. He knew what it meant of course, at least at a psychological level: his dreams were becoming a reflection of the thoughts that consumed his waking thoughts.

His daughter, dead in a place beyond time, dead by his own hand to save her from something that had taken her flesh and skin as a cloak. The stone fragments which were a path to the traveler without shape, the Exile, who could grant any desire.

He turned and pulled a small bundle from beneath his pillow, feeling the reassuring weight and solidity beneath the grey fabric. Placing it down on the mattress, he struck a match and lit the stub of a candle on a chipped plate beside the mattress. The black stone cylinder gleamed in the flame light as he unwrapped the bundle. Letters and formulae crawled over the glassy surface as he turned the cylinder. He let out a long breath which he did not realize he had been holding. The Obsidian Key; the god snare—the means to enslave a being as far beyond human as he was above the crawling lice in his mattress. The fragments were the path to the Exile and the cylinder he held in his hand was its shackle. With both, the barrier between the possible and the impossible would vanish and he could remake the world, could undo the suffering which had heaped high on so many.

It had taken much after his return: the stolen secrets and forbidden books, bringing what was left of the Hand of Solace under his control, offering them hope and direction after their dark messiah, Lemaitre, had abandoned them. Working about the details of what that old monster had been doing, backtracking, questioning, the shock of discovery to find out that Lemaitre had not been alone in his quest to tame the Lord of Nightmares, that there had been rivals that had almost succeeded before him. Those secrets had been the most complex and dangerous to acquire, and it had required sacrifices, both in the figurative and most shockingly literal sense. He had not baulked, even as those faces came to him in dreams as accusers.

I will not fail, he thought. *Not this time, not again.* Gently he wrapped the cylinder back in the grey cloth. He stood, feeling the tiredness in his old muscles and the heaviness in his bones. He would not sleep again, not now. Even without the thunder shaking the roof and windows, the pain behind his eyes would linger for hours and if he tried to sleep the nightmare would come again. Carefully, with the cautious slowness of an old man, he pulled on his clothes. He stood for a moment and closed his eyes, after a second he opened them and stepped forward, all signs of tiredness gone.

The candle flame fluttered in his hand as he pulled open the sagging wooden door. The space beyond echoed with the sound of water pouring through holes in the roof. The building had once been a warehouse and meat-packing store, and squatted close to the train lines which ran along the north bank of the Miskatonic. Its owners had lost their money in the Crash, and the place was falling into ruin, another piece of discarded flotsam on the cruel shore of the modern world. Here and there under its cavernous, patchwork roof he could see the light of small fires burning in scooped out tin barrels in the darkness, and the pitched sides of tarpaulins suspended as tents between jury-rigged wooden frames. The air smelt of dampness and smoke. Chains ran along rails high above, the links stirring in the storm wind that came through the broken windows. Such was his kingdom.

Dr. Fields walked forward and saw faces look up at him from beside the struggling fires. The faces were old, young, tired, and angry, but all saw him and bowed their heads to him as he passed, clasping their hands together in front of them, muttering a greeting. He nodded solemnly back to each of them, keeping his distaste from touching the expression on his face. There were many here, men and women who had seen family die in pain, or watched their lives crumble around them, or who had simply become lost beyond finding. All had suffered at the hands of a universe that cared nothing for them, and all followed him because he had offered them hope. There were others, of course, of his "flock" moving amongst the rest of the world like ghosts, laying the groundwork for what they must do.

He did not much like the trappings of devotion and religion which he had woven into the new Hand of Solace, but faith he had found could carry you further than hope and compel you to do far worse things; it was a lesson he had seen Lemaitre prove when using the original Hand of Solace as his instrument, and one that he had applied to its rebirth.

There were things beyond gods and science and the veil of reality; he knew this, had seen it and touched its truth. He did not need faith, he had bitter experience in its place, but he could not do what he must alone, and those who he had gathered to him needed to believe.

Hands reached up to him as he passed and he reached out to touch them gently. Most wore the frayed clothes of their ordinary lives, but many wore rough grey robes cut from sackcloth with deep hoods over the rags of former prosperity. Ragged firelight caught amulets in the shapes of linked hands hanging around the necks of those that reached to him.

"Soon," he whispered to those he passed. "Soon it will be done."

Above the thunder rolled.

None of it mattered, of course, not the fact that he had sought these people out and twisted their desperation to fanaticism, not what he had done, nor what he would do. When they succeeded, none of it would ever have happened.

"Doctor," said a coarse voice raised loud above the sound of the breaking storm. "Dr. Fields."

He turned to see a figure walking toward him between the fires and tents. Beads of rain scattered from the figure's rough grey robe as it came forward. The hood was pulled high to hide their face, but Fields knew the voice at once: it was called Marrow, and if it had another name, that had been cast aside long ago with its lost humanity. The figure stopped a pace from him and bowed its head.

"You have news of the fragments, or you would not have come at this hour," said Fields. The figure nodded its head slowly.

"Speak," Fields demanded at once.

The figure looked up and Fields saw the vague impression of a face form from the shadow within the hood. "I have seen her; the woman." The voice was a harsh, ungodly rasp, the sound of which still made the others visibly flinch.

Dr. Fields paused for a second, his eyes fixed on the twin glimmers within the cowl that were not remotely those of a man.

"Tell me all of it!" he demanded.

* * *

"You said you are a relative, Mr...." Dr. Zabriski smiled professionally as she let the words hang.

"Raker," he said, smiling back.

She held his gaze for a second, then turned her eyes back to the clipboard. Raker could see columns of names in neat black letters. A frown gathered on her forehead and she flipped a sheet over to scan the one beneath. His eyes flicked from her face down to the sheet of paper on the clipboard. After a moment she bit her lip and looked back up at him.

"I am sorry, but there is no Raker on the patient list."

"No," he grinned. "There wouldn't be. We're cousins—different names and all. The name would be Collins."

She looked back down at the list. Raker hoped that he had read the name correctly and that he hadn't picked some dowager grandmother thrice his age. It had been upside down, in a column of other names and there had been only enough time for a glance.

He had reached Arkham Asylum just as the thin autumn light was replaced by night. The man at the gate had looked at Raker for a long while, and Raker wondered if he had recognized him from his last visit. The fold of bills worked just the same as the previous time and if the man recognized Raker, he had said nothing.

The woman at the desk had asked him who exactly he was there to see, but he had said that it was one of the patients brought in by the police the night before. She had looked like she was about to turn him away when Raker had noticed a note folded beside the visitor's ledger. "Dr. Zabriski" had been scrawled across it.

"I was told to ask for Dr. Zabriski," he had said without a pause, and that had changed the woman's attitude. She'd told him to wait and wait he had for more than an hour. Once the doctor herself had finally appeared with an apology that seemed genuine rather than perfunctory and returned his smile with a broad one of her own, things had become a lot smoother. Raker had followed Dr. Zabriski up to the tile-lined wards, all the while memories of what had happened to him in the basement of the same building creeping into his thoughts. He had had to suppress the instinct to turn and run from the place. The asylum itself seemed somehow darker, worn out, colder even, but that was just as likely his imagination, he conceded, rather than fact. His smile must have been good enough, though, as the doctor didn't ask him anything too pressing about who he was there to visit until they were standing in a wide corridor with green tiles.

"Ah, yes. Collins, Micah," she said, looking up at him. "I'm afraid we have no more on him than that." She looked down at the board again, frowning. "I am sorry, but he is catatonic, has been since we brought him in."

"Cata-what?" he feigned.

"His body and mind have shut down. We don't know why, might be an extreme shock, or something else..."

Raker whispered a brief, silent thanks in his mind that the name he had picked was someone who would not be able to say that they had no idea who he was.

"When will he come out of it?" he said, fixing his face into an expression of concern.

Dr. Zabriski gave an apologetic shrug in answer and it was only then he noticed just how bone-tired she looked beneath the professional facade. "It's hard to say; perhaps it will pass quickly of its own accord, perhaps... I am sorry. Would you like to see him anyway?"

He nodded, keeping worry and gratefulness running through the lines of his face.

"Yes, thank you."

She smiled again. "It's good of you to visit, with the...times being what they are at the moment, the reality of a place like this and those that need to be here is something many people would rather ignore."

Cute smile, he thought as he nodded and made small talk as they walked, deflecting any questions about his "cousin's" past health with vague generalities. He followed her down though a heavy door and into a long ward, suppressing a shiver of nervousness when he heard the orderly close that door behind them and turn the key.

Bars covered the night-darkened windows which ran down one side of the room. Lightning flashed beyond the glass, and for a second he saw Arkham's silhouette captured in the blink of light.

The ward they had entered seemed vault-like; polished wood covered the floor and cold white tiles ran up the walls and across the arc of the ceiling. Electric lights buzzed in their fittings, filling the room with a faded yellow light which struggled to dispel the shadows. Metal frame beds ran down the sides of the long room, and Raker could see prone figures lying on each of them, more than a dozen all told. All were still, some appeared to be sleeping, while others had open eyes just staring blindly, or very slowly blinking as if in constant puzzlement. They were quiet, quieter than anybody would have expected a ward full of mental patients in a thunderstorm to be, and the feeling of that realization struck Raker as a strangely sinister one.

"Are these people all…all suffering from the same thing?" Raker asked, unable to mask his astonishment.

"Yes," she answered simply, "they have all come in at various times and in various circumstances, but they are afflicted with a similar catatonia."

Dr. Zabriski looked around at him as she walked to the side of a man who lay on a bed with his eyes shut. To Raker's eyes, the man looked asleep, the sheet over his chest rising and falling to the rhythm of slow, shallow breaths. The man's skin was pale and seemed to have settled loosely over his thin frame like a shroud lain over a skeleton. Raker noted the hollow cheeks with their coarse grey stubble, the myriad tiny scars and the flaking, discolored nails which spoke of a life lived without comfort and with too little food. A crude tattoo of an angel ran across the man's forearm, its face a blank black ovoid of ink.

"No one has really told me what happened," said Raker keeping his eyes on the man.

"The police brought him in yesterday," said Dr. Zabriski quietly. "They think he and some others were mixed up with some sort of liquor racket gone bad. He was found wandering in the woods the morning after the big raid that was in the papers; but nobody seemed sure what he'd been mixed up in or how. I'm afraid I don't know anything about the incident itself except that several men were badly injured." There were a host of unexpressed questions in her reply and she paused after speaking as if hoping he would answer them.

Raker could see her biting her lip again as if in thought before she continued. "We only know his name because he was wearing old Navy dog tags."

"He was in the war," Raker replied noncommittally.

"There's talk of poisoned liquor," she said.

Raker shook his head as he noted the doubt in her voice. "He wasn't much of a one for hard drink despite what you might think, or crime either."

"It's what the prohibition agents say."

He turned and looked at her, noting a surprising edge of scorn in her voice.

"You think different?"

She glanced around the ward, then at the door before answering slowly.

"He shows the signs of malnourishment and exposure principally, not poisoning. And he's hardly the only case of his kind we've had, of catatonia that is to say."

He took the risk and pushed, edging his voice with what he hoped was just enough raw emotion to trigger a frank response. "Look, Doctor, there's something going on here, something not right. Tell me what you know, what you suspect, please?"

She sighed. It was a sound born more of mental exhaustion than the purely physical kind.

"We've been seeing more cases in the last few months, unexpected cases, far more than you would expect over the given time. Otherwise ordinary people suffering emotional breakdowns, delusions, sudden outbursts of despair or violence, or like Mr. Collins here, catatonia without a determinable physical cause."

Her voice trailed off into silence. Out beyond the barred glass of the windows a sheet of lightning turned the sky to silver.

He could see how weary she was now, how much she needed to tell somebody, and he figured it might as well be him. "But what does it mean?"

"It's like…," she began, then shook her head, unable to say the words out loud.

This was it; she'd either spill it or shut him down. Raker rolled the dice. "What?" he asked with sudden force. She looked up at him, alarmed by his shift in tone. "What is it like?" he repeated more gently, looking straight into her eyes and holding them with his.

She shook her head again, but answered, "It's like a contagious hysteria running through the whole town, striking down seemingly unconnected individuals at random, and it seems to be getting worse with every day." She paused and bit her lip again. "Like a fever or a virus. I've never seen or read about a case like it before."

She drew back and waited for a retort or a denial from him, but none came.

Raker thought of the discord he had seen in Arkham since he had come back, of the sense that the whole place was walking along a cliff edge between stability and panic. He nodded slowly, and then looked back to the man on the bed.

"Where are the things he came in with?" he asked quietly, letting what she had said inhabit the space between them.

"He didn't have much, just the clothes he was in, a bit of tobacco, that sort of thing."

Raker looked down at the thin fingers of the man's hands.

"He wasn't wearing a ring?"

Dr. Zabriski shook her head, looking at him thoughtfully.

"He always used to wear a ring, a family heirloom, I suppose you'd say," Raker added softly, careful to make it sound as if he was both sorry and tired; the last thing he wanted now was to provoke her suspicion. "But it's been a long time since I've seen him."

He shrugged and turned away, noting that she was studying him closely now. *I have to be careful with this one. She's too clever to take for granted.* "Thank you for what you are doing for him, I really appreciate it. I couldn't have hoped to have somebody better looking after him, everything being what it is," he said with as much earnest conviction as he could muster.

Blinking at the sudden compliment, she colored slightly and nodded as if pleased, but her smile was guarded as if she was still unsure of him.

He reached into his pocket, pulling out a square of pasteboard on which he had written the number of a drugstore in town where the owner had agreed to take messages. "Look, if anything happens to him, if there's any change, or you hear of anything, anything at all, you can call this number and leave a message."

She nodded, looking at the number on the card.

He decided that he had enough of an opening. "And if anything strange happens…," he continued.

She looked up at him, eyes suddenly bright and sharp. "Strange? Strange like what?" she asked pointedly.

Raker shrugged.

"I don't know, but you said earlier that what got to Micah and these others is not normal, and I can't help but be curious. I'm a writer you see, always had an interest in things that don't quite fit." He gave her his best smile, the one he had practiced for years in his old life.

She looked at him sternly for a few moments, then her face cracked into an involuntary smile of its own, a smile that said, *I don't believe you, but what the hell.*

"Sure," she said. "Okay. If anything happens, I will let you know. The orderly will show you out, Mr. Raker."

"Thanks," he said, knowing he'd been dismissed. He tipped his hand to his forehead in a salute of goodbye and began to walk away from the bed of a man he had never seen before that night, and the sharp-witted lady doctor with the weight of the world on her shoulders.

* * *

Rain was soon pouring from the sky as Raker stepped through the asylum's doors. Pulling his hat low on his head, he turned the collar up on his coat and made for the outside world. Thoughts rolled through his mind like waves as he jogged down to the gate.

Collins and any others brought to the asylum from the raid's aftermath might be Hand of Solace, but somehow he doubted it; there were none of the signs and symbols that the Hand of Solace normally kept around them. That and the man he had seen close up looked like somebody who'd known lifelong poverty and more recently spent his years as a vagrant, rather than one of the freshly disabused, desperate, and wrung-out ordinary people who came to the Hand of Solace looking for answers. The cult fed on those that had-and-lost, not those that never had at all.

Either way, something was coming, something that had got under the skin of the whole town. Zabriski had summed it up about right: it was like a virus of the mind. He shivered, suddenly aware of the cold rain already soaking through his coat, jacket, and shirt.

The gatekeepers appeared after Raker banged on the window of their little blockhouse. A sour look twisted the skin of the one that came out to him, the rain rolling down his stubble-covered face as he unchained the gate. Raker nodded thanks, but the man just spat, hit up his belt, and slammed the gate shut behind him, fastening the heavy lock.

Raker called sarcastic thanks, pulled up his collar, and turned to begin the long walk in the rain back to Ma's Boarding House.

A car drew up beside him, sliding out of the dark and rain like a polished knife. The beams of its headlights sparkled with falling rain, and Raker could see a softly lit interior behind the slick glass of the windshield. He had just enough time to step back from the curb as it suddenly stopped and two figures stepped out of the gloom behind him.

His hand went to the automatic in his pocket as he twisted around, but he was far too slow. The first punch took him in the gut, and the air left his lungs. The second punch hit his jaw as he bent over. It was not a hard punch, almost casual, in fact, but carefully aimed for maximum effect. Raker felt colors and darkness spread at the edge of his eyes, and his legs buckled. Strong arms caught him as he fell and he was half aware of the sound of a car door opening and his feet bumping against the running board as he was shoved into the space beyond. His last impression before the darkness swallowed his sight was the smell of leather, sudden warmth, and a pair of pale eyes looking down at him from above a reptilian smile.

Chapter Six

Arkham

November 27, 1929

The storm rose above Arkham, shaking rain from its thunderheads in endless strands. Jackie Simmons was curled in the carved lip of a mausoleum. It gave little shelter, but was better than nothing and kept the worst of the downpour from his blanket.

Why did I come east? he thought. *All those weeks in the back of railroad cars just to be shivering in a graveyard in an autumn storm in this God damned town.*

Six months ago he would never have imagined coming east, but six months ago he was still turning enough money in his store to pay for a roof above his head when the rain came. The fat and flesh had gone from his face and limbs since then, and left his skin hanging in grey folds over a body that was forty but now looked sixty. He coughed and spat. He tasted iron in his mouth, and tried not to think of the clicking rasp in his chest. Arkham was a rotten place, no work and less hope than he had seen since he had taken to the road. He'd never heard of it until he'd jumped off the train at Northside before it made the station, and sure as hell wished he never had. Tomorrow he would go down to the train tracks and try and make passage on a freight train when the rail yard bulls weren't looking.

Anywhere will be better than here, thought Jack. The place was not just falling apart physically; it even *smelled* wrong somehow, and the cloying fogs which rose from the river tasted like death in the mouth. The strangest thing, though, was what he hadn't found here: hard times had filled the back roads and the rail yards with men like him looking for work, moving on, but not here, not in Arkham. Instead he'd found the ashes of old fires, discarded bindles in culverts by the roadside, strange noises…old blood stains even. He'd seen the fires of some gang that certainly were not hobos, but something else a lot worse hiding out in a warehouse by the river, the words *The Traveler Comes* carved in a dead tree with bones hung up in its branches like wind chimes. That was when he knew he had to get out.

Still, he would be gone soon, and he would find work somewhere, somewhere well away from here.

He heard a noise like crackling paper and sat up to look across the night-drowned graveyard. Twenty feet away, thick blue sparks crawled across a statue of an angel, writhing like hungry maggots across its green-bronze skin.

Jackie frowned and blinked into the storm. In spite of the rain, part of him was tempted to go closer. He put his hands down to the damp stone and began to push himself up. The air suddenly smelled of hot sugar cutting through the wet, as if someone was burning candy.

The bolt of lightning struck the bronze angel, and Jackie's eyes clamped shut painfully as the thunder roared around him. A high shriek filled the air, growing louder and louder. Jackie clamped his hands over his ears, then felt pain stab through his head as his eardrums burst; the sound of thunder and rain vanished but the high shriek rose through him. He could still see the lightning bolt writhing against the swimming darkness of his eyelids; it had not stopped, but burned as a single jagged line of light cutting into him.

I must keep my eyes closed. I must look away.

He felt his eyelids open, as if peeled back by gentle fingers.

The lightning bolt, still blazing, rose into the night sky, connecting the ground to a turning column of black cloud above. The graveyard was a bleached white forest of stone at the column's base. Slowly, the lightning bolt widened like a crack in a curtain pulled wide, and in the core of the fury Jack could see the outline of a human figure, its edges rippling as if they were fabric caught on the wind.

The figure stepped from the lightning, the black outline thrown into hard clarity, resolving into the shape of a tall woman with green eyes and short, dark hair. The silk of her strange robe billowed in the storm wind. Blackness began to spread once more across Jackie's vision. In the last second before his retinas burned out and blindness took him, he saw the woman raising her face and arms to the rain and laughing at the storm-filled sky.

* * *

The first thing that Raker noticed was the heat. Not a dry heat but a close, oppressive heat that prickled sweat from his skin. With his eyes still closed, it felt as if he was floating in a thick cotton-wool world. He could feel the straps holding his wrists to the metal arms of the half-upholstered chair. *Not good, not good at all.* He tried to open his eyes, found that he could, and looked out at the world again.

A black and white face smiled back at him, a thick mustache held between finger and thumb. "*A Hayden Wax set is the only real set*" proclaimed bold letters from beneath the smile. Raker blinked and looked up from the tin of wax. His own face rose to look at him from a mirror.

No bruise, he thought, looking at his jaw, which still hurt like hell. That meant that the guys who had bundled him had been pros: neat and precise, no muss, no fuss. That meant that he was in a lot of trouble. He let out a breath. The chair was locked in place but he could see the room around him in the mirror's reflection. He was in a barbershop. A single gaslight turned up high burned with a hissing yellow flame in its bracket, and shadows clung to the rest of the shop. Wide windows ran down the front of the shop to his left. Blinds hid the rain-lashed night outside, but the sound of the storm still filled the shop with its sea-surge rumble.

I haven't been out too long then, he thought. Behind him another row of chrome and leather chairs sat beside basins in front of a wall of wide mirrors. Sweat ran into his eyes and he blinked. The hot air smelled of aftershave and hair wax. He could see no one else in the gloom, but they would be there.

"Ok," he said croakily. "Let's talk."

"What makes you think that we have anything to talk about, Mr. Raker." The voice was like dry pages rustling together.

"If you wanted me dead, you would have done it already."

"Would I?" offered the voice, and paused. Raker blinked more sweat from his eyes. "But you are right; I would rather that we could come to an arrangement."

A figure stepped into reflected view behind Raker as if solidifying from the gloom. Raker had to stop himself from jumping with surprise; they must have been there all along standing utterly still in the shadows.

"I have an offer for you, Charles Paul Raker." The speaker was revealed to be a man Raker had never met before. At first Raker would have said that the man was old, but the more he looked at the smooth skin of the man's face he could see no line or mark to explain the feeling. The man's suit was grey, tailored with a smooth perfection that spoke of deep pockets. A grey silk cravat circled the man's throat, its surface broken by the head of a copper pin. The skin of the face and head above was hairless and a pale color that almost matched the grey of the cravat. The face smiled at him in the mirror's reflection, perfect white teeth in a humorless slit.

"You know me?" said Raker.

The grey man nodded slowly.

"I know you. I know the little hole you grew up in on the edge of Boston. I know about the friend you cut out of a deal five years ago. I know about how you broke the fingers of a man called Kelly, and I know why you did it." The man licked his lips, the pink tip sliding slowly over white teeth and grey lips. "There is no inch of your life that I do not know, and there is no part of it or you that I do not now own."

Raker felt cold despite the cocoon of heat. The grey man's voice had not risen or changed from its rustling monotone, but Raker suddenly felt as if he had never been so close to something as dangerous or intelligent as this man. The grey man smiled again, and Raker felt as if he wanted to stamp on his face, stamp on it until it was a crumpled ruin that would not move or speak again. "Your debts in Boston have been taken care of. Your former associates will not trouble you again. All other matters that you have left…" The man trailed off as if deciding on the correct word. "…have left unresolved, have also been settled. That is with one exception, which we will come to. I care not for your past allegiances or the deals you have made. I have done all this, and so I am now your sole creditor in every respect. "

The grey man stopped talking and simply watched Raker in the mirror, eyes unblinking.

Raker opened his mouth; his tongue felt dry. "So you do want to talk," Raker said, trying to edge his voice with strength.

"No, Mr. Raker, I wish to make you an offer."

Raker nodded. *Of course*, he thought bleakly. "A way to clear my debt."

"Oh no, Mr. Raker. That is quite impossible." Another smile like a crack in dry clay. "But I can make you another offer, one which I think you will accept."

Raker said nothing, but the grey man seemed unperturbed.

"I have need of a man like you, Raker, a man of violence and resource, and a man who knows something of what is occurring here and now in Arkham."

Raker felt as if the words had sent an electric shock through his head. *This is no shake down*, he thought. *This is something else, something worse.* He suddenly felt that for all he had been afraid before it had not been enough.

"I see you understand a little more of the gravity of the situation you are in," said the grey man with a nod. "I had an agent acting for me in these matters, but while effective, he proved to be unreliable. I hope that you will be much more efficient and more loyal."

"What—," began Raker, but the grey man carried on without pause.

"There is an object I wish you to find, or to be more precise, a series of fragments of an object. They may be in the possession of a man and woman I believe are hiding somewhere in Arkham, or perhaps their confederates here may have them. Finding this man and woman, or what has befallen them, are your goals also, but it is the fragments, my stolen property, that are of the most paramount importance. I will support any means needed in order to recover them. Do you understand me, Raker? *Any* means. If you succeed in recovering these and returning them to me, I will be in a position to offer you what no other can in return. I shall grant you a miracle, in fact."

"What would that be?" asked Raker before he could stop himself. He should have been incredulous, but there was self-superiority and certainty in that dry voice that he couldn't help but take at its face value.

"Why, Mr. Raker, the return of Miss Vivian Bradbury to life at your side, of course."

Raker could do nothing but stare at the reflection of the grey man in the mirror.

"While you consider this," said the grey man, his image rippling like a heat haze, "you should know who makes you this offer. My name is Shawcross." The reflection of Shawcross nodded as though trying to be reassuring. As if it came from the only part of his mind not ringing with shock, Raker realized that Shawcross had not blinked since he had appeared in the mirror. "Well, Mr. Raker, do we have an understanding?"

Raker felt himself nodding even before the conscious thought of agreement had formed in his mind.

"Good," Shawcross almost hissed. "Then to the details."

* * *

It was quarter to four in the morning when the electric light in the station house gave out for a third and final time.

Wyatt Meeks groaned quietly as the steadily worsening storm that had raged all night rattled the windows and he struck a match with shaking fingers. More gladdened by the sudden flaring light than he would care to admit to any living soul, he reached out and lit the nearby paraffin lamp before setting it back down on the desk and holding his head in his hands.

It was not his desk, just as it was not his office. Instead it had been one in the Arkham police station "commandeered," as it had been put to him, by Roland Banks, the missing federal agent Meeks had been sent here in part to find. His desk, his files, even his portable typewriter Meeks had sat uselessly in front of for hours, hammering out words he'd torn up and thrown in the trash time and again.

Meeks had never actually met Banks, but by all accounts he had been a straight shooter, a rising star in the Bureau of Investigation, a man with an enviable track record of success in difficult cases, and intelligent with a "by the numbers" approach that had earned him favor in the new guard that was now helming the Bureau. From what Meeks had been told before coming here, Banks had actually volunteered for Arkham, the mysteries that were mounting up here attracting him like a moth to the flame, despite subtle warnings from others that the place was a stone better left unturned. And what had Roland Banks's diligence and zeal got him? Dead or missing; after the raid in the woods, Meeks didn't want to try and imagine the particulars.

No, those guarded, yet still insane-seeming reports Banks had tried to file, with their suggestions of "unknown predatory animals" in the surrounding countryside, "un-guessed at numbers of violent deaths unreported to the authorities," and "cultic activity with connections to the highest levels of the town's society" linked to "collusions between criminal gangs and unknown agencies" now seemed to Meeks less like the paranoid ravings of a lawman gone off the deep end, as it was all becoming the very real tip of a black iceberg whose cold, crushing weight he was already feeling for himself.

The empty typewriter mocked him; he hadn't refilled it since he'd torn up an abortive resignation letter that read more like a suicide note. *Who am I kidding anyway? I can't resign, I can't just leave; they'd arrest me for dereliction of duty, incompetence, negligent homicide.*

Either side of the portable typewriter and framed in the pool of light from the lamp sat on the right his loaded revolver and on the left a half-empty bottle of brandy, the track marks of his fingers cut into the patina of dust that caked the bottle. Meeks had never been much of a drinker, having seen it help put his father in an early grave, but sometimes a man just needed a drink and that was all there was to it. Meeks had figured the bottle—a pre-prohibition number he'd stolen from the top of a bookcase in the sheriff's own office, no less—was a damn sight safer than the local poison.

The illicit alcohol brought Sykes unwelcomed to his mind. The prohibition agent with his sly, liar's smile and his wounded arm worn like a badge of courage had stood beside that vacillating, watery-eyed wreck that called himself sheriff and done his best to send Meeks down the river for the bloodbath the raid had turned into.

Well, that at least hadn't gone the way Sykes had wanted it to, and Sheriff Engle, despite the fact he was one deputy crippled and another two still missing, had still been bizarrely reluctant to take Meeks to task, or to even damn Meeks with his superiors over the debacle. Instead, the sheriff had simply accepted that the raid had gone wrong and wanted to brush the whole business under the carpet as much as he could. It had sickened Meeks—even though it had played in his favor against Sykes's case—to see the hollow resignation in the sheriff's eyes, the way he'd just kept saying that things were "regrettable" over and over; it turned his stomach as he remembered it. Since then, Sykes had avoided him as much as he could, and the other lawmen in the town looked right through him like he wasn't there unless directly confronted, meanwhile Engle had remained unflaggingly cooperative, but utterly indifferent to what he was doing. He was a pariah with them now and he knew it, as if he was still carrying the bloody mark of that night on him for all to see.

He couldn't find it in himself to blame them for that, just as he blamed himself for what had happened during the raid.

He kept turning it over in his head, trying to make sense of it. He'd led nine men into Cold Spring Glen: Sykes and three other prohibition agents, three Arkham deputies, and the two part-time constables from Dunwich. All had been well-armed with shotguns, rifles, and sidearms; it should have been more than enough to tackle a bootlegger camp. Criminals didn't want to die, no more than ordinary men did, and only a fool or a madman tried gunplay against odds like that. Going in, his principle concern was that the bootleggers would hear them too soon and scatter into the woods before they could catch them.

How wrong he'd been.

The Dunwich men had lived, of course, and by some miracle Murtry had lived too. *Miracle?* Hannah Whateley's pale face swam up in his mind, but he pushed that thought out of his head and went back to his reckoning instead.

Sykes and one of his cronies had made it out all right, dragging with them one of the deputies who had been badly wounded, but Meeks had heard he wasn't expected to live; the doctors in Boston had cabled he'd developed some kind of rapid gangrene and it was already spreading too far and too fast to stop.

They'd all gone back with reinforcements at first light, and it had taken every shred of willpower and courage he possessed to do so. Meeks had led a posse raised up from Dunwich, and met with Engle and Arkham police coming from the other direction. They'd found the clearing soon enough; the disused still, the trees, the ashes of the fire, spent shell casings, and discarded weapons were all there. And blood, blood everywhere, but no bodies, not a single one, bootlegger or lawman.

They'd searched, but it had been a strangely cursory, reticent affair and had only turned up three men around that wild, desolate place. Two of them were taken wandering in the woods, out of their wits and another crouching in a hollow at the edge of the barrens they called Devil's Hopyard, eating what was left of his own fingers. They'd called the search off then, as the dark was drawing in, though no word had been spoken of it, and equally without comment they had not resumed it the following morning or any time since.

The men that had been taken had been pointlessly and formally arrested before being removed to the asylum for want of anything else to do with them. One, the self-cannibal, had been identified immediately as one Jacob Lime, a farm laborer reported missing from Arkham some three months previously, and one had been named by old dog tags he was wearing but was unknown to the local law. The last was a complete mystery, written up as John Doe of unknown origin, but by the looks of him he'd been living rough for weeks as well.

That left four lawmen missing, presumed dead, and of the bootleggers they had themselves shot down, there was no sign either, nor of the corpse Meeks had seen lashed to the trees, not that he had spoken to anyone about it. The raid was a disaster, a debacle worthy of outrage and opprobrium in the newspapers from here to New York, yet there was no real outcry, no statewide alarm. In Arkham aside from a mangled, half-detailed story in the *Advertiser* there was just wordless, dreadful acceptance, the tragedy swallowed up in silence.

It was inexplicable to Meeks, as if he was in a nightmare from which he could not wake; he couldn't shake the feeling it was all somehow unreal, but knew at the same time it was not.

The guilt and the emptiness gnawed at Meeks, but above all there was the fear; it wrapped him in cold chains, weighed him down, and stole the heart from him, paralyzed him dead. Even now he could only remember what had happened in Cold Spring Glen in snatches, frozen images that became even more disjointed and water-slick as the days passed, like his mind was trying to erase them to protect itself. A ragged man, grinning, coming at him with a broken bottle, heedless as Meeks shouted at him to stop, the shotgun roaring, the flash of flame, the man going down bloody and leaping up again, his jawbone gone, the red mess that remained still laughing as it lurched forward. The shotgun's thunder again and again, but the glistening wreck of flesh would still not stop. The screams all around him, gunfire, the bitter smoke, the blazing light of the bonfire, something moving in the trees, huge and white, eyes like cold stars, so many eyes, burning, burning. The sound of the pipes, shrill and mocking…

Meeks jammed his fist into his mouth and bit down until blood flooded his mouth and the pain shocked him away from the memory. Silent tears streaked his craggy face as he poured brandy on the cut his own teeth had made in his hand and he did not flinch.

Morgan, Walker, Banks, he thought with brute anger. *Real people: two fugitives and one absconder.* They were solid, they were facts, anchored in reality; they were what he was in Arkham for, nothing else mattered now. He would find them.

"Morgan, Walker, Banks," he whispered aloud as if it were a prayer.

Meeks pushed the typewriter to one side and laid his head down on the blotter, his right palm resting on his revolver's cold reassurance, and closed his eyes. Still, sleep did not come until the dawn's wavering light edged through the rain clouds of morning.

Chapter Seven

Arkham

November 29, 1929

The storm that spent its fury over Arkham was like few that any could remember, lasting almost three days and three nights without relenting. The power failed and the darkness was pierced time and time again by flashes of lightning, so close between the savage strokes that it seemed to the people huddled in their homes like some blazing searchlight of the heavens was playing across the town. The storm burned its hard white light through curtained windows and the hauled-up coverlets of children alike, laying bare all it saw to harsh, cold scrutiny; there seemed nowhere to hide from it. The rolling thunder that followed in its wake was for some worse, for it was as relentless and deafening as the trumpet blast of the doomsday that Sunday school had promised them one day would come.

In Arkham Asylum, the windows rattled as if an army of demons laid siege to the Gothic palace that the flashing lightning had transformed its halls into, and every inmate was roused to bedlam. All save for the silent ones of Ward Nine, who, unnoticed in the tumult of the fearful and the enraged, silently turned their heads in unison, and tracked the passage of a solitary female figure as it paced the asylum's outer boundary walls, as if distance and stout bricks were no bar to their sight.

Were any foolish enough to brave the streets against the tempest, they might have seen glimmering corposant light crawling across the ironwork adornments of the Silver Twilight Lodge and the rusted weathervane that topped the university Administration building. On Arkham's Southside, a tenement house that had stood since the revolutionary war collapsed and killed the family that huddled within, although afterward none could say whether a thunderbolt had struck it or the old place had simply shivered itself to pieces in the storm.

Far out on Sentinel Hill overlooking Dunwich, strange fires burned, and the earth whispered in response to the thunder in the valley, but the folk of Dunwich knew better than to look out or to listen.

After the thunder came the rain. Hard and heavy, it pounded Arkham mercilessly, hammering down on the gambrel roofs of the old town so that they seemed to make the buildings sag under the weight of their years, water jetting from overflowing gutters like rent arteries.

Out on the Aylesbury Turnpike, the road had suddenly become a river, and a thuggish black touring car was forced to pull off onto higher ground less it was swamped. Inside, a man tapped his gloved fingers quietly on the wheel to a tune in his mind as he waited; a loaded automatic sat poised on the passenger seat next to a telegram that read simply: *It has started.*

The rain came down and kept coming down. Even though it waxed and waned, it did not stop until it had nearly drowned Arkham. Sewers flooded and the unpaved roads in the poorer parts of town became quagmires. Tombstones in the old cemetery toppled into subsiding graves suddenly keen to give up their tenants, and the Miskatonic River rose high and roared through the town, thundering like a runaway train and threatening to swamp the bridges.

When the rains finally ghosted away toward dawn three days later, Arkham lay shivering in the chill, murky stillness, as if holding its breath for what was to come.

* * *

The storm had passed finally leaving Arkham cold and mist-swaddled in the thin morning light. Raker had been watching the street outside the boarding house since just after dawn. The money in his pocket was unfamiliar, but the weight of the automatic at his waist was more reassuring. Shawcross's influence had been generous, but his latest arrangement felt more like a suspended sentence than a blessing.

A green-painted truck hove into view and then clattered past; Raker shifted the yellowed net curtain to watch it go. It was nothing; just one of the few parts of Arkham life carrying on with obstinate blindness to what seemed to him the slow death-rattle of the place. Raker frowned and unconsciously brushed the metal lump of the automatic. The street looked clear, but the feeling was still there, just like it had been when he had gone to meet Tucker.

"Just a feeling," he muttered to himself without conviction, and turned away from the window to pick up his jacket from where it lay on the undisturbed bed. The suit was new and had come with the thick fold of bills in his pocket, along with two names and dossiers. Of the two, he liked the sound of Tony Morgan the least: a hard man and, if Shawcross had had use for him, probably a sharp operator. The second sounded easier to find by a long way: she was a librarian apparently, and she lived in Arkham. Of course, if Daisy Walker was as easy to find as she seemed, then it begged the question as to why Shawcross had not got to her already, but she was somewhere to start at least that wasn't the trail of a cold-blooded killer.

Raker left the room and went down the creaking stairs, pausing to leave a fold of bills under the vase in the front hall. A flick through the Arkham phone directory told him what he needed, and he memorized the address printed next to "Walker, Miss D." in a few seconds. At the front door he stopped to look through the dusty strips of glass either side of the door frame.

Still nothing.

His hand went to the door handle, and stopped. He glanced back into the dusty space of the boarding house's hall. He could hear the distant clatter of pans in an unseen kitchen.

Nothing.

After a second he turned away, pulled the front door open, and walked into the fog-filtered light of an Arkham morning. The anonymous black Ford car Shawcross had given him was parked farther down the street, its windshield and headlights beaded with moisture. Raker spared a glance up at the boarding house. The simple sign at the front just said "Rooms" but everyone called it "Ma's," though the woman who ran it seemed to be mother to no one but her cats.

Raker frowned, doubting himself, doubting what he was doing, doubting his senses. He was unable to shake the feeling that he had heard someone whisper in the dust shadows of the hallway. He had thought he had heard a word in that whisper he could almost make out. He had thought that un-placeable voice had said, "Wait-something" to him. *Wait*, wait for what? He shivered, turned up the collar of his jacket, and went to find Daisy Walker.

Arkham wasn't that big a town and it took him no more than a quarter of an hour to reach the address. The streets had been far from busy and the fog patchy, but unpredictable enough for him to leave his headlamps on all the way.

Her house smelled of emptiness. As soon as he had forced the back door, Raker had known that he would not find Daisy Walker there. The dust at the edges of the rooms was thick and had spread even to the open surfaces of tables and sideboards. The pantry was bare of all but a few cans stacked neatly into the spider-thickened corners. In the small, neat bedroom, the sheets had been stripped from the bed, and the water jug was dry on the nightstand.

"But did you leave easy, or did you run?" muttered Raker as walked between the cluster of small rooms.

It felt like the kind of place one would find someone who kept their world defined and limited to a deliberate circle of truths and kept everything else at bay, and the trappings were feminine enough for him to have guessed their owner's gender without being overly fussy or folksy. There were plenty of books, stacked neatly on shelves in tight rows, that he did not need to scan to known would be ordered by some common factor.

It was the books that told him he was not the first to have come back to this house since it was first shut up. The gaps in the neat rows stood out like missing teeth in a perfect smile. Someone had taken, no, *chosen* a few volumes from several different shelves and removed them. Once he noticed that, the rest of the signs were everywhere: clusters of empty hangers in a wardrobe, no hats by the door, a line of thinner dust on a shelf that said a picture had been taken from where it had rested, but not before the dust had started to settle.

He paused when he reached the hall. A neat stack of mail sat under a little fossil paperweight. He picked them up and flicked through the envelopes. All were addressed to Daisy Walker and reached back several weeks; most looked to be circulars, adverts, bills, one a banal postcard from Mexico of the inane "wish you were here" variety. He put them down, unopened, and replaced the stone back on the top of the pile.

"You did not run, or if you did, you had time to prepare."

He looked back at the pile of mail. A printed crest covered the corner of the top envelope, the ink and details smudged, but the words "Miskatonic University" were still legible. Raker let out a slow breath. Time was running down and he had the feeling it was going to be a long hunt. The question which Shawcross had not answered the night he had met him rose again in his mind as he left the cottage house to its dust and silence: What did a man like Shawcross want with a librarian?

* * *

The man appeared beside the ornamental stone griffin as if from nowhere as Harvey Walters walked down the steps of the university's Science building. One second there had been no one standing there, just a few students going hither and thither to morning classes, and then Harvey had glanced down to his footing on the rain-slick steps and when he'd glanced back the stranger was there.

It was an older man, close to Harvey's own age or older, although a little smaller in build and considerably more expensively, if formally, attired. The stranger half-raised a silver-topped cane at Harvey in order to attract his attention, and even in the somewhat dim morning light the cane flashed brightly.

Harvey was brought up short, immediately uneasy.

"Good morning. Excuse the imposition, but you would be Professor Walters, would you not?" the stranger asked.

"Yes," Harvey replied. "How can I help you? I don't believe we've met, Mr....?"

"Doctor," the stranger answered with a smile that didn't touch his eyes. "Dr. Lyman Fields. And no, Professor Walters, we haven't had the pleasure of prior acquaintance."

Harvey stayed a step above the man and, tucking the leather book satchel he was carrying under one arm, he offered the doctor his hand in greeting, saying, "Forgive me for asking, but the old brain-box is not what it used to be; so many names and faces rattling round in there when you've been around as long as I have that a few get misplaced from time to time, you understand?"

There was something of a sardonic twist to the man's smile, as if he was amused by some private jest as he reached out a gloved hand to shake Harvey's, but made no comment.

"Are you here for Professor Bright's funeral?" Harvey asked, looking the man up and down, and not imagining for a second that this "Dr. Fields" was.

The man did not let go of his hand and for a moment there was a sudden tugging sensation in Harvey's chest and a flicker of vertigo, but it passed as quickly as it had come and Harvey was suddenly unsure he had felt anything at all.

Fields jerked his hand out of Harvey's as if he had received an electric shock and backed away a step, blinking furiously for a moment.

"Sorry, eh," Harvey offered to cover his own confusion, "as I said, how can I help you?"

The expression on Fields's face went from one of incomprehension to something like fury for an instant before leveling out into something sly and guarded. Watching the play of emotions, Harvey decided to get away from this strange and disturbing man as quickly as he could.

"No," Fields said slowly, "I am not here for any Professor Bright...nor am I here to bandy a charade of pleasantries with you. I require for you to help me, Professor Walters, and you *will* help me."

"Really, well," Harvey said, bristling at the man's impertinence. "I somehow doubt that will be the case, 'Dr.' Fields," he replied, injecting as much doubt onto the man's assumed title by the tone of his voice as only a seasoned academic debater could.

Fields's left eye twitched slightly. *Here is a man*, Harvey thought, *not accustomed to being told no.*

"Where is Daisy Walker?" Fields demanded.

Harvey looked at him for a long moment before drawing himself up straighter and fixing Dr. Fields's gaze with his own. When he spoke, all trace of the avuncular, slightly grandfatherly academic was gone and something considerably sterner and more unyielding was in its place.

"Leave Miss Walker alone. She was subject to great misfortune and you can have no good business with her."

"So you know her," Fields insinuated.

"Of course I know her," Harvey snapped back. "She was a valued member of staff here and I counted her as a personal friend, neither of which can be any business of yours."

"Tell me where she is, Walters. She was seen here; as recently as a few days ago, she was seen!" Fields sneered.

Harvey shook his head firmly in reply.

"My source, shall we say, is unimpeachable!"

"Poppycock!" Harvey retorted curtly. "Miss Walker has not been here for months. Even if she were here, I most certainly would not involve her with some ill-mannered stranger such as you."

Fields was almost vibrating with barely contained anger, his cane clasped in both hands. "You have made a very grave mistake, Professor Walters, a very grave mistake."

The old professor looked down on him squarely and said calmly, "One of the few benefits of getting on in years I find is the luxury of one's follies. As to Miss Walker, I tell you again: she is not here, that is the truth. Now, Dr. Fields, I will have to ask you to leave the university campus and not return. If you do not, I will be forced to have you removed. So unless you want an undignified scene unbecoming to either of our years, I suggest you go."

Fields looked at him incredulously. "Are you threatening me?"

"Yes," Harvey replied with a slight smile, "I rather think I am."

With visible effort, Fields controlled himself, and when he spoke again, there was no anger in his voice, only certainty, but the threat was there like a shark swimming below the ocean's surface. "My quarrel is not with you, nor with this university and its people, not unless you choose to make it so. Daisy Walker has something I need, and I will have it, regardless of the consequences, however unfortunate they might be to others. Think on that, Professor Walters."

With that, Fields turned and stalked off across the misty morning campus. Harvey stood and watched him go. It was only when he was out of sight that Harvey reached into his vest pocket and withdrew the signet ring he kept on the end of his watch chain. He had been curiously aware of its presence, its weight, ever since he had shaken the strange doctor's hand.

Harvey had kept the curious little whitish-copper signet ring with him for more than forty years. He'd found it wedged between the rotted pages of a book tucked into a corner of a decaying wine cellar in Portugal. He'd come across it while cataloguing the contents of a private house whose first occupant had been burned in the *auto-da-fé* and whose last had died a decrepit recluse who'd left the contents of the sprawling pile to the University of Coimbra, where Harvey had been a visiting undergraduate at the time. The band was blank, evidence of writing there long since eroded away, but on the flat seal was the still vaguely discernible shape of a curiously distorted star, with what appeared to be a burning eye at its center.

The old rector, Vesalius, had called it an ill-favored thing and would neither see it in the university's collection nor sold on the open market. He was loath equally to see something so clearly ancient melted down or broken, however, and so grudgingly had made a gift of it to Harvey at his leaving and thus negated the problem. It was not until many years later when Harvey Walters saw the twin of the little ring's symbol graven in John Dee's translation of the *Necronomicon* that he learned it was one of the forms of "Ye Elder Sign," as Dee had called it.

Once the ring had returned to its seemly normal weight in his hand, Harvey pocketed it again, wondering from what fate he had just been saved by this keepsake of so long ago, before turning his mind to more pressing problems. He still found it hard to believe in such things, but he knew they were real.

Matters were moving quickly now, as she had said they might, and it was no longer safe for him to keep what she had entrusted to him here, of that he was certain.

He turned the man's name over in his mind: *Fields, Dr. Lyman Fields*...no, it didn't chime with anything he knew, but the symbol on his cane pommel—the two hands clasped together—that he had seen somewhere; had it been on a paper amongst Daisy's things?

"I must speak with the dean," he muttered aloud, all thoughts of the next lecture he was meant to be holding forgotten, and set out at a pace that belied his years toward the Administration building.

* * *

Raker had stopped off at the Commercial House for smokes and a copy of the day's paper after visiting the Walker cottage. It was there he spotted the man ahead of him in the line to be served and his plans changed. The man was a dour, middle-aged type, heavily built, like he'd made a living with his hands and the strength in his back all his life. Indistinguishable from many in the town, he was dressed in an overcoat that looked like it had seen better days and a two-day growth of stubble on his chin. He'd been unremarkable except for one thing: the ring that had flashed under the store lights as he reached out to pay for his tobacco, a ring bearing the clasped Hands of Solace.

Without giving it any thought, Raker slipped out of the line and followed the man as he left all thoughts of Daisy Walker and Shawcross for the moment on hold; here was a potential main line to the Hand, and he'd lucked right into it.

Raker was a shadow, and the man did not turn; he followed him past what would have been a normal distance to park by car, and Raker felt a surge of triumph. *Maybe he'll lead me right to where they are now.*

The woman came from nowhere, and before he knew it, Raker had clashed with her, knocking her sideways and sending him tumbling to the ground.

He swore under his breath as he saw his quarry increasing the distance.

"I don't know where you're from, but around these parts its custom'ry to apologize to a lady when you walk into her."

He looked up; the woman standing over him was striking, not through any attractiveness she possessed—not that he would have labeled her ugly in the slightest—but by her sheer presence. She seemed almost larger than life, as if the world faded around her, and Raker was caught staring at her as if he'd been confronted by a tiger on a Sunday walk in the park. She was a young woman, despite her matronly tone and old-fashioned dress, and had a mane of raven hair elaborately braided so that it hung over one shoulder almost to her waist, contrasting starkly against her pale skin.

"Sorry." He smiled. "At least I seem to have come off worse from the encounter."

She let out a short snort of derision and offered out a hand to him. "What's a matter?" she asked as he hesitated. "An affront to your chivalry to take a lady's help?"

He took the hand, but was careful not to lean on it as he got up and dusted himself off. He had a curious blank moment, as if he couldn't remember what he was doing exactly.

"You a stranger in town, mister?" she asked.

"Raker," he said reflexively. "Charles Raker."

She smiled again, and it was a strange, knowing smile and Raker found himself suddenly very ill at ease. The hairs on the back of his neck stood up.

He waited for her to introduce herself, but she didn't, instead she asked, "You on business in Arkham, Mr. Raker?"

"I'm looking for someone, someone that doesn't want to be found," he caught himself replying, and blinked at his own candor.

"Well," she said, turning slowly and looking over her shoulder as she began to stride away, her boot heels clicking, "I hope you find them, and when you do, you don't regret it. Goodbye, Mr. Charles Raker."

He raised his hand and looked at it. *Why the hell am I standing in the street? Smokes and today's paper, that was it, and I'd better get some food and some sleep as well before I chase down that librarian anymore. I'm more tired than I thought.*

Raker walked back to the Commercial House, cautiously watching for signs he was being followed.

Chapter Eight

Arkham

November 29, 1929

Meeks watched the psychiatrist closely as he went through the folder the marshal had set before him with pedantic slowness. It was the first time Meeks had set foot in Arkham Asylum and it seemed to him the very acme of somebody's scary story of a mental hospital: a great, brooding, Gothic pile of brick and slate set in its own spare grounds and encircled with a high wall and gatehouse like a medieval fortress.

From what he'd been able to glean from Sheriff Engle, the place was currently under-staffed and overflowing with patients, more than a few of which in recent times had been left on their doorstep by the Arkham Police Department. Even in daylight it seemed to Meeks a depressing, oppressive place, and the staff about as grim and taciturn as he had expected, but once he'd produced his credentials he'd been given unimpeded, if diffident, cooperation by them.

Engle had led him to expect that also; the asylum, it transpired, had long been partly funded by the town municipality, which was also its landlord, and an "understanding" between the asylum and the town's authorities had long been in place. That alone spoke volumes to Meeks, but for the moment, at least, it served his purpose.

He'd come here notionally to check on the men taken in the raid, but in truth he had an entirely different reason.

"You believe that some or all of these individuals are currently, ah, under our care?" the psychiatrist asked without inflection.

Meeks studied the man for a moment before asking. Those thick-lensed glasses of his had never left the file pictures arrayed neatly on the blue leather blotter in front of him. The brass nameplate on the desk between them read "E. Mintz, M.D, A.B, Ph.D."—a full-bore headshrinker in Meeks's estimation, and he took the part well, too, right down to the domed forehead, receding hairline, and slight trace of a home country somewhere east of the Danube lingering in his voice.

According to Engle, Mintz was senior man now at the asylum, which meant if he couldn't help Meeks in what he wanted, nobody could, and so Meeks forced himself to be as polite as he could.

"I think it's a strong possibility, Doctor," he replied. "After all, you yourself said that you had a great many new admissions recently, and not all of them could be identified satisfactorily."

Mintz slowly took off his thick reading glasses and placed them with obsessive care into a black case, and that case into the pocket of the single-breasted starched white surgical tunic he wore, and looked directly at Meeks as if seeing him for the first time. "Yes. Yes, I would say it is not entirely beyond the realms of possibility… Things have been made difficult of late, and at times errors may have been made, or information may simply have been unavailable. It is possible that either of these men or this woman could be under our care," he conceded.

"Then you don't mind if I take a look?" Meeks asked with as much force as he thought was prudent.

The psychiatrist looked taken aback, as if it was a possibility he had not considered before demurring, "Of course, we would not dream of impeding an agent of the law in the prosecution of his business, but I will have to supervise you. Our patients are, of course, highly sensitive to strangers and disturbances."

"I wouldn't want to take up too much of your time…," Meeks interjected, only to be curtailed by a regal wave of the psychiatrist's hand.

"It should not take long. The patients without known identities are largely confined to a relatively small area, and indeed one ward in particular contains several catatonic cases. If your fugitives are among this asylum's charges, they will most likely be there."

And that was how, some quarter of an hour later, Meeks was looking down into one ashen, empty face in a ward full of silent, vacant faces.

"Are you quite sure this is him?" Dr. Mintz asked at his elbow.

"Look at the picture; what do you think?" the marshal replied gruffly, holding out the open folder to the psychiatrist who did not answer; there could be little doubt as to the truth. *Banks*, Meeks thought, *so here you are*, but didn't voice his recognition out loud. "These were the only effects he was brought in with?"

Again Mintz confirmed that this was so. It was a pretty bland series of objects as far as Meeks could tell: an empty wallet and, strangely, two watches, alongside a muddied up suit and an unused matchbook. Meeks picked up each in turn, examining them slowly; the first watch was a Waltham wristwatch, a decent make, but nothing too showy, and the wallet was stripped of anything useful. The second timepiece was a little more curious: a battered and doubtless broken old bronze-colored fob watch that looked like it had been in dropped in a fire at some point. Other than "*E.M.*" visible on the dial, it bore no distinguishing marks at all and had no value that could be readily ascertained; still, it seemed out of place enough that it might have some importance, so he pocketed it anyway. The matchbook, however, was printed with "Sanders Gas & Auto. Arkham. Mas." To Meeks this was immediately more promising, as no matches had been struck from it, which might—if he was lucky—mean that it had been acquired very close to Banks's disappearance.

"The admission records?" Meeks asked when he was done studying the effects.

"The patient was admitted as 'Unknown September 20th'—a 'John Doe' to use the parlance. That would be several weeks ago now. Admitting physician was Dr. Grace Zabriski; she has the night shift currently as the doctor of record."

"Who brought him in?"

"Ahem…he was brought here under the ministrations of Agent Jennings, of the Bureau of Prohibition; the only recorded statement being that he was found in what was initially believed to be a state of severe intoxication but was found quickly to be instead, a form of catatonic nervous collapse. He has remained largely unresponsive since, but has been able to take gruel and water under direction."

"It say anything else?"

"No," Mintz answered without looking down at his clipboard, "it does not."

Jennings was one of Sykes's crew; he went with us on the raid, but he didn't come back—it figures it wouldn't be that easy. Had Sykes seen Banks? Had Sykes known? It was possible he hadn't after all; he wasn't one to get his hands dirty with honest police work if he didn't have to. The answer to that question could answer a lot of others as well, not to mention open up one hell of a can of worms if Sykes *had* known. No matter how much he despised Sykes as a toady little coward, he couldn't just accuse him of having something to do with Banks's state without hard evidence. *I have to tread softly here.*

"The Department of Justice would like to avoid any undue attention around this patient, Doctor; to avoid any embarrassment to his family or scandal, you understand. I'd like to keep his identification strictly between us two for the time being."

"Of course," Mintz answered coolly, as if he had expected no less. "He remains Unknown September 20th with us, so long as you wish it."

That easy, eh? Not even a blink of protest, Meeks thought with a scornful twist of his mouth. Truly he did not like this man, nor what he represented.

"I'll arrange to have him taken back to Boston as soon as it's practical to do so, and I'm sure that the Justice Department will be happy to meet any expenses you have incurred in his care. Thank you, Doctor," Meeks said, pocketing the matchbook and leaving the rest of the catatonic man's effects scattered on the small table beside the bed.

"Just so," Mintz replied.

Meeks looked down again one last time before he turned on his heels. *Well, it looks like you get to go home after all, Agent Banks, but not covered in glory. The Bureau is not going to be all that pleased to find you like this. I'm afraid you're just a potential scandal now, an embarrassment to be filed and forgotten. I'll get no answers out of you, it looks like, and now I've only more questions.*

Chapter Nine

Arkham

November 30, 1929

The first thing Tucker knew was the world being jerked out from under him, and sleep with it. The short, stomach-lurching drop from the bed to the floor ended with the sharp crack of the back of his skull against the rough wooden boards.

His hangover hit him a second after the pain from the blow. His eyes clamped shut again reflexively against the light and his stomach twisted in barbed wire knots. What had been intended as a vitriolic burst of outrage ended up leaving his lips as little more than a strangled moan.

His head was spinning crazily and a pain was constricting around the base of his brain. He knew somebody was looming over him, but still he couldn't manage to open his eyes, speak, or even think straight.

Something wet, stinging, and rankly cold was splashed across his face and he spattered and coughed, but it did the tick and he began to painfully come round to his sense of who and where he was. *Whisky*, that's what it was, stale and flat and chill as the morning; last night's leftovers had been emptied across his face—no wonder he couldn't breathe.

"Good morning... Tucker; that is, I believe, how you prefer to be known, is it not?"

Tucker just nodded slowly in reply, his head throbbing. The voice that drifted down to him from across the room was urbane and almost bored, but there was something else to it as well; something caught at his perceptions, even in his current state, and rang alarm bells. *Malice, real, gilt-edged spider-and-fly malice.*

"The bed," the voice continued, "is behind you and a little to your right, if you need support."

He noted through the painful haze that the voice had circled around to the left as he scrabbled ineffectually at the iron bedstead behind him.

"Help him, Mr. Fetch," the voice almost purred.

Tucker cried out as a metal bear trap—it couldn't possibly be a human hand—fastened around his shoulder, lifted him like a paperweight and dumped him doubled up, knees dangling, on the bed. The sharp pain of the bones in his shoulder grinding together did what the stale whiskey could not and he snapped his eyes open and his mind to full, sickening wakefulness. The first thing Tucker saw was the girl from last night, a little older and a little more gaunt than he remembered her, and a whole lot more frightened. She was sitting pushed back as far as she could get and tucked in a ball, the ratty grey sheet drawn up to her pale shoulders, her eyes as wide as an open sky. With a sober clarity he realized he couldn't remember her name.

"I'm real sorry, honey," he croaked, and was surprised to realize he meant it.

The voice to his left chuckled. "Come now, Tucker, are we brutes? Let's send this little scrap on her way, shall we?"

Tucker turned his head and saw the speaker for the first time. It was a man in his later middle age, robust but unpleasantly fleshy, with a bald head and startling green eyes. He was immaculately dressed in a tweed suit with a pale yellow silk waistcoat and russet cravat—perfect for the country club, and all utterly out of place in the gin-swill back rooms of a cathouse in Arkham's Eastside—with handfuls of rings that made him look like a sideshow huckster. Tucker had the unshakable conviction that he knew who this outlandish man was, that he'd been pointed out to him once in warning, but the name and the reason for the warning fled him as his mind tried to grasp it.

The stranger took Tucker's thick billfold out of his pants pocket from where they hung lopsidedly over a chair back, and casually tossed the money to the girl in the bed.

Despite the serious mess he was clearly in, Tucker's heart still skipped a beat as he saw the money leave him, even though he already knew it was useless to resist. Whoever the gorilla with the bear trap hands behind him was would see to that.

"Take it and run," the stranger muttered, and there was real venom invested in every word, so much so it made the girl flinch as though struck and Tucker's spine crawl to hear it, "and keep running far, far away."

The girl's thin fingers swept up the money as she was gone in a flash of bare skin and flapping blanket, her feet staggering and tripping as she fled, slamming the flimsy door behind her.

Tucker pulled himself slowly up the bed and half rolled over, enough to catch a glimpse of the man standing at the foot of his bed and wish he hadn't. The man was twice his size and stood almost hunchback-stooped with a narrow, chinless face the color and texture of chopped liver, and tiny glassy-black eyes.

"A little bird tells me you've been tattling tales, Tucker, and by the looks of it, making a tidy penny while doing so."

Tucker's heart sank and he felt his teeth start to chatter involuntarily; inside he was already screaming in panic. He needed time to think, time to get his story straight, but his mind was racing in a hundred directions at once, questions and answers balled up like a car wreck. "Look, I'm…I'm a reporter." It was all he could think to say.

The stranger snorted as if insulted, and impatiently examined a pocket watch as if he was already running late for a more important appointment. "I have little time or patience for this, Tucker, so let me explain it to you. In a moment, I shall ask Mr. Fetch here to hurt you. And he will go on hurting you. And nobody will come, nobody will help, nobody will stop him, no matter how long or loud you scream. And afterward what is left of you will beg to be truthful with me, just so that I allow you the luxury of dying."

Tucker talked then; in fact, once he began he couldn't stop. He told the stranger everything, everything he knew, everything that seemed important. He told him about every dirty deal he'd done since coming to Arkham; about families he'd blackmailed over scandalous secrets of incipient madness and degeneracy he'd uncovered, about taking bribes from bootleggers to feed false information or rat out their rivals to the prohibition agents, about how he'd stolen from crime scenes, and when that wasn't enough, he told them about the Hand of Solace and about Raker, and about how he'd no sooner found him before selling him out to the real score, just as he'd intended all along.

Through it all, the stranger listened disinterestedly, lighting a cigarette from a white-enameled case, while "Mr. Fetch" stood silent and still as a statue, so still in fact that Tucker could have believed he'd never even drawn breath.

At last Tucker ran out of his sordid parade of confessions, and the stranger paused thoughtfully, as if mulling over whether or not Tucker had successfully bought his life. It was in those long, murderously tense moments, the longest of Tucker's sordid life, that his mind fastened on the rings on the man's fingers and he realized in growing horror who he was.

"Well," the man said, "that's quite a tale, and does indeed shine a new light on things. Come, Mr. Fetch," he pronounced, and went to leave, his business concluded, the hulking Fetch falling in step behind him.

"You're not…not going to kill me?" Tucker's words rushed out before he could hold them back.

The man turned around in the doorway and placed a sable fedora on his head, saying with some amusement, "Oh no, Tucker, I'm not going to do that for you. I rather think that your 'Mr. Shawcross,' as you call him, will manage something for you that would make even my imagination boggle in payment for betraying him, when he finds out, which I am sure he will. Oh, that is to say if dear Dr. Fields and his congregation don't find you first."

Tucker collapsed back on the bed and covered his face with his hands as the cruel laughter of the man from the Silver Twilight Lodge mocked him in a fading echo.

* * *

Wyatt Meeks looked at his stern countenance in the cracked and misted mirror above the equally battered porcelain sink in the jail cell, straightening his black tie and pulling his cuffs right. The pink water gurgled as it disappeared down the plughole, taking with it the flecks of blood that had been on his hands, and long after it faded away into the distance, Meeks stood still and silent, staring at his reflection in the cloudy mirror, the only sound in the holding pen of the Arkham police station the labored breathing of the man he'd just beaten and broken. The smattering of other prisoners—two sobered-up drunks, a petty thief, and a whey-faced commercial traveler who'd tried to pass a bad check at the station—watched on with blank, terrified eyes, and kept as still and quiet as they could manage. They were like rabbits caught in the headlights of an onrushing motorcar, or lambs cast into a lion's den.

Meeks paid them no mind as he donned the suit jacket he'd left on the back of a rickety chair. "They'll let you out in the morning, Sanders. Needless to say, you want to split town and talk to nobody, understand?"

The battered man in the cell nodded his bloody head very slowly, fixing a watery eye on Meeks in understanding, his other swollen shut and purple-black already. Sanders was an ex-con who worked as a motor mechanic in downtown Arkham. Meeks had found his auto shop on a matchbook in Banks's gear; it had been a small enough lead, but a look at Sanders's rap-sheet had immediately made it worth paying attention to. Meeks had sent the two deputy marshals they'd sent him from Boston to pick the mechanic up, and they'd brought Sanders back to the station for a private "interview" with Meeks before the marshal sent them off again to find some lunch. The two deputy marshals, middle-aged veterans who had already ascended about as far as they would go in the service, had just nodded and left, knowing full well what was about to follow and not to question it.

Once Meeks had been left alone with his suspect, Sanders's other activities had soon come to light. It soon became quite clear that the ex-con didn't much care who he fixed cars and trucks for, where those cars and trucks came from or went to, or whether their real owners knew about it, for that matter. As such, he was also a sometime confederate of the Sheldon Gang, and thanks to a string of bad habits, his trade, legal and otherwise, couldn't quite keep up with him, so he moonlighted off and on again as a paid informant to the Arkham sheriff and the prohibition men. As well as, it had transpired—once a few teeth had been loosened by Meeks's persuasion—Federal Agent Roland Banks, who was now rotting in an Arkham Asylum ward. Once Sanders had broken all the way down, he'd told Meeks everything he could about his dealings with Banks and Sykes—which in truth wasn't much, but Sanders knew it was enough to mark him as a stool pigeon, and that was a kind of bird with a very low life expectancy.

The door to the small cell block rattled open and the overweight, middle-aged, and mustached cop, whose name Meeks couldn't ever seem to remember, was standing there nervously. When the cop's eyes fell on the battered Sanders, they went wide as saucers and his mouth started to open and close uselessly like an aquarium fish.

"What?" Meeks barked at him.

The man juddered as if startled and looked at Meeks blankly for a moment. "Oh, sorry, Marshal…" He stopped abruptly as if he was about to say something he should not, but just caught himself in time. "…eh, there's a visitor for you upstairs at the front desk."

"A visitor?" Meeks demanded. "Who?"

The fat cop shifted uncomfortably. "From Dunwich," he added at last, as if that was all the explanation that was needed, and for Meeks it was.

The grim marshal jerked a thumb toward the cell behind him. "Clean him up and get him some hot coffee, a doctor as well if he wants it," he pronounced coldly before pushing his way past the cop.

The front office of the police station was silent and still in a way that closely resembled the heavy, threatened quiet that Meeks had left behind him in the cells; the typist behind the desk was still, her head bent low over a report she wasn't seeing, while the officer behind the desk just looked fixedly ahead, a bead of sweat trickling visibly down his temple. It was all because she was here, Meeks knew.

She stood patiently by the front desk in a forest-green overcoat over a long rust-colored dress and a white lace underskirt that fell down over the tops of high button-hooked boots of a style that had gone out of fashion when Meeks was a boy. She had skin so pale it seemed translucent, hair the color of a raven's wing tightly drawn back and plaited; she seemed at once both young and old, and entirely self-possessed in a way that was flatly intimidating in its certainty. She also did not take kindly to waiting, as could be seen in the hard line of her humorless mouth. Meeks had met her only once before, the night of the terrible raid gone awry. Hannah Whateley was the woman's name, and beneath his iron façade, he was as frightened of her as everybody else was, and just like the rest of them, could not have said precisely why.

"Marshal," she said, folding her arms across her chest and fixing him with her dark eyes.

He was suddenly rooted to the spot by those eyes, held like a butterfly on a pin, but he let no hint of the sudden panic he felt show upon his face as he met those eyes, or enter into his voice as he replied, "Miss Whateley, how can I help you?"

She sniffed sharply. "It's more the case that I'm here to help you, Marshal. The phone wires and telegraph poles are down between here and Dunwich, in case you didn't know, main road's gone to hell besides, so I thought I'd come see you in person to tell you how your man's doing."

"Murtry." Meeks nodded. "How is he?" His concern was genuine, although the young prohibition agent was nominally one of Sykes's people; he'd been one of the men brought in from outside to reinforce them for the raid and not one of Sykes's own crew. He'd also stayed and fought when the others had run, and in Meeks's book, that counted for a whole hell of a lot.

"He'll live all right. Fever's broke and he's awake, and what's more he'll walk—may even dance given a few more weeks." There was a wild pride in her look when she answered him. "Reckon you can move him back to the city as soon as the roads dry out some—best thing for him, being back among his own."

"Thank you, thank you for everything," Meeks said quietly. The irony was not lost on him. Murtry, with his chest flayed open so you could just about see his heart beating, Murtry, bled lily-white; he'd live, he'd be fine, tended to by—what had she been described to him as? "The village midwife"? Whereas the prohibition agent Sykes had pulled out with a leg wound had been seen by a surgeon that night and then shipped off to Boston where the best care available had seen him eaten alive by infection and fever in a matter of hours.

She'd been waiting for them that night as the truck had slewed into Dunwich. Hannah Whateley had stood sentinel between the lights of two swinging hurricane lanterns outside Osborn's General Store on the village commons, men and women of the village gathered around her at a respectful distance.

She'd taken immediate charge of things: sent out men to watch the edge of the town for strangers, taken care of the wounded, taken care of him. He'd been in shock—he recalled the unpleasant memory of it well enough—it had been like he was walking in a sickbed trance.

She'd told him what to do, and he'd obeyed without thinking, sitting him down and tending to a cut on his thigh he hadn't known he'd taken, forcing a hot tin cup of coffee laced with something mint-and-cloves tasting in his hand. When he had woken the following dawn, it had been in the shack of a local man called Harney Jones at the border of the blasted heath, with no idea how he'd got there. There'd been fresh clothes, breakfast, and men with guns and dogs waiting for him to lead them back into that wilderness; she'd arranged it all.

He'd summoned the courage to ask old Harney about her later that day when their fruitless search had been done. All he'd said was that she was a recent arrival in Dunwich, which had surprised him at first, adding that she was down from the north to sort family business after her kinfolk had passed, and had stayed on to help out around the place. Adding cryptically that she was a "Whateley, of the un-decayed Whateley's" as if that both answered all questions and ended the conversation.

And here she was standing before him again, like a figure from a strange dream come to life.

"He's awake?" he asked her cautiously after he had gathered his thoughts again.

"And talkin'," she replied. "He don't recollect much, though, save that you carried him out and he wanted me to pass on his thanks."

Meeks didn't know whether he was relieved that the other man couldn't remember, or infuriated that it was the case, and only nodded in reply.

"There's been no more signs of them bootleggers, nor of the men you lost, I'm sorry to say," she said in response to the unasked question that hung in the air. "I'm guessing any signs went with the rains; there's been mudslides, broken trees fallin', and thunder-strikes all along those old thickets, Harney tells me, made it very dangerous. My guess'ed be that the camp you found has gone right under by now, and any hope of tracking those boys with it."

"Too dangerous to go back there then?" Meeks asked, cold sweat pricking down his back.

"Oh, I'd say so," Hannah Whateley replied, and it was as if all the air in the room had frozen solid. "Any of those bad men left alive down there probably went for higher ground way back in the hills when the storm came, if they was able, and you could lose an army up there. That, or made the road here to Arkham, in which case I'm sure they'll turn up, up to no good.

Any that didn't make it out of the glen, well, I doubt they lasted long that night."

Meeks nodded slowly, not trusting himself to speak out loud.

"Well, Marshal, that'll be about all. I have other errands I need to be about, and I'm sure you have important business of your own to pursue," she said knowingly.

Meeks stiffly showed her to the door and opened it for her before retreating swiftly back inside the police station, his right hand convulsing uncontrollably for a moment.

She was right of course; he did have business to attend to, and thanks to Sanders he had a tangible lead to start with.

* * *

The monster that wore the woman's skin sat alone in the dimness of the day, rainwater still dripping from its fingertips. He had drawn the old overstuffed chair into the center of the abandoned shop facing the half-boarded-up storefront window and watched as dawn had risen over the town. From the street its bedraggled, storm-lashed, and ragged figure, still as it was, might have been mistaken for a distressed old manikin cast aside when the place was boarded up and left vacant, but the few who had walked by on Arkham's streets offered no glance within on the misty morning after the storm.

Piercing the veil and forcing a breach through which it might pass bodily and intact—and doing so here and now, in this place—had cost it dearly indeed, and it had wandered at first, all but mindless and disorientated, with only blind instinct and need to guide it.

While the storm raged, it had been ever driven on, the wrath of the tempest itself hounding its heels, and any unfortunate enough to encounter it in that first hour had been burned and blinded by the terrible strength of where it had been and what it had been in that far place beyond space and time. But soon, as narrow and parochial as this petty realm of matter and force was, it sought to exert its patterns upon the monster, and sheathed in flesh it could not resist them, so it became once more certain and solid; once more as it had been.

The rains came and with them the whispers of Arkham bleeding into its reforming mind; all of the ancient sins and secrets this shadowed place held, all lain open and proclaimed for its consciousness to witness in a cacophony that assailed its mind as the rain assailed its body.

From the bricks and mortar of the asylum came a thousand petty figments, shouted and moaned, nightmares and revelations, scorned fancies and horrific truths peeled from the lips of madmen and men others wished were mad.

From that evil-ridden place men called the Witch House it could feel the passageways of time twisted and tangled like the knots of a hangman's noose, and hear the chitterling obscenities of rats with human faces as they coursed along them in legions.

From beneath the fetid ground came the worm-sign of the jackal-god, which rose up as the ghouls swam slow and cold through the earth, writhing at each thunderstroke.

From behind the closed doors and weakling wards of the Silver Twilight Lodge, the craven thoughts of plotters and schemers revolved in a vortex of mistrust and moral degeneracy, each prideful and terrified—all as hopeless as chaff before the reaper's scythe for all their coiling lies.

Somewhere an old serpent watched patient and cold for its prey to show itself, for what had once been his to become his again, for his vengeance to be served and his foes and pawns devoured alike.

And more and more, from locked attics and bricked-up basements, from bookcases and padlocked tombs, they spoke to the monster in blind, idiot outcry: sins and phantoms, ghosts and never-born things, concealed murders and pacts unspeakable; a chorus men could not hear, but only feel as a morbidity in the air, as a shadow on their dreams—this was Arkham and all its secrets. All were bestirred by the coming of the Exile as the hurricane rents up the sea bed and spews up its secrets, for it was the Hungering God; that which is to come and always was, the traveler whose shadow plunged all into darkness before it.

It was the self-same siren song that had called him forth, the beacon he had followed from across lightless vistas and dimensions of madness uncounted, back to Arkham from whence he had once passed beyond, here to wander insensate and lost.

On the second night in the waking world, the gnawing in its stomach and the aching in its bones grew to become intolerable. *Hunger*...the word floated in its mind... *Cold* came upon the heels of the first.

One thread in all the whispers—close, warm, alive, foolishly calling attention to itself, muttering words it did not understand, an unguarded spark in the darkness.

In the basement of an old run-down house off Independence Square a woman had been laying out her cards for a man whose fear and apprehension had been strong enough to bring him out in the downpour and the night, and through the door with its painted plaque reading "Anna Kaslow, Mystic" beneath the sign of the all-seeing eye.

The Kaslow woman had looked up as she turned her final cards: The Magician and The Broken Tower. She had time to scream before the end, but the man died before he knew that his questions would never be answered, and soon the needs of the body had been dealt with, save one: sleep.

After that deathly oblivion, a great deal more had become clear, but memory floated like broken fragments of a shattered mirror, memories not only of its own, but of lives it had stolen, and of bodies it had worn. With an instinct now as human as it was otherworldly, it knew it needed time to think, to remember, and a place of safety away from the now red-smeared basement room with its reek of the abattoir. The Kaslow woman's clothes it had taken to replace its own perished rags; for it knew now that the flesh it wore was female, and the still falling rain had washed clean its hands and mouth.

The abandoned store had been familiar, reeking of ancient things that had left their ghosts echoing in the dusty outlines on the emptied shelves, but also in the mind of the body it now sleeved itself in; before he'd claimed it. The woman had visited this place and here felt the future-echo of what was to claim her, a circle broken and unbroken.

"Jacqueline Fine," the monster whispered in the remembered voice of the woman that had once owned that name. The words fell into the musty air of what had once been Arkham's pretentiously named Curiositie Shoppe, as the dim day passed by and the broken mirror was slowly reformed. "And I am the master," Lemaitre whispered, "and I will have my due."

Chapter Ten

Arkham

December 1, 1929

Leaves and cold rain scudded through the university's courtyards. Raker pulled his hat low as a gust of sodden rain tried to lift it from his head. The windows of the grey stone buildings watched him pass. The sounds of Arkham had faded as soon as he had crossed onto the campus, as if silence clung to the old stones. It felt as if he had stepped into another, older world where the only noise was the whip of the wind and the patter of cold rain drops. No one else crossed his path, and for a moment he wondered if the buildings had been deserted, shut up to gather dust and secrets. He shivered, half at the cold and half at the thought that this was a place apart in Arkham, a cyst of silence wrapped in the corpse of a city.

He shook his head, trying to put aside the black melancholy he felt, but he couldn't quite do it. *I have to keep my mind clear, or I'm going to miss something.*

It took him some time to find the library, partly because there was no one to ask, and partly because he mistook it at first for a church. It was a huge, Gothic monster of a building whose long windows spanned three floors, and gargoyles guarded its corners. The steps up to its arched double doors were wide, and their worn treads glistened under a skim of rainwater.

He'd left this place to last; instinct told him that if there was an easy lead here, somebody would have found it by now, and from what he'd heard from Tucker and Shawcross, he was likely to receive a cold welcome to his questions.

Stillness greeted him as he pushed the door open and stepped inside. It took a second for his eyes to adjust so that he could see more than soft shadow shapes and the dim glows of weak electric lights. When the door clicked shut behind him, he almost started. If the rest of Miskatonic University felt deserted, then the library was a vault of cold shadows at its core. He realized that he could hear the blood pulsing through his ears. Impressions of spiraling staircases and dark avenues of shelves coalesced in front of his eyes.

"Can I help you?" The voice drifted out of the dark. Raker squinted and then saw the figure standing behind the wide desk of dark wood. He took three steps forward and the figure became a woman, a thin face narrow behind glasses, hair drawn back into a neat bun. Her hands rested either side of a ledger, thin fingers splayed like pale spiders on the dark wood.

"Hello, there," he said, smiling, but the woman did not smile back. "It's a bit dark in here, isn't it?"

"The power's low," the woman replied in a clipped voice. "It's like this all over the campus—probably the storms. Can I help you?"

Two young, bookish men appeared without warning between the stacks, muttering to each other in low, earnest voices, and were gone again just as quickly behind another row of bookcases. Raker found himself suddenly pleased that there were people about the place somewhere going about their business.

"I was looking for a friend who I think worked here." He tried the smile again, focusing back on the woman. "Daisy Walker?"

He could tell he was going to get nowhere even before the woman opened her mouth.

"I am afraid I can't help you, sir," she said with precise coldness that left him in no doubt that further queries would be met with equally firm refusals.

As expected, he thought.

"I am guessing no one else would be able to tell me where she is?"

The woman behind the desk gave an icy smile.

"Like I told the others: no. Now please be on your way."

Raker tapped his fingers on the wood of the desk, his eyes skating over the woman's unmoving stare. Then he nodded and turned to the door. He had taken three steps when he turned.

"What others?" he asked.

"All the others who have come asking the same question as you," said the woman with an edge of iron in her voice.

Raker did not press the point, but opened the door and stepped back into the damp daylight. Shaking his head, he fished a cigarette out of his jacket pocket. He would need to find a way of finding out what the hard-faced woman in the library knew; without it, he had nothing but cold leads leading nowhere.

"Do you have a light?'"

Raker turned to see a pair of grey eyes looking at him from beneath a rain-spattered hat. The girl had a coat pulled close around her, and she had a pre-rolled cigarette held between slim fingers.

"Sure." Raker struck a match and lit the girl's cigarette, then his own.

The girl blew out a low plume of smoke.

"You're not supposed to smoke out here," she said. "But I guess I will let you off." Her mouth twitched into a grin.

"Thanks," he said.

"It's okay, it's a dumb rule anyway. I wonder if the university has thought where would be a better place. The library stacks maybe? A room with lots of old paper sounds like a perfect place to strike a match." Raker laughed, and the girl smiled wider. "You aren't a student." It was half statement, half invitation.

"What gave it away?" He grinned.

"Oh, just about everything. You aren't another marshal are you?"

Raker's skin prickled and he felt his face become still.

"No," he managed, hoisting an amused smile into place. "Nothing like that, just looking for an old friend."

"Daisy?" said the girl, and Raker felt his surprise crack the mask of his face. The girl grinned a clever and satisfied grin. "Thought so. Popular girl." She smiled again at the look of confusion he deliberately offered her. "That's who the others were asking about, too. I'm Sarah Danforth by the way." She held out a gloved hand. After a second, Raker shook it.

"You work at the library?" he asked. Sarah nodded and exhaled another cloud of smoke.

"I'm a student really, archaeology, but yeah, I'm a librarian part-time." She snorted. "Part-time and unpaid."

Raker's smile was genuine this time.

She is smart, he thought. Sharp enough to most likely cut apart any soft lies he might try, and clearly already suspicious of anybody interested in Daisy Walker.

"So other people have come looking for Daisy?"

Sarah nodded and shook the ash from the tip of her cigarette.

"This morning—a big U.S. Marshal." Her lip curled. "He was frightening, just mean, and he wouldn't believe anyone that told him they did not know where Daisy was. In the end, the dean had to come and tell him he would phone friends he had in Washington if the man did not go and stop causing a scene. Everybody on campus is talking about it."

Sarah paused, frowning at the rain splashing the puddles at the base of the library steps. "Then there was an old guy the other day. I never saw him, but the other librarians said that he was very polite." She looked back to Raker. She took a careful drag of her cigarette and raised an eyebrow. "And then there's you."

"So do you know where Daisy is?"

Sarah shook her head as if disappointed.

"No. None of us do and that is the truth. I," she said with comic self-importance, "have not seen her for months." She dropped the cigarette and ground it into the damp stone with her foot. "The only thing I know is that Daisy got mixed up with something in Kingsport last year. That's what everybody says anyway."

"What kind of thing?" he asked, trying not to sound too desperate to know the answer.

Sarah gave him a sharp look.

"Something unpleasant, tragic," she said cagily. "It was in the papers, I think. That and she knows that Whateley woman from Dunwich who comes to use the library sometimes. She's a bad sort; the locals say she's a witch, but that's just Yankee tommyrot."

"Daisy Walker?" Raker asked, not following the sudden turn in the conversation.

"No, the Whateley woman, but that's just the natives for you, still stuck with Cotton Mather and seeing goblins in the woodpile." She chuckled. "I miss Providence; that's where I'm from, you understand?"

"Yeah, thanks," said Raker with a sigh, sensing that was all he was going to get of use, and he didn't have the time or the inclination to flirt for the sake of it. "I have to run, but maybe another time?"

"Thank you for the light," she replied, and the clever smile flashed across her face. She turned and walked back toward the library doors, making sure it was she, not him, who walked away first. Raker watched her go, then turned up his collar and walked down the steps and away from the university.

* * *

The un-breathing man watched Raker reach his motor car. It was not his purpose to intervene, only to watch, to be the eyes for his master. He kept those eyes fixed on Raker while the man got the motor car started and drove out onto the road. The un-breathing man watched until it was out of sight, noting the second car followed a few moment later, its slick black and chrome flanks beaded with rain, those inside hidden by darkened glass.

Neither Raker nor those in the black car had noticed the un-breathing man, but then why should they? In these times he was just another figure in stained and torn clothes folded into the margins of the town like a pile of windblown leaves, even had the mists that lingered not concealed him.

For a pained second the un-breathing man wondered if he should care what had become of him: a ragged, bearded creature in sodden cloths, wrapped in the reek of the streets, the canker that had been planted inside him growing, feeding. The thought vanished.

For him to care would have to mean he could remember who he was, and that, like breath in his lungs and the beat of his heart, was gone. All that was left to him was his purpose, that and the image of a frozen lightning strike burned into his mind.

Slowly and patiently, he turned his milk-white eyes back to the university and his vigil.

* * *

Grace Zabriski dreamed. It was the most vivid dream she had ever been subject to in her life, and the most terrible. She knew both at once that she was dreaming, but at the same time experienced all as real and as inescapably solid as stone.

It began in a playground, one as familiar to her as her father's face but one she had not seen in many years—a figment of childhood memory. The sparse little playground was near Coney Island, by the side of the beach and in sight of the turning sea. It was no more than a few fairground castoffs given a home, a rusting slide, and a rickety old merry-go-round whose wooden boards were at last succumbing fatally to salt air and the endless abrading grasps of countless children's hands. Her aunt Miri used to bring her here on late summer Saturdays come rain or shine while her father worked on in his tailor's shop. They would ride the trolley bus there and back and eat pastries and hot dogs in sight of the surf.

The playground was empty now, its sandlot cratered and uneven, as if things had been buried there better left unseen. On the near horizon the sea turned over red-black like spoiled wine and a purple sun hid behind monstrous thunderhead clouds as frozen and still as an ice sculpture.

I am dreaming, I am not here, but I am cold and I can feel the sand shift beneath my feet.

Nearby, the familiar old swing creaked and she turned to see a little girl sitting dolefully in its seat. She was pale as winter with a cascade of black ringlets for hair and wore a fine filigreed dress of black lace; slim hands sheathed in grey silk gloves gripped the swing ropes tightly. The girl was beautiful and terrible all at once, and pain stabbed into Grace's heart to see her.

She called out to her, but the pale girl, as silent as a funeral portrait, stepped down from the swing and walked over the dune. Grace followed her, unable to do anything else, unable to conceive of anything else but to follow as they set out across the sand.

Buried things pressed on the edge of her sight, but she didn't want to see them; she stumbled around a broken car axel, a shattered hurricane lantern with a long hank of hair caught in the crazed glass, and a twisted skeletal arm up-thrust from the ground as if imploring mercy, threads of red flesh still clinging to it. She called out again in fear, but the girl did not stop.

The sea was close now, an ocean of cloying blood in which dark leviathans heaved and murmured as if trapped just below the surface. Ahead across the beach was a vast promontory of rock topped by a strange high house, and out to sea the jagged spar of a lighthouse swept its beam across the world like a sword of cold fire. *This is wrong; there was no rock, no lighthouse… Where am I?* Then came a flash of recognition. *Kingsport, this is Kingsport.* She had visited once, not long after she came to Arkham; bought a painted china cat from a street vendor, ate candy floss on the beach…the beach…but it wasn't like this… Where was the rest of it, the town? Gone, plowed under, destroyed, she somehow knew. Something terrible beyond comprehension had happened here.

She was no longer alone with the girl. There was a forest of men and women on the shore with her now, surrounding her. They were standing rigid and still as statues save for their lips which blurred with the speed of their droning chant, the sound of which rose in her ears like the buzzing of flies. Each looked blindly out to sea, horrible words forming and un-forming too fast for her to understand.

The pale girl wove between them, as if she were playing a game with her pursuer, and Grace was compelled to follow, even though the figures filled her with dread.

Ring around the rosy, a pocket full of posies, ashes, ashes, we all fall down, she thought wildly, seeing the pale girl bob and weave between the droning figures. She knew why—a splinter of knowledge she'd never known when she'd sang the rhyme as a child—it was a poem about plague, a nursery rhyme about death and futility, the end of the world.

She followed, stumbling and frantic. In the manner of her dream, she knew as she had not before the identity of some of the taunt, wide-eyed faces of the watchers. They were those of her patients; her silent ones no longer silent. She tripped and fell at the feet of a young man whose face she knew. He had been handsome, clean-cut, but was now gaunt and lost, one of the nameless ones, turning something over and over in his pale hands, blood flecking his lips.

A sand dune's crest robbed the girl from sight as she raced ahead, and panic took Grace fully then, a dread too vast and absolute to express exploding in her mind. She screamed out for her to come back, not to leave her in this terrible broken memory. She ran up the dune crest, away from the forest of men and women, stumbling and staggering in the sand. She fell. Cold paving slabs bit into her palms, arresting her fall. She looked up. Arkham lay smashed and murdered around her. There were mangled, half-dissolved bodies everywhere, overturned automobiles and blind, broken windows, burned trees, and poisoned earth. The sky was the same frozen purple-black canvas, but against it dark shapes like tortured scarecrows drawn in blood and spilled ink cavorted and wheeled. The words of Poe came to her again unbidden.

"...evil things, in robes of sorrow..."

The girl was gone and she was alone with the dead and the shadows wheeling overhead. Again she ran, this time in a nightmare of horror she could barely comprehend. It was endless; vistas of carnage and destruction, massacre and dissolution, it was Arkham and it was New York, it was all cities and everywhere, death was all around her. She ran until her muscles throbbed with pain, until her bones cried out in protest and her lungs were filled with broken ice. At last before a white-faced building spattered with sprays of gore she could go no further. She was on her knees, begging to wake up, knowing she could not.

A hand touched her shoulder and an electric shock of contact surged through her. It was the girl, right beside her, looking down at her with empty eyes that stretched on forever into the abyss of night.

"Do you want this?" The voice echoed in her head like a scream of despair and mockery.

The shadows coiled and thickened around her, but she could not answer.

"The Exile, the Black Traveler, the Hungering God."

Grace tried to crawl away but her bones had turned to rotted sticks and she went nowhere as the pale nightmare child stood over her. "I don't know what you mean!" she heard herself cry out.

"He comes, he is very close now, and this is what he shall make."

The dark shapes were circling closer now and she could see the coils of cold fire which coursed at their hearts, the endless stars that glimmered like dead souls deep in their writhing darkness; she could feel their malevolence, their need, like razors slicing into her skin.

"Do you want this?" the nightmarish figure asked again.

"No!" Grace screamed, blood flecking her lips.

"Then stop it."

Pain like nothing she had ever known blazed in the palm of her hand; she looked down, expecting to see a scattering of charred bones, but instead she saw her fingers fastened around a shard-like chunk of glassy black stone on which strange figures blazed in a color her mind couldn't name. Hungering blackness shrieked soundlessly down upon her and blotted out the world…

…and she woke screaming, writhing helplessly off her bed.

She slid hard to the floor, her thrashing legs tangled helplessly in her sheets.

She lay sprawled, helpless, panting, terrified. Her empty hand ached furiously as she stared at it, her fingers ignoring her desperate mental commands to move, to flex, anything.

There was a knock on the door of her little apartment, and a moment later a second knock and wavering voice inquired if she was all right.

Grace Zabriski almost cried out in relief that there was another soul alive in the world. With effort she found her own voice, and the lie came without any forethought. "Yes…yes, Miss Teague. I trod on something…something sharp and I fell over. I had an accident, but I'm all right… I'm sorry to have caused a commotion."

"Well, if you're sure that you're all right, dear?" came the thin reply, and Grace answered again in the affirmative and let out a sobbing breath when she heard footsteps receding away.

It was as well. Her own voice had sounded broken and terrified to her own ears, but the old landlady had accepted it nevertheless. She almost sobbed in relief because even as sprawled half-naked, awry, and tangled up as Grace was, she could not have moved if a hundred men had barged in to see her distress.

Slowly, very slowly, she regained some movement and was able to half crawl her way across the rug to her divan chair and pull herself up. Her muscles ached and cramped so badly it brought tears to her eyes and dragged out her breath in wet sobs as she pushed her cold, sweat-sodden hair out of her eyes and attempted to regain some composure.

As the physical anguish faded, the mental turmoil took charge. Unlike almost every dream she had ever had, each detail of her nightmare vision remained crystal clear; every chill barb of cutting wind, every reek of carrion, the fathomless night in the girl's eyes—all of it.

Her gazed roved around the room. She came to the realization that it was twilight. The clock struck four and she knew that in little more than two hours she would be expected to be at work. The photograph of her father looked down at her from the mantle, stern and proud, gone to his grave and blessed of memory for six long years. Her framed doctorate and certifications flanked his image; they were the campaign medals hard-won in the quiet war that was her life, emblems of achievement, of order, of safety. All useless now as she stood on the brink of an abyss of unreason.

The Exile, the Black Traveler, the Hungering God—all words that she had heard before, heard them on the lips of the patients she had treated for months, patients whose minds had been blasted and splintered by unknown causes, as perhaps her mind had almost been. With those words, heavy with fear in her mind now, were others she seemed to know, but the meaning of them she couldn't quite grasp, though she felt she ought to know, like a memory caught on the tip of her tongue: *Sutter, Stonegroves, Cormac, Walker, Damascus.* Their meaning and context was lost to her utterly and yet they seemed to be savagely important somehow, as if the sheer weight of them wanted to crowd out everything else on her mind. But what could it be? What could it mean?

Coincidence, incorporation, contrivance, extreme stress, unconscious absorption, nervous exhaustion, and sleep deprivation, her training and her reason countered weakly in return to the turmoil in her mind. Weakly, because all of it failed to account for two things: the first was the pattern of lines and strange symbols scored in pale lines on the palm of her still useless hand. Patterns that conformed to her dream image of the un-colored radiance on the stone fragment. The second and far worse was the blood on the walls of her apartment. They were blood-blotches soaking through the wallpaper from beneath like a repeating series of Rorschach tests showing the faces of the damned.

The night was coming sooner than she would have liked, and she was very cold, very cold indeed.

* * *

Raker flicked his eyes to the rearview mirror. The car was still there. He had spotted the black sedan with the smoked glass after he had driven only a few streets from the university; it had hardly been anonymous. He had slowed down and sped up to see if they pulled past him or dropped back, but they had held the same distance, never letting him out of sight, never coming close, and in traffic this thin it was more than suspicious.

Who are you? he thought, glancing back to see the darkened windows still looking back at him like a pair of holes in a skull.

The rain started to come down harder, hammering on the windows and roof of the car like the endless tapping of small fingers.

It wasn't the local cops, that he was sure. None of them would drive a car like that, and why would they be following him even if they did? He had been careful to stay out of the way of the law in Arkham since coming back, and had not heard their heavy footsteps behind him.

No, he thought. *This is nothing to do with the law.* Shawcross perhaps? But why did the dry man want Raker to know that he was being followed? Whoever was in the car wanted Raker to know that they were there—that or they were the most incompetent tail he'd ever seen. So who? If Shawcross wanted him to feel his eye upon him, he'd have found a less clumsy and far more sinister way of doing so. Maybe it was someone from his days in Boston? The girl at the library had said a marshal had been asking questions at the university, but that didn't seem like a likely candidate either.

It did not matter, though, ultimately—that question might answer itself later; all that mattered for now was losing them.

Raker yanked the wheel hard and his car skidded as it cornered, but the auto Shawcross had given him was well-made and well-maintained and it didn't stall as he feared it might. He hit the accelerator and felt the engine roar through the car's frame. The black and chrome tail car took the corner behind him in a spray of water, struggling to keep up. Raker took the next corner and swerved as an old man pushing a barrow shook his fist, only to have to jump back in panic as the black and chrome sedan exploded around the bend after him.

"Come on," snarled Raker. "Keep with me. Keep with me."

The polished radiator of the tail car loomed large in his rear window. Raker took another corner, cutting the curb dangerously close, wondering if his shadow knew Arkham, and if so, did they realize where they were going?

Raker took the final corner and stood on the breaks as he swerved to a stop. Behind him the black and chrome car took the bend, began to break, and then jerkily accelerated past him. Raker watched the windows of the long car as it slid alongside. For a second he thought he saw the shadow of a pale face through the darkened glass.

He glanced up to the side of the road where the building he'd avoided since he had last walked from it sat with rain washing down its grey face. The glass sphere of its street sign was not lit, but the word "Police" was still visible. Raker allowed himself a half smile before reversing the car and turning to accelerate the way he had come.

* * *

Tucker took another discreet swig of gin from the small brown bottle in his inside pocket, but kept his eyes firmly on the door to the church. From his position nestled in the far corner of one of the rear pews, and concealed from much of the rest of Arkham's South Church by one of the wooden pillars that upheld the roof, he felt safer than he had done all day—which wasn't saying much.

His nerves were shot and he hadn't eaten, and the gin—which was about all he could afford after that evil bastard from the Lodge had given his stash to the girl and left him flat broke—was doing little more than keeping him awake from the raw burn it spread in his throat and guts. He rubbed his face, trying to stay alert, and his own flesh felt as cold and clammy as a dead fish.

This had been without a doubt the worst day of his life, and he had never been so afraid; he was sick with fear and sick with running. The irony wasn't lost on him either; he didn't believe in God, he didn't believe in much of anything except the church of George "Tucker" Adams Esquire and its needs, and yet he had ended up here in a church, based on the half-lie that he might be safe here for a while.

He figured the place would be busy somehow, given all the strange happenings of late, the deaths and disappearances, but it wasn't so. He'd finally made it here about three o'clock and seen no more than half a dozen people since he'd arrived, old folks mainly, lighting candles and praying alone. After an hour or so some younger guy, not a priest but a groundskeeper or caretaker maybe, had come up and fixed him with a stare and told him the place was being shut up at six on the nail and he would have to be gone then. There had been an implied threat to the man's tone and Tucker, wired as he was, made some crack about the church being meant to offer sanctuary that he couldn't quite remember, but he could recall the man's response clear enough. "Father Michael would have said so, but he's gone, and you be gone as well by six." The "or else" hadn't been spoken aloud, but it had been there all the same.

So he waited, and as he sat nervously fidgeting in the dim and drafty church, he kept turning his situation over and over in his mind. He had to get out of Arkham, far out, certainly a lot farther than the few dollars he had dug from the nightstand in his rented room would take him. And to think, only last night he'd been rolling in dough; selling out Raker to Shawcross had been his biggest score of the year, but he'd ratted Shawcross out now and maybe signed his own death warrant in the process.

If Shawcross found out he'd talked about their arrangement, he was a dead man, and if the Lodge told the crazies from the Hand of Solace he'd set Raker and Shawcross on them, who knew what they would do? He was up against the wall, and knew bitterly that he was alone; no help, no friends, nobody to lend him a hand or even a kind word. He called himself a reporter, but what was he really? "A third-rate garbage-sifter, too scared to make it as a crook and too stupid to make it as a real newsman"—that's what his old boss on the *Tribune* had called him before he'd kicked him out on his heels. He'd played both sides then and got burned for it then, too, but at least in Boston that had just meant he was finished in the newspaper racket as far as the city went once the word got round, but here it was going to cost him his life if he couldn't get out.

What's keeping him? Tucker thought furiously, and glanced again at his watch. *Quarter past five—he said he'd be here an hour ago!*

Tucker was starting to come to the dreadful certainty that he had been abandoned when the church door eased open and a young man in a fancy overcoat with a fur-edged collar crept slowly into the church. Tucker's heart leapt and he cried out before he could control himself. "Sykes! I'm over here." The shout echoed in the stillness of the church and Tucker bit his fingers in alarm at the volume.

Sykes flinched and with a look of anger on his face waved Tucker back to his seat and swiftly joined him, his eyes darting round the all but empty church as he did so.

"Oh boy," Tucker began, "you've no idea how glad I am to see you!"

"Keep it down, Tucker," the prohibition agent whispered harshly. "Whatever kind of mess you've got yourself into, I'm here to tell you I don't want any part of it, okay?"

"Sykes, buddy, don't be that way. I helped you out, haven't I? Haven't I always helped you?"

Sykes put one hand on Tucker's shoulder and gently pushed him back down from where he was starting to rise up in the pew, an edge of mounting hysteria in his voice.

"Easy, easy," Sykes said in alarm, one eye on Tucker and one eye on whoever might be watching them. "What the hell's gotten into you?"

In a whispering, half-coherent ramble Tucker told him the fill of it, Sykes's expression looking increasingly grim. "…so you see, Sykes, I'm in bad. I need a way out, some dough, I figured you…"

"Hold on, Tucker," Sykes interrupted harshly. "We aren't exactly friends, you know. Sure, you've helped me some in the past, and you took my money too as I recall, that's all there is between us."

"But it was you that put me on to Shawcross in the first place. I figured you…"

"Figured I could what? Put in a good word for you? Are you mad?" Sykes shook his head in fearful disbelief. "All I did was pass on word, that was all; I got nothing to do with Shawcross or any of them. Every guy on the make from New York to Maine knew they were looking, and the kind of money that was on the table if they found what they were after."

Tucker couldn't take it in; Sykes had been his last hope, the only one in Arkham that maybe owed him something.

"I got my own problems," Sykes muttered. "This town's gone all to hell. I got that son-of-a-bitch marshal breathing down my neck, and what I've seen here I don't ever want to see again, understand?" Tucker stared at him uncomprehendingly as he got to his feet and looked round, saying, "I'm getting out myself. Just got to square it with the Bureau back in Boston. Something's coming; can't you feel it? Something bad."

"But, Sykes," Tucker whined, "what am I going to do?"

Sykes looked down at him with something like a touch of pity. "Call Shawcross," he said.

"What!" Tucker hissed.

"Tell him that 'Sanford' whoever-he was from the Lodge was nosing around. Tell him he threatened you—tell Shawcross Sanford mentioned him by name, which is at least half-true anyway; put the blame on him, make him the problem, not you."

"You mean lie?"

Sykes sneered in surprise. "Sure, it's what you do, isn't it, Tucker? Sell the dirt; make it work for you if you can—lie. It's your only play as far as I can see it."

Tucker just blinked at him, comprehension slowly forming in his mind.

Sykes reached into his back pocket and peeled a ten dollar bill from his money clip. "Here," he said, "get a hot meal in you and shower first. Pull yourself together; you look like one of the town crazies and you're starting to sound like one, too."

Tucker scrambled for the bank note as it fell underneath the pew, mumbling his thanks.

"And that's the last cent you're getting out of me as well. I don't want to hear from you again."

Tucker looked up and began to assure the prohibition agent he'd do as he was asked, but Sykes's dark-coated figure was already half way to the church door.

* * *

Outside, Sykes put his hands in his pockets and almost skipped down the steps of the church whistling merrily, tipping his hat as he jaunted by the groundskeeper who was already preparing the padlock and chain for the main gate.

A little further down the street he opened the door of a parked green Ford and slipped behind the driver's wheel. He looked over his shoulder to the back seat where a hulking figure cradled the faceless, half-naked carcass of a dead man as if lulling a sleeping child.

"Well then," he said, smiling, "that went splendidly, Mr. Fetch. Mother will be pleased," and started the ignition.

Chapter Eleven

Arkham

December 2, 1929

Candles burned low in the basement of the disused Curiositie Shoppe. Amid a twisted series of wildly curling spirals and clusters of symbols—still shining wet in the flickering light—sat the cross-legged figure of a young woman, emaciated and drawn. From this slight body a sonorous and ancient voice intoned a repeating series of maddening phrases that twisted and looped around themselves like a mantra for the damned.

The body was that of Jacqueline Fine, but the voice was that of Lemaitre, who had walked a bloody trail through history, bringing himself to this moment, and buying the alien words he now incanted with the lives of the many he had led to their deaths down the centuries.

Jacqueline's eyes had rolled up white in her head, and blood trickled from her nose and ears, but Lemaitre's voice remained strong and insistent as it wormed away at the barriers between worlds.

Around him, the cement floor of the basement began to shudder and ripple like pond water at the approach of a colossal tread, losing cohesion, becoming other than solid, other than real.

The inhuman chanting never misplacing a beat, Jacqueline's arms reached out imploringly and the ground began to surge and crest like a turbulent sea around her, worm-like forms pushing and distorting its surface, struggling to break through.

Between the blood-flecked spittle of the words, Jacqueline's mouth jerked into a distorted smile. A master needed servants, but this time, mere human lackeys would not do. There was much blood to be shed if he was to herald in the coming lord, and little time to do it. So he called them, and they came.

Chapter Twelve

Arkham

December 3, 1929

Having been to the university for a second time in search of the woman that morning and got exactly nowhere, just as he had expected, Meeks had spent the rest of the day running down fruitless minor leads and dealing with pointless paperwork before filing a report with his masters that was nothing but a concoction of half-truths and generalities. The report, empty as it was of substance, detailed all he was willing to say about his investigation so far as the department was concerned, at least until he could show some tangible results and some cold, hard proof. Unlike Banks, he had no intention of letting his superiors doubt his sanity.

It was getting toward sundown when he judged it was time to run down the next link in his chain. Unlike Sanders, he judged this man needed a visit in his place of business and threats more implied than visceral to extract what he wanted to know, and unlike at the university, he could be as direct as he wanted in his search for answers.

This time it was a man named Ryan Dean—an individual who previously Meeks had not so much as heard of—but who thanks to Sanders's information had become the next domino he had to make fall if he was to reach his quarry.

Dean wasn't so much a mobster, but what his more desk-bound colleges at the Department of Justice would have called a "fellow traveler." His legitimate business was as manager of Hibb's Roadhouse—which Dean had "acquired" little more than a year ago—a place that passed for the raucous end of Arkham's nightlife at the east end of town. A low, sprawling building, it was a gambling joint masquerading as a pool hall with, as he had come to learn, a basement speakeasy for the hardened drinkers and table-service booze provided in brown paper bags for those of a more taciturn disposition, while the basement was kept private for high stakes card games and dice from time to time. What went on at Hibb's was an open secret in the town, and aside from a spattering of token arrests and the occasional half-hearted raid for appearance's sake, it had never been shut down. Meeks knew why even if he didn't exactly agree with the reasons: it allowed for somewhere for the town to let off steam, and an unpopular law that wasn't likely to last much longer on the statute books anyway to be flouted somewhere out of sight and out of mind. This tacit arrangement hadn't been one Meeks had been part of, however, so it didn't mean that he needed to play nice.

He and his deputies simply walked on in to the half-empty joint and paid no heed to anybody who tried to stop them from pushing past behind the old bar, his two guns holding station downstairs and keeping anybody else at a distance while Meeks simply barged into Dean's upstairs cashier's office and sat down without a word, the butt of his revolver plainly visible in its shoulder holster as he reclined in the leather chair.

Dean took the sudden intrusion well; Meeks had to give him that. He didn't look alarmed, he didn't rant and rave, didn't demand to know who he was. He just got up and walked over to a roll-top bureau by the wall—open-handed and easy so Meeks could see he wasn't reaching for a weapon—calmly retrieved a whiskey bottle and two glasses, and set them on the desk between them.

Meeks studied the man; he was a stocky, square build under a gilt-and-blue pinstripe suit that spoke of money and not a whole lot of class; slick-backed hair and a pencil mustache topped him off. He didn't look like a local and certainly more Mediterranean in ancestry than his name suggested. When he spoke however, his accent was pure gutter-Chicago. "You'll take a drink? It's good stuff, Canadian, right off the boat."

Meeks expressionless, answered, "I'm not here for whiskey."

"Suit yourself, Marshal." The double meaning of Meeks's reply was not lost on Dean, and an eyebrow rose quizzically as he poured himself one anyway and casually sat down, just as if they were two friends talking.

He's a cool one, Meeks thought. "So you know who I am?" he said flatly.

"Heavyweight law from Boston," Dean said conversationally. "This town isn't so big that when a man like you rolls in, a man like me doesn't get to hear of it pretty soon."

There was also the unholy mess of the raid gone bad in the woods, Meeks had no doubt Dean had heard about that too, but at least he'd had the sense not to hurl that in Meeks's face.

"You I hadn't heard of before, Dean, but it looks like you've got a pretty nice setup here, a real dollar-press."

Again Dean caught the implied threat without Meeks having to spell it out. "Oh, I pay my taxes, Marshal, just like a good citizen. I make sure I'm squared away with the sheriff and the local prohibition boys both; I cause no waves for them, and I don't want to cause no waves with you either."

Meeks's rocky countenance finally cracked a half-smile. "This isn't a shakedown, Dean; I'm not interested in your money either."

"When a lawman comes to me and he doesn't want my money and he doesn't want my booze, then I got to wonder what kind of bad news he's bringing to my door. So, Marshal, what is it I can do for you?"

"You can talk, Dean, you can talk. I have it on good authority that one way or another you know just about everything that goes on in this town; so you can talk."

Dean threw back his whiskey and let out a hollow laugh, saying, "Anybody that thinks he knows everything that goes on in Arkham is a fool, Marshal, and anybody that flaps his gums too often around here is looking to commit suicide, and I don't fall into either category."

Meeks's thick hands curled and uncurled reflexively into fists, but his voice remained level and gravel-pit deep. "Let me explain something to you, and I'm only going to do this once because I'd rather have your full cooperation, it's quicker, and I could do without having to listen to you speak through a splintered jaw. I don't care about the local law or what deal you have worked out with them or the damn Bureau of Prohibition. I don't care who your backers are or who you owe. I'm going to get what I want out of you and I don't care if I leave this place in ashes and send you to the hospital in order to do it, or for that matter, the morgue."

A sour look crossed Dean's face for a moment, but then he leaned back in his chair and sighed. "You don't give a body a break, do you, Marshal, but that's fine with me, that makes things easy. What I was trying to say wasn't that I wasn't going to help you, but that there's some things, a hell of a lot of things in fact, that go on round here that I make it my business not to know too much about. It's a whole lot healthier that way. I may not have the answers you want or the answers you like, that's all."

"You haven't heard my questions yet, so convince me. Give

me what you've got and convince me you're not holding back, and I walk out of here and you can go back about your gutters, picking drunks' pockets and such. Like I said, I don't care about your booze and I don't care about your racket; I've got bigger fish to fry."

Ryan Dean nodded; he was backed into a corner and he knew it.

"Ask away then, Marshal, that's the best deal I'm going get today, it looks like."

"The Sheldon Gang, Sykes, Banks, Morgan, Walker." Meeks rolled off his list, looking closely at Dean for his reaction to each name in sequence.

Ryan Dean laughed again, bitter and low; the laugh the kind of man might make if he'd just bet his last chip on a turn of a card and lost, just as he had expected. He paused for a moment, visibly putting his thoughts in order and refilling his tumbler to the brim from the open bottle.

"Well, you don't ask for much, do you, Marshal? You sure I can't interest you in a stack of sawbucks instead?"

"Cut the bull."

"Well, it's your party," Dean said resignedly. "Sykes, Sykes is easy. He's the kind of lawman I like."

"Corrupt," Meeks snarled before he could stop himself.

"Weak," Dean countered with a sly smile. "He comes, he takes his cut, he chases some tail, plays the big man, and then he leaves thinking he's doing well. Truth is, I'm nickel and diming him and he doesn't even guess at it. And if I'm doing it to him, I dare say others are, too. Unlike you, Marshal, that fella never met a dollar he didn't like the look of and he's very cheaply bought. Nothing much else to say."

"What about the rest?"

"As for Banks, you mean the missing G-man dontcha?"

Meeks nodded.

"Well, not guilty, if that's what you were wondering." He paused, but plowed on when Meeks didn't so much as blink in response. "I didn't have much to do with the man. Came in the joint once or twice, spoke to me one time, asked a few questions on the Q.T. to the staff and the barflies. Same deal always: trying to get a lead on the Sheldon Gang, some of the…crazier stories around town, same as you are now in fact. Difference is he didn't get very far; everybody he spoke to made him for a fed as soon as he walked in the joint and clammed up. That and he didn't have your…direct approach. I haven't seen hide nor hair of him for weeks. From what I hear, this wasn't the only place he poked his nose in, looking for answers to the wrong kind of questions."

Dean was dancing around something, looking for a cue that Meeks already knew just what he was talking about; the only problem was, Meeks didn't. "Go on. Spill it."

Dean took another strong draw on his whiskey. "Like I say, Marshal, I'm a businessmen, liquor and entertainment, that's all; I don't like gunplay and I don't like trouble in my place if it can be avoided, 'cause it's bad for business, but sometimes you can't get by without trouble finding you. Most times if a man's willing, if he's got some muscle and some dough and the will to use it, trouble can be faced down; it can be beaten down or it can be bribed—I don't have to tell you that. But some kinds of trouble, the bad kind, it don't bend and it don't bribe and it don't break; instead it breaks you—that's the kind of trouble Banks was heading for."

"I'm getting tired of this bull," Meeks growled.

Dean carried on regardless, his voice wavering, "That boy-wonder fed had gone and bitten off a damn sight more than he could chew. Don't ask me what, 'cause I don't know, and I'm not sure I want to, but he'd got the smell of it all over him.

Something unnatural had gotten its claws into him—he was marked. That boy was already in the grave pullin' the dirt down over him and he couldn't see it."

"God damn spook stories," Meeks muttered angrily. "All I've had since I came to this rotten town is God damned spook stories." But behind his challenging tone was the edge of fear, the confrontation of something he didn't want to confront head-on.

"I'm leveling with you, Marshal, like we agreed, but like I said, you might not like the answers, but it don't change what they are."

"Then say what the hell you mean, or so help me I am going to spoil that nice blue suit of yours!" Meeks growled.

"You ever heard of the Legion of Rapture, Marshal?" Dean retorted angrily. "Or the Order of Dagon, or the Hand of Solace—how about them?"

Meeks looked at him coldly, but didn't answer.

"You ain't got a damn clue, no more than Banks had, and you've got about as much chance as he had if you walk that road." Dean shook his head grimly. "Arkham, Dunwich, Innsmouth; all round here, it ain't like the rest of the world. Deep down in the out of the way places, the old places, it's bad, bad like you don't want to know. Like I say, there's trouble a man can get into round these parts that just being a lawman ain't no help against, or being a gangster for that matter; understand? Mad dogs, mad dogs and worse."

Something running in the dark, snarling—dogs? Somebody had shouted that: "Dogs!" But they weren't dogs—one of Sykes's men, open-mouthed, screaming, being snatched...upward?

For a moment Dean's words had put him right back in the night of the raid, and a shock of cold sweat rippled down Meeks's back as he snapped back to reality. He fought to let no sign of his sudden, nightmarish fugue show on his face. But he saw he needn't have bothered as Ryan Dean seemed in equal unquiet reverie himself.

"As for the Sheldon Gang, that's the biggest damn joke of all: there is no Sheldon Gang, not anymore," Dean pronounced, emptying his whiskey tumbler in one last swallow.

"What the hell do you mean?"

"They're gone. Dead and gone, Marshal; scattered, running, whatever's left of them. Months now I haven't had a single one of that crew through these doors, not trying to sell me bad liquor, not trying to fence what they'd stole, not to drink or chase tail or any other damn thing. They've gone."

The human carcass tied to the dead tree trunk with coils of rusted barbed wire like a monstrous scarecrow, its skull emptied, its skin like parchment, the flesh withered. How old? Days? Weeks?

"I don't understand," Meeks muttered, his own voice sounding strange and faraway to him.

Ryan Dean shrugged, as if he didn't really know how to begin. "Let me tell you a story, Marshal, a true story, not some he-said-she-said, 'some guy I know heard it from a guy' bull, but the straight dope. I'll tell you what happened to Blackie Sheldon; he was one of the first, oh, about a year and a half back now."

Meeks cocked his eyebrow in surprise. *A year and a half? Just how long has this been happening? Just how long has this town been sliding into hell?*

"He was Royal Sheldon's youngest cousin," Dean continued. "Backwoods trash like the rest of them, no-account thieves and moonshiners before prohibition came along. But then they get money rolling in. They know the out-of-town roads like the back of their hands, you see, they've got the contacts and the experience, and the ban on hooch was like a gift from heaven for them. Soon they were going up in the world; fast cars, Boston-tailored suits, and ideas above their station like they're gonna be the next Chicago Outfit or something. But they're still just poor, thieving trash on the inside, understand?"

Meeks nodded. He did know the type; they were a breed he was more than familiar with from Colorado to Maine: local rogues and two-bit cutthroats bloated fat on prohibition and the crime wave it had fueled.

"Soon enough Blackie's rolling around Arkham lording it over everybody in silk ties with hundred dollar gold stick-pins and packing pearl-handled pistols, but he's still housebreaking for kicks and stealing autos for strip parts—no imagination." Dean's voice took on a reflective tone, and Meeks realized he wasn't even really talking to him anymore, but caught in remembrance. "Then the stupid sap got to hearing that one of the old, deserted houses on French Hill had treasure hidden in the walls—treasure! Crazy story peddled to him just to make him look a fool for believing it. Well, he fell for it, hook, line, and sinker; reckoned he was the big man now, that he wasn't afraid of the spook stories about the place anyhow, they were just there to frighten off the rubes.

"You know what they call that place? They call it the Witch House. Blackie went missing for days and they found him in there after some old dame walking her dog smelled something awful from outside one morning, a chemical smell she said, like ammonia." Dean swallowed hard; a haunted look had come over him. "I saw the body in the morgue; it looked like somebody had taken a giant ice-cream scoop to his face, and well…scooped it out. Spook stories, who'd believe them?"

It went quiet in the room for a time, neither men speaking.

It was Meeks that finally broke the silence. "What's that got to do with the rest of them?" he growled with a forced distain he didn't truly feel; what he felt instead was fear, fear creeping across him like a cold night descending.

"Nothing…everything, who knows?" Dean offered noncommittally. "Except maybe those backwoods the Sheldons were so well acquainted with got other tenants coming along in the last year or so, and they were a lot worse than bootleggers."

"But the lie keeps going," Meeks said, catching on. "I've heard nothing but them blamed for everything since I've been here."

"Oh yeah, blaming a gang nobody can seem to catch is a lot easier that trying to handle the truth. Even saying it out loud."

"Mad dogs," Meeks replied, and Dean only nodded.

"You know, people keep saying they see lights in the Witch House most nights these days, and nobody goes there, nowhere near, not anymore. I wouldn't go back," Dean said as if to himself.

"Morgan and the woman Daisy Walker?" Meeks pressed, bringing the questions back to saner territory.

Ryan Dean looked at him again directly, sneering something like a smile. "Morgan: the meanest sum'bitch I ever met. Bounty hunter, got a lot of enemies, but I'd think twice before becoming one of them as that seems to have a real short future in it from what I hear. Mixed up in a bad mess a while back out in Kingsport with some lunatic religious group; left most of them dead, so it goes, been hunting the rest of them down ever since. Bang, bang, bang," he said, tapping the table with each faked gunshot. "If you're looking to take him down, I hope you've brought an army with you."

"He around?" Meeks asked.

Dean shrugged. "He comes and he goes; I don't know where he's at right now, but I could maybe find out for the right price. He's another kind of trouble I don't need. I don't know where he stays regularly when he's here, which means it isn't anywhere on my side of town. But I know he's been seen around here and Kingsport since."

Meeks let Dean's offer lie unanswered for the moment. "What about the woman?"

Dean raised his hands. "I got nothing."

He was lying, flat out lying; Meeks knew it in his gut.

Meeks slowly pulled his .38 from its shoulder holster and pulled back the hammer to prime it. "I told you what would happen if you weren't straight with me," he said, and leveled the pistol at Ryan Dean's face.

Dean looked back at him, one of his hands trembling on the table. "You've had your answers, Marshal." His voice was a broken thing.

Meeks paused, the long seconds ticked by. Slowly he eased back the hammer and replaced the service revolver in its holster. There were some lines, he discovered, he was still unable to cross.

"You see or hear anything, *anything*, about Morgan or the Walker woman, you get in touch, because if I hear otherwise, even if I suspect it, I'll tear this place down around you and bury you alive in it."

Dean just nodded slowly and steepled his fingers to stop them trembling.

Meeks got up and left without another word, and at the desk behind him Ryan Dean slumped slowly like a puppet with its strings cut.

Long minutes and another tumbler of whiskey later, Dean picked up the candlestick telephone on his desk and got the operator to put him through to an unlisted number.

"He's been here… No, it was Meeks, the U.S. Marshal… Yes, I told him, like you wanted, now just…just leave me alone."

The line cut into dead air.

Chapter Thirteen

Arkham

December 4, 1929

The little kettle whistled tunelessly as it came to the boil. Harvey Walters went through the small ritual of making coffee almost mechanically, his mind distracted and wandering. It had been a particularly trying day and he had an important decision to make.

He brought back his coffee tray into the sitting room of the little Miskatonic University campus guest house which he had made his home for several years and sighed deeply. The place had been ransacked that day while he lectured and the job had been quite thoroughly done and the results very messy. Books were strewn, papers scattered, pottery smashed, drawers forced, and locks bust open.

Harvey had for many years previously lived something of a rootless existence; he'd jokingly called himself an academic vagrant on many occasions, moving from one post to another, relying on his body of work and his reputation to carry him through the doors of a string of institutions as an invited guest. But still, this place had been his home, or the closest thing to it he'd had for a long time, and the sense of invasion and impotent anger at whoever had done this was palpable and galling. The one consolation he had was that whoever they were they had not found what they were looking for; because it had not been here for them to find.

Nothing had been taken—no money, none of his valuables (such as they were), which combined with recent events made him certain about the matter: this was about Daisy Walker and the broken tablet.

She had been right, of course, right all along. She had said they would come for it and for her; that it was as inevitable as the turning of the seasons. An appointed hour approached and only the broken tablet could tell them exactly when. The attempt by the Legion of Rapture cult to use it at Kingsport had narrowly been averted by her and the gunman Morgan at great personal cost, and even that abortive ritual had ended in utter carnage, madness, and destruction he knew he could barely comprehend. What would happen should they have it in their hands when that true appointed hour came—what Daisy had called the moment "when the stars were right"—would be immeasurably worse. Kingsport had changed her, set her upon a course Harvey could not fully fathom, but he himself had been dragged along in its wake. *No*, he conceded, *that's not right. I could have turned my back on her, on this madness too terrible to believe, and walked away. It has been my choice to stay, to be part of it.*

He had not been privy to the true nature of her plan and he had accepted that. In truth, he'd rather not know it, as it was safer that way both for her and for him, but he and the inner cabal of the university faculty had helped, some more grudgingly than others. They had granted her full and private access to the true restricted collection—not the one the library made available to outsiders (the incident three years ago had shown them all the disastrous naivety of the older practice when they had been one and the same). What she had learned she had shared with no one.

Through his own exhaustive connections and contacts he had been her go-between in tracking down even more, both in written form and in strange artifacts and relics, all to her hidden purposes, all to her plan, and with every day the clock ticking, counting down to what? Armageddon? *Perhaps*.

There had been suspicions that they were being observed, watched, of course. It was not for nothing that Daisy had become a recluse after the Kingsport affair, effectively in hiding; enquiries from reporters and police alike, as well as more dubious characters, had been deflected and rebuffed, and things had seemed to quietened down after a time. It had been the federal agent—*What had been his name? Yes, Banks; that was it*—he had heralded the change, the acceleration of events. That had been three or four weeks ago, just as matters in Arkham, which had been becoming more sinister for months, had begun to get palpably worse. Banks had had a haunted, hunted look to him; his questions had rambled across a dozen different incidents and events of the previous year, the Kingsport disaster as it had been reported in the papers only one of topics he had raised. Harvey had spoken to him in this very room, answered his questions with the vaguest suppositions, his hints of macabre import with the most banal explanations. Satisfied or not, Banks had not returned. After him had come others: strangers spotted hanging around the campus that needed to be rousted off by the staff and night watchmen, suspicious requests for information by strangers with dubious credentials, and all in all a growing dread. And Daisy—Daisy had gone.

Afterward there had been his encounter with Dr. Fields, then another government man, this time a U.S. Marshal, had come and had attempted to bully his way to what he wanted, and it had taken both Harvey and the dean to face him down and send him packing. And now, now there had been this break in—this ransacking. What would they do next, and indeed, who were "they"? The symbol on Dr. Fields's cane he had seen before, he had been right about that, "the Hand of Solace" just another of the fringe religious groups that had sprung up offering hope to the hopeless in hard times. But then, hadn't that been exactly what the so-called "Legion of Rapture" had been as well, at least on the surface? The trappings appeared quite different, as did their promises, and if Daisy was right, after Kingsport the driven, insane members of that strange church had scattered, leaderless and damned. But what if this Hand of Solace were simply another head of the same monstrous hydra? Harvey did not truly know; like so much else, he had only suspicions to go on, and they were enough to keep him awake long into the night with worry.

When Daisy left she had taken a fragment of the tablet with her, and had given the greater part to him to hide; he had been simultaneously pleased by her trust and the responsibility she had given him and terrified of the consequences of it. She had told him that she must be ignorant of where he hid it, just as he would be ignorant of where she herself would be going, except that it would be "out of sight, rather than far away." Whatever her plan was, it required her to be close to Arkham, it seemed.

When he had concealed the tablet, Harvey had believed he had been quite ingenious, but now he wasn't so sure. Whoever was insane enough to want such a thing as the tablet would not stop at mere housebreaking; violence, coercion, murder were all likely their next acts in order to get at it. On reflection, in staying in Arkham and in keeping up a pretense of normality, Harvey Walters now feared he had put not only himself but everybody else at the Miskatonic University in danger, and that he could not continue to do.

You'll have to go, Harvey old boy, he thought ruefully, *and take the bloody thing with you—that's the only thing for it.*

He would go, and go later tonight. As soon as the university library was shut to visitors and the campus had quieted down from the end of the day. He would recover the broken tablet from its hiding place and catch the night train to New York, and just to cover his tracks, leave an entirely misleading letter for the faculty to boot.

His decision made, he found himself suddenly raring to be on his way, but prudence forced him to wait, and after gathering a few things, including a few volumes from his own shelves to reread certain passages, he packed a traveling valise. After all that, through which he'd nervously rushed, Harvey realized he still had more than two hours left to kill. Lost momentarily for something to do, he found himself suddenly very cold, and banked up the fire in his grate, settling down beside it with the dullest book he could find to calm his nerves.

"*A Discourse on Ecclesiastic Architecture in the New England Colonies*," he said aloud, pulling an unremarkable grey quarto from the pile beside the hearth, "that will do nicely."

Outside the neat little red-brick house, black frost crawled like spilled ink up the walls and across the windows, as a thing that cast no shadow watched and waited with inhuman patience.

* * *

The old man looked up as Raker pushed the door open. The store was shadowed and smelled of old leather, tobacco, and paraffin. The old man behind the counter looked up from the paper spread across his counter. Age had curved his shoulders and bent his back, but the brown eyes beneath the white eyebrows gleamed with undimmed intelligence.

"Got some messages for you. I stayed open late, 'case you'd be by," he said without preamble.

Raker glanced around the clutter of the ill-lit drugstore. No one else lurked amongst the stacks of canned goods, coils of rope, and boxes with faded and peeling labels. He walked to the counter and held out his hand for the messages. The edge of the old man's mouth twisted up, and he gave a small, slow shake of his head. "Cash first, friend."

Raker met the old man's steady gaze, and reached into his pocket and peeled a pair of bills from the fold. "You're welcome," he said, as the bills vanished into the old man's hands.

"Two calls for you," said the old man, pulling a folded sheet of paper from a pocket. "One was the paper, the other was a doctor lady." The old man leered, gold winking from amongst the stained yellow of his teeth. "Sounded nice." He held the folded sheet up between two fingers and Raker took the paper without replying.

One was a message from the *Arkham Advertiser*'s back-issue morgue; Raker had paid for a check through their back issues and they had issues for him to review. The second was just an Arkham telephone number and a single line: "Please call Dr. Zabriski." He frowned at the message, then looked up at the old man.

"How much to use your phone?"

The old man grinned and quoted a figure that raised Raker's eyebrows.

"You trying to keep this place quiet, or trying to retire?"

The old man's eyes glittered darkly.

"This place is quiet because this town's finished, if you ask me. Been waitin' for you to come back, but after you've paid me, I'm closin' up and getting a train out, goin' out to my sister's in Connecticut. As my last customer, you get my preferred rate."

Raker ran his tongue across his teeth as he counted out the bills onto the counter. The old man watched him, and then indicated the phone attached to the wall behind the counter. Raker moved behind the counter and took the receiver from its hook. The old man stayed where he was.

"That price included privacy," growled Raker.

The old man snorted, but moved out of sight. Raker watched him go and then turned back to the telephone. The receiver clicked and whined with static, and Raker had to repeat the number to the operator twice before she could understand him. When Dr. Zabriski picked up, he could tell that something was wrong.

"Hello," she said. She sounded strange, disorientated almost.

"It's Raker. I got your message. Has something happened to my cousin?"

"Look, let's not play each other for fools," she replied with a strange flatness. "I don't know who or what you are, but I don't buy that you are related to any of my patients."

Raker paused for a second as the line popped and hissed between them. He was half tempted to smile.

"Okay, you got me. So if you know that, why did you call?"

"I still want to know who the hell you are first."

Raker thought about just telling the truth. He liked Dr. Zabriski from his one meeting with her; she was sharp and seemed to genuinely be trying to help those unfortunate enough to fall into her care, that and she trusted him enough to call even though she knew he was a liar. She deserved the truth, maybe, but he had learned that the truth in this case was a poisonous thing. He let out a long sigh.

"I'm a private eye," he lied. "I was employed to find a girl who went missing here in Arkham a while back. She was mixed up in some fairly strange things." He paused, letting the importance of what he was trying to say sink in, as if this were a confidence he were betraying with her. "Things that most people would not consider sane." He let the last half-lie hang in the phone line's electric crackle.

"Thank you," said Dr. Zabriski quietly.

"So what did you want to tell a liar like me?" he said, trying to sound charming.

"Something tells me you might be the only person who I can talk to freely." She gave a dead-sounding laugh that held nothing of humor. "I tell anyone else and it will be me locked up in here."

"What's happened?" He was almost frightened of the answer.

Dr. Zabriski did not say anything for a time, and a swell of background noise buzzed from the phone.

"I can't say now. It's strange." She paused, and when she spoke again there was a strained, strangled quality to her voice, as if she was speaking words that were not her own. "I'm in the middle of some research right now, but I need somebody to talk it through with me when I'm done, but I don't want to talk about it here, not now. Not in Arkham." Raker was about to reply when he heard voices in the background on her end of the line, another woman calling her name, and when the doctor spoke, she sounded herself again, sure and authoritative, the woman who knew her own mind and whose judgments, once made, were certain. "Say we meet over the weekend, Saturday next, that should give me enough time," hissed Dr. Zabriski in a quick whisper, "at the Kingsport train station, midday."

He was about to reply when the line went dead. He looked at the receiver for a long moment before replacing it on its cradle. Something in Dr. Zabriski's voice had made ice roll across his skin, and the whole deal seemed off to him; first an urgent call, then a delay nearly a week long before she wanted to meet with him—it just didn't add up, but really, what choice did he have? Storm into her office and demand she speak to him? He doubted that would get him far, even without the small matter of the asylum's brick walls, locks, and burly orderlies to contend with. The game was the game, and he'd play along for now, besides which he had legwork to do in the meantime. If he was lucky, he'd find what he was after without meeting the young doctor out of town, or without having to drag her further into this mess. *Not that I believe in luck anymore*, he thought sourly, *except the bad kind.*

He looked up as the shopkeeper appeared again.

"Anything else I can get you?" asked the old man.

Raker shook his head, turned toward the door, then paused. He thought of the black and chrome car gliding past in the rain, and the impression of a pale, watching face behind the darkened glass, the near-riot he'd seen earlier and the blood on the sidewalk. The shop keeper grinned at Raker when he turned back.

"You got a gun?" he asked as calmly as if he had enquired about a packet of smokes.

The old man's grin faded and anger clouded his face.

"I ain't got a license to sell things like that," said the old man in a low, hard-edged voice.

Raker stepped back to the counter, pulled out his fold of bills, and began to peel off ten dollar bank notes.

"Place like this, man like you; I am guessing you keep something near at hand just in case." The old man's gaze wavered as Raker put the bills on the countertop in front of him. "Not much need for an equalizer anymore if you're shutting up for good."

The storekeeper reached for the cash and Raker's hand clamped over the old man's wrist before his hand could close. Their eyes met. For a second Raker thought the old man was going to spit in his face, and then he looked down and nodded.

Raker let go of his wrist. The old man reached under the counter and brought up a scattergun. It was clearly old, but the sawn-off side-by-side shotgun barrels looked oiled, and the cut-off grip looked worn like it had seen some use. Raker took it from the old man's hands before he could get any ideas. He broke open the breach and checked the barrels were clear, snapped it shut again, then cocked and dry-fired the hammers.

The old man looked at this pantomime with bland indifference.

"Shells?" said Raker. The old man bent down and brought up a ripped cardboard carton. Raker emptied the handful of mismatched cartridges into his jacket pocket before wrapping the gun in a dishcloth from a nearby shelf and folding it under his jacket.

"Thanks," Raker said without sincerity, and turned toward the door.

Behind him, the old man scooped the cash off the counter. Raker was at the door when the old man spoke. "Free advice, friend." Raker turned to look at him. The old man was sneering, gold teeth and pale skin making him look like the leering skull of a dried-out corpse. "It won't help you. Not guns, not money." The old man seemed to be gloating somehow. "My family's been around these parts a long time, so I know, but it's never been as bad as this before; this is the end."

Raker gave a tired smile. "I know," he said, and stepped out into the gathering gloom.

* * *

The little clock tower on the Liberal Arts building chimed out nine strokes of its bell across the eerily quiet campus. Harvey Walters huffed his way at a brisk pace across the central courtyard of Miskatonic University toward the library building. The mists that had been temporarily banished by the storm and the rains had been edging back all day and now darkness had fallen they had thickened again, deadening sound and blurring the borders of sight. Harvey knew this was the best time for what he wanted to do; an hour after the library would have been completely shut up and an hour before the night watchmen started their rounds of the university buildings. The fact he had carte blanche from the higher faculty to go where he wished without questions from the night watchmen was neither here nor there; he wanted nobody to know what he was doing tonight.

The electric campus lampposts, an addition of recent years, seemed low and hazy, their sodium-yellow glares struggling against the wispy darkness. It was cold enough for Harvey's breath to paint the air before him as he walked. Suspecting that the weather would be foul one way or another, he had dressed accordingly in a heavy Chesterfield coat and a pair of knitted woolen gloves he'd had for so long he'd utterly forgotten where he'd acquired them. He had a leather satchel slung crosswise over his shoulder and a stout walking stick tucked under his arm. The walking stick had been a concession to self-defense, although he felt vaguely foolish for carrying it as such.

The dark bulk of the library building loomed spectrally out of the night mist and Harvey cut sideways, taking a path around one of the neatly trimmed ornamental hedges and toward one of the side entrances.

The heavy, cold silence weighed on him and he felt partly foolish, partly frightened and wholly out of his depth. *You're too old for these capers, Harvey, too old and too ordinary. What on earth are you doing out here in the middle of the night like a spy in a cheap novel?* he asked himself pointedly, but his step didn't falter.

He reached the side door and looked around but could see nothing; for the chill air and gathering fog turning the darkness grey-white, he might have been the only man in the world. He drew his duplicate key from his coat pocket and went to the door, realizing just as he reached out with the large iron key that the chink of light at the edge of the doorframe was larger than it should be, that and that there should be no light at all. Tentatively he reached out with the key and prodded the heavy door.

Slowly it moved inward a fraction of an inch, but it was enough to be sure; it was already unlocked and left ajar.

The fear that he felt at that moment was genuine and unexpected; it was a visceral thing, a sudden pounding of his heart and an almost physical need to run quite alien to him. The entire matter frightened him, of course—what was happening in Arkham so much as he pretended to understand it, the thing he had been asked to hide and those that were after it—but up to now that had been a different kind of dread, almost abstract, spiritual even. This was much more immediate; it was the unaccustomed fear of deliberate harm, of pain and of death.

Harvey took a deep, icy breath. *Calm down, old boy, let's see this thing through.* He took hold of his walking stick by its base, brandished it somewhat self-consciously, and pushed open the door as slowly and quietly as he could. There was nobody waiting for him on the other side, no brigand or monster, just the empty foyer and the corridor beyond. *Monster, now there's a thought. What should I do if I actually meet a monster? I'm an old man with a walking stick, not Beowulf.*

He pushed the door closed behind him, but from some instinct did not shut or lock it, and then advanced cautiously into the library. He paused frequently and listened but heard nothing, sensed no movement; the silence was utterly oppressive and the air still. The electric lights in the side corridor he had come through had been left on, and as he slowly turned through an archway into the library's main open floor he saw that one of the large bar lamps on the check-in desk had also been left on, creating a pool of light around the lamps and spreading the dim edges of their radiance across the high-ceilinged chamber to where it was swallowed in the darkness of the stacks and bookcases. The light reached the two floors of mezzanine not at all. Harvey waited there cautiously for a moment, his eyes straining at the darkness at the edge of sight, his ears alert to anything that might betray the presence of another in the vaulted library. Aside from the pale mist curling slowly beyond the high arched windows there was no movement, and aside from the beating of his heart there was no sound.

Willing his legs to move he began to cross the open reading area at the center of the room and walk toward the check-in desk as briskly as he could, reasoning that the quicker he was done and gone the better, regardless of why the door had been left open or whether or not there was somebody still here. *Occam's razor: the simplest explanation is that somebody just left the lights on, and one of the staff left by the side door and didn't lock it, perhaps expecting somebody else to follow behind them.* But it sounded pretty thin reasoning indeed.

"Professor Walters," a voice called out calmly from above.

Bugger Occam, Harvey thought sourly, and turned as calmly as he could to look up toward the voice. "Hello, who's that?" he called.

"Please stay where you are, Professor Walters, I'm coming down." It was a woman's voice; the speaker sounded young but very certain of herself, and the diction had something of Long Island in it, he thought. It was not a voice he recognized.

There were quiet steps on one of the small spiral staircases that led down from the stacks on the next floor.

Harvey did not quite know what he was expecting, but the girl who almost seemed to materialize out of the darkness at the foot of the staircase wasn't it. She was slight, no more than five feet tall, and could not be more that twenty-one years of age. She had a pinched, freckled face and copper-red hair cut in a fashionable bob. She was wearing a demure, dark woolen dress, and had a book satchel of her own slung over one shoulder. She was a student then, not one of his but vaguely familiar from around the campus, although he could not place a name to go with the face; Harvey felt suddenly very foolish, particularly as he realized he was brandishing his walking stick across his chest. He lowered the stick immediately and actually felt himself blushing under his whiskers.

"You gave me quite a start, young lady. I'm afraid the library is off-limits to students after hours. You really shouldn't be here, you know."

She smirked; it was an ugly expression and it turned her face into something unwholesome to look upon. "You stupid old man," she laughed, and reached into her satchel. She withdrew a heavy stub-nosed revolver from the bag and leveled it at him. The gun looked almost absurdly large to him grasped in her two small hands, like something from a cartoon drawing, but the sound of the hammer being pulled back had a grim and very real finality to it.

Now the danger had become a real and tangible thing to him, a calm settled over Harvey. "This is a very serious matter, young lady. Are you sure you know what it is you are doing?" he said levelly and without threat.

She spat another laugh at him. "Of course it's serious, this is a real gun, you fool, and I really will use it to blow bloody great holes in you if you don't cooperate with us."

"That wasn't what I meant," he replied, and then the penny dropped. *Us, she said "us."*

"It's fortunate that you came, it will save us a lot of trouble and time, you being here."

"I'm not going to help you."

Her face twitched at his words, and the gun shook in her hands for a moment.

She wants to kill me, she's shivering with rage, he realized with a surreal shock. *She actually wants to kill me, but she can't yet; she needs me to find the broken tablet—they haven't got it yet!*

"Drop the stick and get over by the desk," she snarled.

Harvey's heart skipped a beat. Did she know where it was, that it was within a dozen paces of them both right now? She couldn't, surely?

Harvey slowly did as he was told, the walking stick clattering to the floor as he back-stepped away from her and toward the desk.

Three figures walked out into the library from the same side corridor Harvey had entered by, and the door left ajar made a sudden, sickening sense to him. *Why didn't I lock it behind me?* he admonished himself. *Because you wanted to be able to make a quick getaway, and she'd still have been here,* he answered himself just as quickly.

Two of the men looked like they were trying to maintain at least a facade of respectability: rumpled overcoats and mismatched suits, one was youngish and blond with day-old stubble and hard eyes, and the other was middle-aged and balding with an ugly burn-scar on the side of his head. Both carried crowbars like they were weapons and they did not speak. The third figure was the strangest and Harvey felt a feeling of dread coming off him in waves. He wore a long, ragged leather duster over what appeared to be a thick, grey robe, the hood of which was pulled up over his head like a monk's cowl, completely losing his face in the blackness of its recess. He carried no weapons, but Harvey could see his hands and fingers were swathed in dirty bandages, except where long, blackened fingernails jutted out like a bird's talons.

"What do you want?" Harvey asked as firmly as he could, swallowing back the fear he felt as the hooded man advanced on him.

"You know what we want." The voice that came from beneath the cowl was like wind-scattered gravel across a tomb stone, without accent and inhuman. "We want what she left here. I can feel it is close, the Exile's stone… Give it to us."

"I don't know what you mean," Harvey managed as his back contacted the check-in desk; he hadn't been aware he was still backpedalling away from them.

There came a dry, rattling sound from beneath the hood and Harvey realized with a start that it was laughter. The black-nailed fingers reached up and pulled back the cowl.

"Oh my," Harvey heard himself whisper.

In outline the thing's head suggested a human skull, something left to parch and dry in a desert; the eyes sunken deep in the sockets were points of amber swimming in darkness. Its grin was a lipless, skinned-jackal snout filled with jagged, broken teeth.

"It's in the restricted collection," Harvey lied, "on the third floor, behind the vault door, just don't hurt me."

The skull-faced thing roared in anger.

"Liar!" the girl shrieked at him from one side. "The giver has told us there is nothing there but tatters and counterfeits!"

His head snapped around toward her, and he looked down the looming barrel of the revolver, mere inches from his face. On her hand was a signet ring, unnoticed before but now hideously clear, the symbol engraved on it was of two hands clasped together.

"Fields," he gasped. "Fields was here earlier; you're with him!"

"Give it to us!" the girl screamed, pushing the gun at him.

"No," he said, and lunged forward at her. She was too close to react to his sudden charge and he cannoned into her.

The girl fell, the gunshot exploded like thunder, the skull-faced ghoul howled in pain. Harvey staggered on, his ears ringing painfully. With one hand he pulled himself round the side of the check-in desk and lashed out with his arm, sending the solitary lamp crashing to the floor. As the green shade shattered, the library was plunged into darkness.

Harvey ran on blindly into the darkness, painfully grazing his elbow on the edge of a bookcase. Behind him were shouts of confusion and a bestial roar that ended with the sound of wood splintering. With his hand on one of the bookcases to his left, Harvey ran on blindly, panting, his heart hammering in his chest. He turned and turned again, trying to make a random pattern in the darkness to shake off pursuit without actually doubling back on himself.

"Find him! Take him!" the inhuman voice howled somewhere in the blackness.

There were running footsteps, the overhead lights came on, flared, flickered, died, then came on again but very dimly, turning the library into a twilight shadow play. Harvey was glad of it, for he'd already bashed and scraped himself a dozen times in mere seconds, and he knew he could not have gone much further without nearly killing himself in the dark.

"It's here!" the thing snarled away in the shadows. "I can smell it!" and again the sound of raking impacts and splintering wood came.

He's tearing apart the check-in desk! Harvey thought wildly. *But he won't find it there!*

Running footsteps thudded somewhere nearby, but it was impossible to tell how close. Somewhere there was the dull, heavy thud of a bookcase toppling over and the flutter of papers flying through the air. Harvey tried to get his bearings, but he couldn't fathom just where he was. He'd walked around this library hundreds of times but his panicked memory refused him. *Where am I? Where is the nearest way out?* He forced himself to breathe calmly, focused his thoughts, and did his best to ignore the staccato of footsteps, the inhuman snarls.

Philology! He blinked, catching sight of the brass plate on a nearby shelf. He knew where he was, not far from the stairs to the rotunda. If he could make it there, he could make it to the upstairs offices, shut himself in; there were telephones—he could call for help. Harvey was suddenly aware of how cold he felt. *Am I going into shock?* he thought, but then realized that his breath was frosting the air again as it had done outside. *How is it so cold in here?*

Harvey turned just as the scar-faced man rounded the end of the corridor of bookcases. The ragged man grinned savagely and slammed the crowbar into the bookcase to his right, scattering volumes explosively. Harvey knew running was useless, he was already exhausted. *And too damn old*, he thought bitterly. Harvey stood his ground as the grinning man came at him; he raised his hands up to fight, but never had a chance. The first blow was a sideswipe that sent him sprawling sideways, moaning in pain as the back of the steel crowbar caught his shoulder. The second missed his head by a fraction of an inch as Harvey slid down the face of the bookcase to the left of where he had been standing.

Clasping his arm against the pain, Harvey looked up at the scarred man towering above him, expecting death to fall on him at any moment. *I will not look away; I will not give him the satisfaction.*

The scarred man twitched and shivered. The crowbar tumbled from his limp hand and clanged dully on the polished wooden floor. Harvey saw that his eyes were bulging from his sockets, and stared open mouth as just below his sternum his shirt seemed to push forward and then retract, and a heavy dark stain quickly spread outward. The scarred man sagged to one side and began to fall in slow motion, and it was only then that Harvey realized somebody was standing behind him, gripping the back of his coat, and slowing the scarred man's descent to lay his corpse on the floor.

The man was revealed to be a lean, dark figure with a face too hard to be called handsome, dressed in a black topcoat and vest over a white wing-collar shirt open at the neck. In his hand was a bayonet knife with a foot-long blade which he wiped perfunctorily on the dead man's coat.

"Upon my soul," Harvey breathed with a gasp of startled recognition. "Mr. Morgan!"

Tony Morgan raised a finger to his mouth to indicate silence. "Quiet, Professor," he breathed barely above a whisper, his words misting the chill air in front of his lean face. "I have a feeling this situation is about to get a whole lot worse."

"What do you mean?" Harvey whispered, and Morgan reached down and helped him to his feet.

As if in explanation, Morgan blew out a long streamer of fogged breath. "Something else is already here, something very unpleasant, and very dangerous."

Harvey leaned on the bookcase wall for a moment, regaining his breath. The pain in his shoulder had settled into a nasty, dull throbbing like a toothache, but when he tried he found to his relief he could still move his elbow and fingers without making it worse.

"One of them wasn't…wasn't human. His face—like something from a medieval woodcut of Hell," Harvey struggled to explain. "He was tearing the counter apart, looking for it."

Morgan slid the knife into a scabbard under his coat and took a night-black Colt automatic from his shoulder holster; it barely made a sound as he worked the slide. "You mean that fragments are here? And no, I don't think that ghoul, or whatever he is, is why the temperature's dropping like a stone," he whispered harshly at Harvey.

"Par-part of it. I thought you knew? I thought that was why you were here?" Harvey asked, suddenly confused.

"No time," Morgan shot back. "Where is it?"

The footsteps were getting more frantic, another bookcase toppled somewhere, and the growls had subsided to a vicious low whining.

"On-on the wall." It really was getting very cold now. Harvey's teeth were starting to chatter. "Be-behind the library reception desk there are three bronze busts—they're hollow. The one on the left, Hawthorne, it-it's inside."

"You've got to be kidding me," Morgan muttered.

Somewhere in the library glass shattered and a woman's voice cried out in alarm. A gun boomed three times in rapid succession and the woman screamed—and was abruptly silenced.

Morgan and Harvey exchanged glances, the import clear: whatever had just happened, it had nothing to do with them.

"Come on," Morgan whispered, starting toward the center of the library, pistol raised with Harvey following unsteadily behind.

The air was so cold and still now that tethers of mist had begun to drift across the floor of the library, lending it an even more macabre and surreal aspect.

"Do we have a plan?" Harvey whispered at Morgan's elbow.

"We move quickly, I distract them, you get the fragments; can you do that?"

Harvey swallowed reflexively. "Well, I ca-can try."

"Well, you're a game old bird, I'll give you that," Morgan replied, then quickly held up his hand for silence. They'd reached the end of the row of bookcases where it came to the central reading area, at the far side of which was the library check-in desk, its mahogany boards looking now like somebody had let off a stick of dynamite near them. Harvey was surprised that he had managed to run so far from where he had started, almost in a complete circle around the ground floor of the library, but the tableau that greeted him now was not the one he had expected. It was deserted, there was no sign of the skull-faced ghoul, the young woman, or the other ragged man, but descending down the spiral stair from the mezzanine above was another, unfamiliar figure.

If Dr. Fields's men had been ragged, then this poor fellow was truly destitute: an old, dirt-slicked raincoat hung off his thin frame in tatters, showing pale, emaciated flesh through rents at the shoulders and across the chest; his face seemed bloated, almost puffy, however, and the halo of unkempt hair that surrounded his head was matted and filthy. But it was his eyes that arrested Harvey and caused his heart to skip: they were white—not the white of some blindnesses he had seen, but shining like pearls in the moonlight, shining cold. The figure stepped off the stairs and with a clattering series of thuds something fell out behind him; it was the body of the red-headed girl, her limbs and head at unnatural and sickening angles to her body.

Harvey gasped out loud, and the cold, pale figure turned to face them and began to walk unhurriedly forward. With horrified fascination Harvey stood paralyzed watching the hoarfrost glitter on its skin as it walked through one of the dim pools of electric light cast by the overhead lamps.

It opened its mouth as if to speak. Morgan stepped forward and shot it point-blank in the face. The back of the pale man's head came apart like clotted mud and it staggered three steps backward and righted itself. Morgan paced forward and fired four times directly into its chest, toppling it onto its back, the reports of the .45 deafeningly loud in the echoing library.

The pale figure's arms shot out at right angles, fingers digging like coffin nails into the floorboards, its elbows bending back as if hinged the wrong way, and then it began to slowly haul itself back up. Morgan stepped over it and emptied his pistol into the spindle-limbed creature, the heavy bullets splintering one arm and crashing it back to the ground where it immediately began to crawl on its side, undulating like a worm.

Harvey looked on aghast, utterly unable to comprehend the horror he was witnessing, as the bones of the pale thing, no longer remotely human, seemed to elongate with a series of wet snapping sounds, and inky black smoke started to stream from its wounds, coiling like serpents.

Morgan stepped four paces back, ejected his spent magazine, and slammed a fresh one home into the Colt. "Move, Walters!" he growled, never taking his eyes off the nightmare thing crawling across the floor between them.

Harvey snapped to his senses and began to run round the reading tables toward the librarian's station, keeping a wide berth between himself and the shuddering, twisting pile of flesh on the floor. The air now so cold it felt like needles in his lungs, with clarity it came to him in that moment that the creature was drawing off all of the warmth, the life even from everything around it, and somehow consuming it like fuel, fuel for the change into whatever terrible thing it was becoming.

He made it to the splintered wooden mass of the check-in desk and threw his head backward at the sound of a grating roar echoing through the frigid air. Skull-face leapt from the top of the library stacks, talon fingers raking the air as he plunged, leather coattails flapping, toward Morgan. Primed by some hard-won instinct of life of battle, Morgan was already turning as the ghoul sprang, the Colt snapping up and firing wild as he threw himself to one side. The taloned fingers missed their mark by inches, shredding the hem of Morgan's jacket, and the jagged broken-glass teeth snapped shut on empty air. Lithe as a panther the beast sprang up from its hands and scissored a kick at Morgan's back before he could recover, crashing the bounty hunter over a reading desk and to the ground, sending his pistol spinning off across the polished wooden floor.

Harvey was torn for a moment between what he was meant to do and going back to help the man who had saved his life only a few moments before. Words and half-formed memories of scraps of lore and mythology tumbled through the professor's head as he shouted, "Dog, jackal, curs'd get! Hated of Ra and Tsathoggua! Worm of the Earth! Here!"

The skull-faced thing spun on its heels, the fog of cold air enwrapping it spiraling away at the speed of its movement. It lowered its scabrous head and fixed Harvey with its pit-like eyes with their blazing amber points.

"You would bait me, old man?" the terrible voice rattled as a long purple-black tongue lolled out from between its dripping teeth. "I will smother you with grave dirt and plant maggots in your belly to eat you alive!"

Harvey blanched and took a step back, falling over backward and landing painfully amid the wreckage of the check-in desk as something glittering blackly like a winter moon shadow on a fathomless lake rose from the white fog behind the ghoul. A flickering multitude of tenebrous wings unfurled from a shimmering black coil of a body, topped with a fungous mask of writhing fronds like some feeder of the deeps.

Skull-face turned, and the shadow thing spat a gushing stream of hoarfrost and ink which engulfed the ghoul, who reeled back, spasming soundlessly as its head and shoulders half-dissolved, half-crumbled and the steaming wreck of what it had been collapsed, still jerking, to the floor.

Harvey's world greyed and faded. He was dimly aware that he was on his back, helpless as the thing blotted out the world above him. There was a sound like hissing fire and breaking ice and the distant rumble of thunder.

Harvey Walters awoke to a burning, stinging heat in his mouth and his eyes watering. He sputtered as the haggard-looking Morgan who was kneeling beside him took the little silver flask away from his mouth.

"A little whiskey to bring you round. Can you stand?"

All of Harvey's aches and pains, and they were not inconsiderable, came back to him at once, and he winced but answered, "I think so if you can help me up. I think I fainted, oh my, oh my…," he began as the realization of what had just happened flooded back to him.

"Easy, Professor, stay with me," Morgan said sternly as he pulled Harvey to his feet.

"What happened?"

Morgan sighed and pointed behind him, making Harvey turn. "We lost," he answered simply.

The wall behind the librarian's station was a blistered and fractured mess of scorched plaster and withered bronze.

"It took the tablet fragments! No!" Harvey said grief-stricken.

"Yes, it did. Then flew straight up and smashed through the windows and was gone. I put five more bullets in it and it didn't care a damn. I am getting bloody tired of things that just won't die when you shoot them," Morgan replied bitterly. "One of the men got away, I think, took off during the commotion; the others, however, are very dead."

Harvey looked round the library and took stock. "I'll have to call the Dean of the Medical School, get the night watchmen to take the cadavers there, seal this off, and get it cleaned up. We'll say it was storm damage, or an accidental fire, and shut the library while it's repaired. We will be believed; nobody wants an irrational explanation, particularly not in the current times."

Morgan gave him an appraising look. "Are you serious, Professor?"

"Oh, yes," Harvey said with a troubled expression. "I'm afraid this won't be the first terrible thing the faculty has had to deal with without causing…undue disturbance."

Morgan arched an eyebrow but let the comment pass. "I'm

not sure it will matter. Whatever that monster was, whoever it served, they have the fragment now—and that means I'm not sure anything matters anymore."

Harvey made the decision to sit before he fell down, righting a toppled chair and dropping heavily. "Perhaps…perhaps not," he said cagily, never feeling more his years than he had at that moment. "The fragments here were incomplete, and there is another part that Daisy took with her. Besides…" Harvey's voice trailed off and he looked very unsure for a moment.

"Besides what?" Morgan pressed; he could almost see the wheels turning in the older man's mind.

"I'm not sure," Harvey replied uncertainly, "perhaps nothing. But I fear that it is not all over at all. I fear it's still just beginning. Beginning at last."

Morgan just shook his head wearily. "Make your call, Professor, and let's get out of here. It's too damn cold in here and we need to talk."

Harvey merely nodded.

"What's more," Morgan muttered, flexing his shoulder painfully, "we could both do with a proper drink."

Chapter Fourteen

Arkham

December 5, 1929

Raker sighed and rubbed his eyes. Night had crowded into the attic offices above the *Arkham Advertiser*, reducing Raker's world to the sphere of light cast by the hooded reading lamp over the battered desk at which he sat. The dry leaves of paper lay in drifts around him. There were issues going back over two years, each one picked out for him thanks to a hefty payment to the *Advertiser*'s archivist, a grey man named Soamcroft who seemed utterly oblivious of anything outside of his shut-in world of yellowing proofs and copy-files.

Raker had spent hours picking through each issue, reading everything from front page news to obituaries. As local news-rags went, the *Arkham Advertiser* was a curious mix of the deeply parochial and the wildly sensationalist. As he rubbed his hands across his eyelids, the headlines of articles spread months apart drifted through his mind:

METEORITE SPOTTED ON BLASTED HEATH!

MYSTERY MURDERER AT LARGE—CITIZENS URGED TO LOCK DOORS

POLICE STEP UP PATROLS IN NORTHSIDE!

BIZARRE DREAMS PLAGUE CITIZENS!

THREE YEARS AFTER DEADLY DUNWICH DISASTER, HEIR CLAIMS WHATELEY INHERITANCE

HUNTER MISSING IN ARKHAM WOODS—FOUL PLAY SUSPECTED

FISH DEAD IN RIVER—CAUSE UNKNOWN

ILL WIND GRIPS ARKHAM!

The purple prose too wild to be more than scoffed at by anybody who didn't know better, here it was slapped in next to reports of the town council meetings, weather reports, local trivia, and banal, out-of-date, copy-culled national stories from the wire services. It was in the back pages the real stories crept in: death notices and suicide inquests, waves of funerals and sudden estate sales, and worst perhaps of all, in wrenching little appeals privately lodged for missing loved ones to come forward and be found, but these were swamped and buried by the garish and the mundane. Accustomed to a diet of "news" like that it was no wonder that the people of Arkham just carried on while it all fell apart around them, like the boy crying wolf too many times, the newspaper could be safely ignored.

He opened his eyes, reached out to take a gulp of coffee, and made a face when he found it was stone cold in the cup. He had reviewed perhaps half of the issues provided, but already he had a feeling that they would provide few answers; the truth was so buried that it would take a wiser man to exhume it. He had found a few stories, a few vague references, which related to the Hand of Solace, enough to confirm that they had survived the loss of their master. Nowhere could he find anything about Stonegroves, the Bradburys, or the atrocity that had happened there this past summer. Just as everywhere else, it was as if the places and people involved had never existed, as if the tides of time had swept the shore clean of their footprints.

He had known that he would not find anything, but the reality hung around his head like a leaden weight. He thought of Shawcross's promise to return Vivian to existence and life. Was it possible? And if it was, would Shawcross honor his word? Most likely not, but if there was even the thinnest hope, he had to follow it. He had run from Stonegroves as it collapsed into a vortex, dragged into the beyond, and he had woken in a world he did not know, a world where the only thing that had made him feel like a better person had never existed, and the comfort of old delusions could not exist either.

What choice do I have? he thought. And what if it was true? What if he could get what Shawcross wanted? What if the strange man had the means to deliver on his promise? Raker had seen enough to know that the boundaries of possibility lay well beyond what most would consider sanity. *This is the hope I am reduced to?* Did the Hand of Solace believe something so different? Perhaps they had not; perhaps they had felt the same dread as the question coiled around their dreams: *What if the impossible is possible?* He shook himself and turned back to the paper spread out in front of him.

TRAGIC DEATHS AS FREAK STORM LEADS TO COASTAL COLLAPSE

The headline was proclaiming above a densely printed article and a picture of a tangled spill of blackened debris lapped by waves at the base of a cliff. This was the unpleasant incident out at Kingsport that Sarah had alluded to. It had only been covered in one issue but it had not been difficult to find. Kingsport, no more than a name on a road map to him before, and here it was twice in one day: first Sarah and then Dr. Zabriski; it seemed just too much of a coincidence.

The "tragedy" had apparently been a violent storm that had caused a coastal landslide killing an unknown number of people belonging to a small "traveling religious congregation" known as the Legion of Rapture. The congregation had been encamped on the coast during the storm. The Lighthouse Inn, a local landmark of note according to the article, had also suffered storm damage which caused a gas leak and explosive fire. A number of people had died here as well, including New York socialite Miss Annabel Ryan and the Inn's night manager. Daisy Walker was not mentioned until near the end of the article and then just as a survivor from the fire at the hotel who just happened to be an Arkham local (and therefore of interest to the *Advertiser*), who was now recovering from shock and smoke inhalation. Of the man Morgan, there was no mention at all.

Raker did not buy it; the whole story was riddled with details that did not add up or seem to make sense. No attempt had been made to try and explain why the Legion of Rapture was camped on the coast, or who they were, much less how the apparent hurricane level of damage had seemingly been confined to two very specific locations in the seaside town. It just didn't bear up to scrutiny; Raker had come across press smoke screens before and this read like one thought up by someone in a hurry. Had this "Legion of Rapture" and the Hand of Solace been somehow one and the same, something different entirely, or maybe rival groups even? There were just too many questions and no clear answers.

He rubbed his eyes again and flicked the next paper onto the pile. Outside the windows of the newspaper building, he could see the fog curling up in the night air and sighed, not looking forward to the road trip home. He would be lucky to be done by midnight. What's more, he couldn't shake the feeling there was something important staring him in the face, and yet he just wasn't seeing it.

* * *

The ragged man fled in terror through the dark, the night fog rising up around him like the windings of a funeral shroud. Running, stumbling, falling, the dark shapes of the university buildings were lost behind him, yet the dim lights of the town seemed too distant, like phantoms, never closer despite how far or fast he ran.

Something shrieked high in the black skies above him and turned his blood to ice and he threw himself on the sodden ground in panic, whimpering.

"Well, this is a very poor show, I must say," a voice mocked him.

The ragged man started in terror, looking frantically around into the fog, but the voice had seemed to come from everywhere at once.

"Cowardly little man left before the main show, Mr. Fetch," the voice continued. "Didn't even see anything useful to take back to dear Dr. Fields."

The ragged man scrambled to his feet and tried to run, but got no more than a few steps when an arm like a battering ram shot out of the dark fog and smashed him onto his back. He lay there helpless, his lungs filing with blood from his shattered ribs.

A shape still wearing the face of the dead prohibition agent, Sykes, reared up out of the fog above him. "Still, don't worry, I'll make sure you have a few interesting stories to tell."

* * *

Harvey Walters looked down at the half-eaten basket of fried chicken in front of him and sighed. It wasn't that it wasn't any good, in fact he'd been quite surprised given their surroundings just how good the food here was, or even that a notorious speakeasy served it, but he found he had very little appetite after the evening's horrors and stresses. Instead he reached across the table for his glass of supposed brandy, flinching when a sudden stab of pain from his upper arm caught him by surprise.

"How's the shoulder, Professor?" Morgan asked, looking up from his own basket of little bones.

"Oh, not too bad," Harvey demurred. "I shall have a bruise the size of a dinner plate in the morning, I fear, but Dr. Stanton said the bone was unbroken, for which I am very grateful."

"Very lucky, but you've got some grit as well," Morgan replied, considering the older man closely. "I've seen younger men deal worse with the kind of shocks you've had tonight."

Harvey shrugged self-consciously under Morgan's questioning gaze. "Well, I don't know about that."

Morgan reached for his own drink and started the conversation that Harvey knew they had been deferring for the last several hours while the mess in the aftermath of the nightmare at the library had been dealt with and they'd driven off into the Arkham night. They'd ended up here at Hibb's Roadhouse, sat not in some smoke-filled basement as Harvey had expected, but in a booth off the main floor where slow jazz oozed over the room, and he could see a score of other people seated at tables or slouched against the bar, all lost in their own concerns. It was a dose of normality for which Harvey Walters was profoundly grateful.

"Those…things tonight? Is it the first time you've seen something like that?" Morgan asked.

"Outside the pages of some old worm-eaten book I once had the luxury of believing were some fabrication of medieval superstition? Yes, yes it was. But before now I've seen the aftermath,

I suppose you'd say, the consequences of them more than once. Enough to convince me that such things were real in the literal sense. Even though I won't pretend to understand what they truly are."

"But Daisy does, doesn't she?"

"Yes," Harvey said, his heart heavy in his chest, "yes, I think she does, at least more than you or I, or even old Armitage, more than any of us."

Morgan looked at him questioningly, and Harvey continued, "Oh, before any of this mess really began, Armitage and the university was mixed up in an affair that brushed against, well, something as bad or worse than what we have on our hands now. They beat it by the skin of their teeth, but it ruined his health and he and his wife moved away to convalesce not long after. It was as a result of that horror that Daisy Walker first came into contact with…I'm still not sure what to call them—the outside forces—in dealing with the aftermath along with me and several others from the university faculty. But we all underestimated the poison these things, these events, seem to leave lingering in the world around them when they pass. We were colossally naive, us grey-haired wise men, and Daisy suffered the consequences." Harvey saw the look of intent interest on Morgan's hard features. "She never told you?"

"No," Morgan said gravely. "I'd never met her before Kingsport. And while we've had dealings since, I'd hardly call us friends, not in that way. I'd come at the whole matter from a different angle. I was sent after her friend, Annabel, and those damned fragments, and walked into this whole nightmare business of monsters, walking corpses, magic—if you can call it that—and all."

Harvey nodded. He'd considered Morgan something of a paradox since first meeting him not long after the tragic massacre at

Kingsport; he was clearly a ruthless man of violence—more than that, he was a killer. But he was also clever, clearly educated, and formidably self-possessed, facts which had no doubt contributed to making him extremely dangerous. He also gave very little away of what went on behind those cold eyes of his. Harvey had already realized that in the aftermath of what had occurred he had no option but to trust Morgan, trust his intent to be the defeat of the dark forces that circled them all, regardless of the price of such a victory. It was a price that Harvey feared would be very high indeed.

"This is very important. I know you want some answers, Mr. Morgan, about what happened this evening and what has been happening ever since you got involved in this ungodly mess. You want to know where Daisy is, and who or what has taken the fragments and to what purpose, but first I'd like you to answer some questions for me if you would, fill in the blanks for me, so to speak, things you know that I may not. Could you do that for me? And then I will tell you what I know, or at least what I have come to surmise."

Morgan agreed, and at his prompting told the professor the story of his involvement from beginning to end. He told him of his imprisonment after a shoot-out gone bad in New York, and of the strings the mysterious Shawcross of Copperhead Industries had pulled to set him on the trail of a missing artifact of great value to him. He spoke of his tracking down of Daisy's friend Annabel Ryan and her own pursuit of her missing lover, Maxwell Cormac, the thief who had stolen the fragments in the first place, and the vortex of madness and death they had drawn after them in their wake. The whole affair had turned out to be lie woven upon murderous lie, a plot set into motion by a doomsday cult, the Legion of Rapture, who sought the fragments in fulfillment of the dream of ending the world in a nihilistic orgy of violence under the agency of a force from beyond they knew as the Lord of Nightmares. The means they had were Annabel herself, marked by this terrible being years earlier as a child when her family had unwittingly unleashed the malevolent entity and laid waste to an entire mining town in the process, her blood and destiny ever-entangled with the nightmare from then on. The fragments that made up what Cormac's co-thief, the sorcerer Henri Damascus, called the *Valusian Book of Days* were nothing more or less than a prophetic calendar marking when the stars were right and the Lord of Nightmares could be summoned to walk the earth to grant dark miracles to those that propitiated it with sacrifices of murder, betrayal, and anarchy. On Kingsport Head the whole bloody business had climaxed in a ritual-turned-massacre, and ultimately it had been Daisy Walker, Daisy and the things she had known that had saved her and Morgan while everybody else was destroyed utterly, including Annabel, Damascus, and Cormac.

Morgan had been torn up pretty badly by the end of it, so he'd spent months afterward recuperating in secret and incognito at a private hospital Daisy had arranged for him up in Maine. As for Daisy herself, the experience had changed her on some fundamental level, caused a shift in her that none of them fully understood.

"I should have died," Morgan said with bleak certainty that chilled the professor as he finished his story, "and it's not the first time. And I wonder why," he said, raising his own glass to his lips.

Harvey didn't know how to answer that, so instead he carried on, "That was the true start of it, I think—the ritual at Kingsport; something broke with the world at that moment, a stone fell that began an avalanche. Arkham, Dunwich, this whole area of New England has always sat perilously close to an abyss; that much is apparent to anybody who has come into contact with the strange forces that have been at play here down the centuries and has the wit to see it. Orne, Curwen, Sutter; the past is littered with great and terrible men who used the secrets they knew about this place for their own ends, and most often perished by them.

"But this past year has been worse than anything I can find on record. A great many terrible things have occurred here...forces have been awoken you might say...or drawn here from the outside—madmen, monsters, cults. I don't pretend to know the full extent of them, but I have an idea that Daisy did. She said that they were the shadows before the storm. I think she knew very well what was coming."

"The Lord of Nightmares," Morgan said darkly.

"Perhaps," Harvey replied, fidgeting at his own answer and taking another drink to hide his disquiet.

Morgan saw his unease, but chose to ignore it, asking instead, "Time for my answers now, Professor: What about Daisy and the rest of it, where is she? What's she been doing? And what the hell was she doing leaving the fragments with you?"

"One last question first, please, Mr. Morgan. How did you come to return to Arkham now? I'm very thankful that you did, you saved my life, but how?"

Morgan paused for a moment, before shrugging. "Daisy telegrammed me, told me it had started." Seeing the look of surprise on the professor's face, Morgan smiled sardonically. "She kept you in the dark as much as me, didn't she? Just told us each what she wanted to us to know? Well, after I pulled myself out of my hospital bed, I came looking for Daisy to try and make some damn sense out of it all, that's when we met first time round, wasn't it, Professor? You were playing gatekeeper at the university, weren't you?"

Harvey nodded and Morgan continued, "Shawcross still

didn't have his fragments, and after I saw what they could do, he wasn't going to get them either. That made me a marked man. I'd already decided that I was going to move on, stay ahead of the hunt, but Daisy told me it wasn't over, told me it would all come to a head soon, and if she didn't stop it, it would be over for everybody."

Again Harvey nodded; Morgan had put it succinctly, but it was more or less just what she'd told him as well, and like Morgan he had believed her without question.

Again Morgan smiled that cold, bitter smile of his that made Harvey fear for his life just sitting there, and said, "She pointed out that I owed her my life, and I always pay my debts, so I agreed to come running when she called. I couldn't stay in Arkham, so I've been on the road ever since, keeping ahead of Shawcross's dogs. That and running down the last few scattered stragglers of the Legion of Rapture who didn't make it to the showdown at Kingsport—let's just say I'm not a forgiving man.

"I turned up a day later than I meant to because of the storm, and finally made it onto the campus tonight looking for Daisy, not you. That's when I saw those three creepers in the fog. I thought they would be after her, so I followed them into the library to spoil their evening, and lucky for you I did. Your turn, Professor."

"Indeed," Harvey said, and poured himself another measure from the brown paper wrapped bottle left between them on the table. He'd never been much of a hard drinking man, even when in his youth—more because he had a tendency toward awful hangovers if he overindulged rather than any moral standpoint—but it was helping with the ache in his arm, and numbing the slow sense of panic that had been with him since the things he had seen in the library. "She's gone, as I have said, and I don't know where, other than I have a very strong suspicion she has not left Arkham. Until a few weeks ago, Daisy was still staying with us at the university, but now surreptitiously, you understand. Not long after you yourself recovered after the Kingsport business we started to tell people she had left us, gone away and left no forwarding address. We had to because some very unsavory types started to poke their noses about the university after her."

"Shawcross?"

"Perhaps, perhaps not," Harvey replied.

"You're very fond of that word, Professor," Morgan commented with just a hint of threat in his voice. "You use it like a shield to hide behind."

"Perhaps I do," he countered with an apologetic smile, "but I come from that branch of learning where if you are not certain of a fact, you don't pretend to be."

"Then favor me with supposition, Professor. I'll take your caveat of uncertainty; after all, we're all through the looking glass, aren't we?"

Again Harvey was brought up short by the erudition he found hiding behind those killer's eyes; what a strange man this was, with his not-quite-English accent, his manners and his diction that an assuredly hard life among evil men had not quite managed to abrade away. "Yes, Mr. Morgan, I rather think we are. Some of them may have been connected with Shawcross, separately both I or the dean rebuffed a private investigator and a Boston lawyer, both with impeccable credentials and veiled promises of large bursaries of cash should we cooperate in tracking down certain 'relics' in connection with Daisy Walker, after she herself spoke with them and would not give them what they wanted. Those two I think must have been ultimately connected with your Shawcross fellow."

"That certainly sounds like his style, operating through others, never getting his hands dirty, and he can afford the best, by one means or another."

People like you. Harvey thought, but did not voice it aloud. "There were others as well, less...well less well-heeled, less persuasive, and altogether more directly threatening. In some ways they were the easiest to deal with and gave us ample excuse to have them removed and barred from the campus, with the threat of the law over them."

Morgan studied him closely. "How did Daisy take it?"

Harvey Walters chose his words carefully; he trusted Morgan with his life as matters stood, but if he lied to him directly, there was no telling what might happen. "In her stride, I would say; she was, not unconcerned, but not surprised either. She was engaged in research, coming up with a solution, exactly what I wasn't privy to; she said it was safer for me and her that way, and I didn't have cause to doubt her. I assisted where I could—she used my name and reputation, and that of the university to access certain libraries, academics, and museums all around the world. Her research also concerned her with Arkham's history and with Dunwich's and Kingsport's as well. As time progressed, she also obtained certain rare antiquities and books for very large sums of money from some very unsavory quarters. I don't know how she made contact with them or where the money came from; all I know is that they came in furtherance of her plan. I remember one package: it came from somewhere in South Africa of all places, a copper disk of some kind the size of a coffee saucer; it came wrapped in the most unpleasantly textured sheet of leather with strange, irregular stitch work on it. It wasn't until she unwrapped it that I saw that the leather laid out flat had eyes and a mouth sown shut."

Harvey felt a hollowness in his chest, his mouth strangely dry. He felt as if he was at once betraying her, but at the same time as if he were experiencing a form of déjà vu, as if he'd had this conversation before, as if he were a puppet suddenly aware of his strings. *Get a grip, old man*, he told himself as Morgan mulled over his words in silence.

"But why didn't they find her?" Morgan asked.

"What do you mean?"

"You know what I mean, Professor. I don't care how good a job of hiding out she did in the university, they had more than long enough to find her, so why didn't they?"

"She came and she went, about town I think, out to Kingsport once or twice, I'm sure, spent time in Dunwich as well, I think," Harvey said with unease. "But I confess, I wondered that myself; I wondered if she wasn't using some more…esoteric means of concealing herself and what she was doing…or…"

"Or what?"

Harvey sighed and said what he had never let himself say before, never allowed himself to think about head on, "Or perhaps they did find her, and got more than they bargained for. I confess, when she went away, a part of me was relieved that she had gone."

Morgan nodded slowly in understanding. His own memory of what had happened at Kingsport, at the end, was hazy at best; there had been a nightmare in the sky, twisted flesh, a slash in reality like a bleeding wound in the face of the world and Daisy had stood at the heart of it all. Daisy with nothing to save them but the things she knew and the will to use them.

"Things had grown far worse in Arkham as the weeks passed, and I knew she had been right, that some terrible thing was about to be born, like the Yeats poem, you know?"

"'What rough beast,'" Morgan answered with one of his chilling smiles.

"Just so; you are a very surprising man, Mr. Morgan," Harvey answered; he was starting to feel light-headed, the drink and the exhaustion piling up on him at last.

"I'm a waste of an education and a cruel disappointment to my family, I assure you," he answered wryly, seeing that Harvey was composing himself for the rest of it.

"Daisy," Harvey said faintly. "It all does come down to Daisy. She's a genius, you know?" His voice was wavering. "Of course, we all knew she was very clever, that much was obvious from the start, had such a fantastic gift of recall: every line she read, every word, it stayed with her perfectly, but it was far more than that.

"Oh, there were those that dismissed her intelligence on account of her sex, but I was never one to subscribe to that poppycock, nor was old Armitage, for that matter, but I don't think any of us really knew what her mind was capable of, the conception, the correlation. After Kingsport, I don't know, her intellect grew stronger. She consumed everything with frightening speed: dead languages, geology, physics, astronomy, cartography, whatever she needed, even genealogy for a time, tracing the old Miskatonic Valley bloodlines in all directions. She learned and understood more in a month than I dare say I have in my forty-five years as a historian, you know?" His voice trembled and trailed away.

Morgan carefully reached out and laid his hand on the older man's shoulder. Harvey blinked rapidly and let out a tired chuckle. "Sorry," he said, "I was rather rambling there, wasn't I?"

"The fragments, Professor, what about the fragments?"

"The *Book of Days*? It had been in five pieces before, I was told, but after Kingsport the sections Cormac had, they had fused somehow, forming a tablet; it was only the splinter Annabel Ryan carried with her to her death that remained separate. That splinter Daisy took away with her; she said she was going to hide it 'where many would not go,' whatever that meant. She said that was the key and that it had to be 'brought willingly to whoever wanted its use, but that it could be taken neither by master or servant'—though that I confess made little sense to me. The larger tablet portion she gave me to hide until she called for it, and I was not to tell her where.

"But in the last couple weeks since she's been gone, the sense of growing dread has been palpable, like the whole town is hanging on a knife-edge. There were more strangers around the campus, break-ins, trespasses, first a federal agent asking questions and then this man, he called himself Dr. Lyman Fields, only a few days ago. Him I did not like at all; there was a sinister power to the man, and I was right it seems to have worried about him."

"How so?"

"Those people tonight, the human ones at any rate, and one of the university's students it seems, they were his people, the Hand of Solace, another cult. But as for the other…creatures… whatever we are to call them, I don't know. But I'm getting ahead of myself; before that there was a marshal, asking for Daisy and you as well, by name. I decided then it was just too dangerous to have the thing at the university, that I was jeopardizing the lives of everybody on the campus. I don't know how I didn't see that before. My cottage was ransacked and that was the last straw; they were too close."

"So," Morgan asked, "what were you going to do, try and find Daisy?"

"No," Harvey said with a sigh, "I was going to leave Arkham; I had a foolish plan to take the bloody thing from where I'd hidden it in the Orne Library and get on the night train to New York. Then get on the first steamer across the Atlantic I could find; then, I don't know, drop the damn thing in the middle of the ocean, or carry it to Vladivostok, something," he said sheepishly. "I have no idea really. Just get it far away from here."

Morgan laughed. "You really are a tough old bird, Professor, I'll give you that. Might not have been a bad plan either, come to think of it."

Harvey shook his head, wondering. "Then, well, what happened, happened. If you had not appeared when you did, I would have surely died and the tablet would have been in the hands, so to speak, of the Hand of Solace. Instead..." He let his voice trail off.

"Something else took it. Something from beyond, and it butchered its way through the Solace goons and whatever that skull-faced thing was to do it."

"Do you think that thing belonged to Shawcross in some way?"

Morgan shook his head. "I don't. Somehow I don't, and if the Rapture could...I don't know...what's the word, 'summon' a creature like that, I think they needed the preacher for that, and he died at Kingsport. And if they could, why didn't they do it before?" Morgan shrugged. "Why didn't they send it after me when I declared open season on what was left of them?"

"Then there are other forces at work, other factions?" Harvey said emphatically.

"It would fit the facts of what we experienced," Morgan replied. "Why, Professor? What do you know?" Morgan asked, seeing the look that crossed Harvey's face.

"Sacrifices of blood and treachery...I wonder... Could it, could she...?" Harvey muttered aloud, but did not get the chance to finish his thought.

Morgan was on his feet, the table thrown over, scattering chicken bones and bad whiskey, the Colt automatic already in his hand. People screamed, people panicked, ran. The music jerked and stopped. Harvey saw dark figures pushing through the crowd. He distinctly heard the hard mechanical snap of the bolt of a Thompson submachine gun pulled back and loosed.

Morgan snarled and Harvey clambered to his feet and grabbed onto his arm. Morgan turned to look at the old professor and

Harvey saw death in his eyes. "Please!" Harvey shouted. "There are innocent people here, don't!"

Morgan pushed him away and he fell, tumbling over his chair.

"Anthony Morgan!" a voice boomed from the still-panicking crowd. "Lay down your weapon! You are under arrest! Do it or we'll cut you in half!"

Morgan laughed, and for one terrifying moment Harvey thought he was going to open fire, die in a hail of bullets taking God knew how many others with him. Then Morgan visibly relaxed and dropped the pistol onto the chair he'd vacated and raised his hands slowly.

Meeks came out of the crowd and roughly manhandled Morgan to the floor, pulling his wrists behind his back and snapping the cuffs shut and locking them. "I've got you, Morgan," he growled from behind Morgan's ear.

"Good luck with that," Morgan offered back wryly.

As he was dragged away, Morgan looked back to where the startled professor was still sprawled on the floor, utterly overlooked by the men that had come to apprehend him. He could see Harvey Walters trying to mouth something so he could understand it. *Which house?*

Chapter Fifteen

Arkham

December 6, 1929

The knock on her office door brought her back to the present. Her mind had been wandering. *No, more than that; you were asleep sitting up*, Grace Zabriski realized ruefully. She leaned back in the swivel chair and stretched, popping her back audibly and pushing out a hard breath. "Come in," she said loudly, stifling a yawn.

It was one of the older orderlies, Williams, who had intruded on her accidental slumber. He was carrying a clipboard with a docket for her to sign, medication inventory for the night shift in this case, she noticed. *At least it's not just me,* she thought, looking at him. He looked like he hadn't slept properly for days himself, and the white tunic of his uniform now seemed to hang on a frame that while never exactly robust, now seemed almost fleshless.

"Thank you, Williams. Just put it down and I'll attend to it shortly."

He looked uncertainly at the desk, covered nearly two inches deep in places with reports and documents, chits and patient records. "Err…where abouts, Doctor?"

"Oh, just give it here," Grace said more sharply that she'd intended, holding out her hand.

If he had been in any way surprised or offended by her tone, he gave no sign, just handed over the clipboard and walked out clumsily, like a sleepwalker.

Grace stifled another yawn, thinking, *At least the patients have been quiet tonight; that at least is a silver lining to this strange somnolence that seems to be blanketing everybody this evening.* In fact, the whole place seemed to be wallowing in a deep, narcotic slumber that the staff's ministrations, chemical or otherwise, for once had nothing whatsoever to do with.

On her rounds of Arkham Asylum an hour earlier she hadn't encounter a single patient still awake; even those to whom the night was usually their time to be most active either by cause of habit or malady. But to her it seemed a dead dreaming, grave-like and unwholesome, though of course she expressed this to no one and more than half-considered that her perceptions had been colored by her own terrible dreams of late. *More than just dreams—dreams don't make your walls bleed,* she thought coldly.

Grace was well aware that if it had happened to anybody else she would have found the idea absurd, even comically unbelievable, something she would have put down to exhaustion and misinterpretation at best, and at worst delusion brought on by mental illness or delirium tremens. But it had not, it had happened to her, and she was not laughing or even really doubting her own sanity. In fact, part of her wasn't even surprised but simply accepted it as real the more she considered it, and that was perhaps the most sinister thing of all. She considered herself above all else to be a rational being; to her the human mind and brain were ultimately indivisible, the one the engine to drive the other, and they both existed in a reality objective and absolute which obeyed observable and constant laws. She had always subscribed to the conviction that there was no such thing as the supernatural, but instead only conceded that there were elements of nature that human reason had not yet discovered or explained. As such, Grace had done a lot of thinking since the terrible dreaming at her lodgings and the strange phenomena that had accompanied it, and had done her best to incorporate what had happened to her—the fact of it—into her worldview as best she could; and while she was still mentally rocked by their implications, accepting what she had experienced as being real was shining a far more malevolent and disturbing light on many things she already knew about Arkham and the unfortunates that had most recently come under the asylum's care.

It was as if…as if something in Arkham was happening or had happened that had somehow damaged reality in some way; changed the rules of what she had known, of what she had believed possible in some macabre and poisonous way, but this dangerous phenomena was somehow localized. That at least made some kind of sense as a premise, and was to her mind better than the alternative explanation: that the world as she understood it, that science, rational thought, all human experience as she had known and believed it, were itself a delusion.

With her hypothesis in place, she had determined to find the cause of the breach in normality; that, she felt sure, was the first step in understanding it. *Then what?* She didn't know, but any facts would be the first step; it would be something, a rock to cling to in a world that was slowly sliding into madness.

To the cause of finding out the truth, she had now committed her efforts. In every working moment her duties could spare her, she now attacked both the old records and details of the asylum's most recent glut of cases, pulling records, and even telephoning next of kin where possible and even outside physicians whose names had been attached to the cases, until the lateness of the hour had rendered that course of action counter-productive. She soon widened her efforts to not merely those on the catatonic ward but others who seemed to fit the bill: delusions and hallucinations, attempted suicides and violent episodes, and they were many. Madness and macabre happenings had stalked Arkham as far back as the records went, it seemed, beyond what any ordinary town might endure; it was a fact she had known, of course, but to see the facts laid out before her in cold print and in the light of her own brush with that darkness was profoundly disturbing. It was only her own willful self-possession and the anchor of scientific methodology, in which she held her greatest faith, which kept her from recoiling from her path and walking away from the terrible truths she felt she was on the edge of discovering.

But despite her diligence and perseverance, her researches had thrown up nothing new by way of answers, only brought home the terror of what was happening even more fully: the same familiar themes again and again, sudden breaks with reality, talk of monsters and calamities, nightmare visions, horrors seen and horrors yet to come—talk which now seemed not so febrile to her than it once had, to be sure—and the same phrases over and over again. Why had they not seen it? Seen just how concrete those commonalties were? Mass hysteria they had labeled it, or rumor or folklore reverberating in the collective psyche of myth-haunted Arkham, and the delusion had been their own.

Had the facts been so blindingly obvious and yet so unpalatable that they had all willfully ignored it? The answer was simple: yes. There was some sole cause, there had to be, and that was what she needed to find: the common element that might have been overlooked, simply because it wouldn't be a rational cause of the kind any psychiatrist would have looked for—commonalities of location, habit, travel, even if they might have drunk water from the same well. But it had been useless; there had been no factor common to them that had not been common to hundreds of others who as of yet had been unaffected. She had looked for physical causes as if she were dealing with a disease vector or a poison, but she had found none of those either. *Am I wrong? Am I no closer to knowing what is happening?*

Self-doubt gripped her. Madness to the modern psychiatrist was not something you caught like a germ from the environment; it was not a typhus of the brain…

"Typhoid Mary," she whispered aloud. *Could it be that simple? Have I been going at this from entirely the wrong angle? Instead of a cause, should I be looking for an individual?*

She recalled the facts of that infamous case to mind, reeling through them almost by rote. Her lessons from medical school come back with vivid force: Mary Mallon, better known as Typhoid Mary, had been an asymptomatic carrier of typhoid fever. Although she was herself immune, she went through her life as a cook in New York unwittingly spreading a trail of sickness and death across unknown numbers of people she came into contact with and those she worked for. Discovered by an investigating doctor, she refused responsibility and attempted to evade recognition, causing further suffering and fatalities until she was discovered again and, as a walking contamination without a cure, was condemned to lifelong incarceration in 1915 for the safety of others. Could it be that simple? Could there be a hidden progenitor to the dark forces that had afflicted Arkham—that had afflicted her? Or if not that exactly, if they had not spread the malady, had they encountered it somehow at its source? Could it be tracked that way?

Grace's mind reeled with the possibilities; she knew she was now Alice through the looking glass, and on the other side of that pane lay things too ugly to imagine.

Immediately she began to backtrack through her records by

date, sorting them and discarding the most recent, going backward in the hopes of discovering the first encounter, not with mere sudden madness, but with the imagery that defined the worst of the cases—the imagery and nightmarish experience that had touched her directly. It was then that the same name, hidden in plain sight all along began to appear again and again. The name not of a patient, but of a psychiatrist, here at Arkham Asylum, and to her surprise one she was completely unfamiliar with: Dr. Joseph Lemaitre. She had known there had been an unusually high turnover of clinical staff at the asylum in recent months—it had been, after all, the opportunity that had enabled her to get a position at Arkham—but unlike the old head physician, Hardstrom, she had never met or even heard of this Lemaitre from any of the staff. And yet here he was, listed as principle psychiatrist on each case, here right at the start of the nightmare, which seemed to have occurred only a few months before his sudden and as yet unexplained departure. What was more, now she viewed the numbered files in order, there were several completely missing from that period, sequences of files omitted from the records, names of patients referenced in files that were present, but were nowhere else listed.

Dr. Mintz would know; he was the oldest serving and most senior of the staff—he would have worked with this Lemaitre and surely be able to put her in contact with him. She put her hand on the phone receiver to call him immediately despite the lateness of the hour but froze suddenly. *No*, she thought suddenly. *No. I don't trust him,* and though she had never cohered it as a thought before, let alone admitted it to herself, she knew it to be true. She didn't trust Mintz; the man kept too many secrets, was just too cold, too devoted to keeping the ship afloat, no matter the cost. Truth be told, she was more than a little frightened of him and what he might do if she made too many waves, not physically of course, but he could end her career at Arkham very easily if he chose, and given the state of affairs and the reputation of the place that now tarnished her, where else would she go? But that parochial concern aside, she needed answers for her own sanity's sake, and this was the only place she would find them.

Instead of dealing with Mintz directly, and knowing she was still taking a chance, she decided there was only one course of action left if she wanted to know about this "Lemaitre." He would be the key to unlock the answers that she sought. She picked up the phone and connected to the internal line for the asylum's main nurses' station. A few minutes later, Nurse Heather, who like Mintz, predated anybody else she knew here on the clinical staff, was standing before her.

Grace Zabriski did not dissemble, instead she fixed the older nurse with her most inflexible expression, the one she used with the type of violent patients with whom kindness would have been little more than a bared throat. "There are files missing from the records. Do you know who is responsible?"

Nurse Heather stammered, and began to get angry, but Grace simply bullied her down, defeated her excuses, and backed her into a corner where she feared not only for her livelihood but that criminal charges might well be leveled. Even though some small part of her took pleasure in seeing the often haughty woman humbled, she did not like it about herself that she found it so very easy to do to her what male colleagues who disapproved of her gender in the profession had so often (and unsuccessfully) tried do to her—overawe and brow-beat to achieve what they wanted. She felt a pang of regret and guilt as soon as she saw the woman's composure crack and the glisten of tears form in her eyes.

"Those-tho-those patients were Dr. Lemaitre's, and...," Nurse Heather stammered.

"The doctor that left suddenly? Him?" Grace cut in, trying to sound as if she knew more about the mysterious doctor than she did. "But surely somebody would have ensured he didn't remove records when he left. Surely there was some oversight…" Grace's voice trailed off. Nurse Heather was looking open-mouthed in genuine panic, her eyes darting around frantically, her hands wringing. She looked as if she had been caught revealing some awful secret she had not meant to, and with a startle Grace realized that was exactly what had happened.

"Tell me about Lemaitre, Heather," Grace said, deliberately making her tone calm and open. "Really, I don't want to get you into trouble. You're hugely important to the staff and patients here."

The older woman looked like a frightened animal, her breath hitching in her chest; she looked like she was about to collapse into tears at any moment, and if she did, Grace knew she would lose any chance of getting the answers she sought. Grace took another gamble. "I won't tell Dr. Mintz that we've spoken."

"You…you won't?"

"No, I won't," Grace replied calmly but firmly. "But you can see how I have to look into this, I have to know; it would be impossible to do my job professionally otherwise. But once I'm satisfied, it needn't go any further."

"You promise?" The woman, twenty years Grace's senior, sounded to her like a frightened child.

"I promise," Grace said, and her own smile felt like treachery.

"They…the files…they'll be in his office; that would be it, I'm sure. I really don't know anything else."

"Whose office?" Grace asked, suddenly confused. "Dr. Mintz's?"

"Oh, no," Nurse Heather replied, taken aback. "His—Dr. Lemaitre's office." The last words had been barely spoken above a whisper, as if she was frightened to say the words aloud.

"His office is still kept?" Grace asked incredulously, she had certainly never seen it or any room it could be.

Nurse Heather nodded vigorously. "It was sealed up…after…after he went away. It's up on the old eleventh ward, on the fourth floor. The patients up there were relocated, you know, afterward, but they just locked up his office, left everything in there. Dr. Mintz—it was him, he saw to it."

Grace blinked, trying to comprehend what she was hearing.

Looking at the disbelief evident on Grace's face, Nurse Heather fidgeted and said, "I can get you the key, I mean, if you want it."

Chapter Sixteen

Arkham

December 7, 1929

Jacqueline watched as her hand trembled as though she were suddenly feverish—*No!* he thought angrily. *Not hers, mine! Lemaitre's!* He squeezed the fingers shut painfully, the tips of the nails drawing blood against the palm. This body was far from the first he had worn in the long centuries since he had asked his question of the Lord of Nightmares amid the blood and dust of a lost age, but it was causing him far more difficulty than the rest. That it had been female was likely little to do with it, but that the mind he had displaced had been possessed of certain psychic gifts was more likely the cause, that and the murderous strain he had been putting it under in his secret work scratching and gnawing at the fabric between worlds. Regardless, he would have mastery, he would be obeyed; he was close now, so close to gaining what he sought, close to meeting with the being that had cruelly granted his once fervent wish and unmaking it again. He would not be denied.

There was a rasping, insectile rattle and the abomination of flesh and physical form that the ancients named a shambler from the void gave up its squirming, shuddering prize, which collapsed to the floor with a pained grunt.

The hulking, bear-like mass retreated from sight into the darkness, halfway outside the corporeal world so that only its burning, three-lobed eye gleamed dimly to signify its presence. Its alien gaze was not something even Lemaitre cared to look upon for long, and he harbored no illusions that without his incantations and formulae configured for the purpose of constraining such a creature, the otherworldly predator would instead tear him limb from limb or drag him into the blackness between the stars as a short-lived plaything rather than obey his will. Even now Lemaitre's control over it, just as it was over the other servitors he had bound or summoned, was far from certain, but the risks were necessary, and the barriers were wearing thinner all the time.

"Wake up, Sanford. You live, for now." The woman's voice still sounded foreign on his lips.

Carl Sanford, master of the Silver Twilight Lodge, shuddered and moaned as he tried to pull himself together, although the source of his distress was obvious; he was half-dressed in undershirt and trousers, hoarfrost rimed his hair and skin, and the tips of his be-ringed fingers were a frostbitten black. The entity that had abducted him at Lemaitre's command from his apartment rooms on the uppermost floor of the Lodge on French Hill had done so by pulling him through the void between the worlds, and the passage had not been kind to him.

"Wh-what is the meaning of this?" Sanford managed through chattering teeth, his eyes blinking, night-blind as he raised his head toward his interrogator.

Lemaitre laughed, even so humbled Sanford managed to sound the potentate, but here there was another master.

"You know me, Sanford, although I wore not this body when

last we met, and no doubt you thought well rid of me and my followers from Arkham when I tore Stonegroves loose of this world."

Sanford struggled to an ungainly sitting position, his legs refusing to obey him, his hands curled inward to his chest.

"Lemaitre," Sanford pronounced heavily, a bleak resignation in his voice.

"Yes…yes, Sanford, I, the deathless one, the master of massacres. Once you armed a weak man against me in hopes of my destruction; now you meddle again in my affairs. Did you think I would not find out?"

Sanford shook his head slowly.

"Do not trouble to deny it; the petty schemes of your cowardly society are laid open before me, you who would squat here like toads in this benighted town content with your rotting books and your paltry secrets. So jealous of any other that might threaten you, so afraid to dirty your hands directly. "

"What do you want of me?" Sanford growled defiantly. "If it is my death, then get on with it; your gloating bores me."

Again Lemaitre laughed. "Kill you, Sanford? Why I have saved you! You owe me your life and yet you do not know it."

"What…I don't understand?"

"Your incompetent meddling has brought down more than my wrath upon you, fool. What care I for your fate when the Lord of Nightmares will walk soon. Your life is dust to me, Sanford, worthless, beneath my trouble to take, save for what you know, that alone may spare your miserable life."

Sanford did not reply, but instead shook his head as if trying to clear it. Lemaitre, his patience wearing thin, stalked over to the half-kneeling man and with a strength that Jacqueline's body should not have possessed, grabbed him by the shoulder and hauled him staggering across the room to a low dresser sprawled with scrawled papers and bloody signs daubed on the wood. At the center of the dresser inside an eight-sided arrangement of fresh rib-bones was a greenish-black tablet of volcanic glass standing on its edge, about the size of a pocket Bible, its symmetry marred by a missing wedge-shaped shard making it look as if it had been cleaved by an axe blow.

"Where is the rest?" Lemaitre demanded, forcing Sanford's face within inches of the artifact so that he could not recoil away. "Tell me or I give you back to the shambler for a sweetmeat."

"We do not have it… I…I do not have it!" Sanford stammered.

"Bah! I know that, imbecile! I would smell it on you, just as I smelled out this, but the other is hidden from me."

Lemaitre let go of him and Sanford sprawled backward to the floor, groaning in fresh pain as his legs buckled beneath him.

In the darkness of the room, a terrible malignity stirred in anticipation and the temperature plunged so that when Sanford spoke, the words rasped out in chilled fog from his lips. "You said it…you said it yourself: the Lodge coverts knowledge, yes… power…but security…not…not Armageddon… Too dangerous…too dangerous a thing to possess… We have no desire to bring about…the end of the world."

Lemaitre smiled and cold madness glittered in his stolen eyes. "But I do, and others, it would seem. Arkham has changed in my absence; powers move here I do not know, murder rises, can you not feel it? The Ancient One walks soon, but I must know—know for certain when and where! I am the master, Sanford, and I will have my due."

"Fields…the woman in Dunwich…Walker; she had it, she had it after Kingsport, I'm sure; it could be any of them…"

"Fields!" Lemaitre spat, investing the word with lethal venom. "Yes, Dr. Fields, my would-be assassin, usurper of my treacherous, misguided flock…I have plans for them already. But the rest, Sanford, tell me of them, tell me of all of them; tell me what your toads have seen?"

Sanford rolled painfully to all fours, his head down. "If I tell you, you'll let me live?" he whispered hoarsely.

"Yes, yes, worm, what is your life to me? I spare it for all the good it will do you, but only if you tell me all."

His face pressed close to the floor and unseen, even by the otherworldly horrors that stood about him, Carl Sanford's face twisted for a moment in a mocking smile that was not his own. "I'll tell you…," he began.

* * *

Raker heard the two engines' growl before he saw the head-lamps cutting through the fog, before he caught sight of the glow of the fire, before the fraught bells of the ambulance; before any of the rest of it. Afterward it seemed almost choreographed for him, as if it had been meant to be. It was a thought that would drive him to the bottle long before dawn when sleep escaped him, but that would come later as he turned the events over and over again in his mind.

He'd spent the full day and into the evening visiting some of the places he'd read about in the newspaper morgue the night before, using a fake press card as the only cover and excuse he'd needed, and all the time keeping an eye out for signs of the elusive Morgan, for Daisy Walker, and for the Hand of Solace. He'd found nothing concrete, but his sense of dread about what was going on in Arkham was getting worse—if that was possible—and the fearful silence and reticence to talk he'd found was, if anything, more disturbing than the few who'd been forthcoming with their stories, as bloody or strange as they had been.

His last stop had been in a basement speakeasy at the foot of French Hill that made Hibb's look like the Ritz, but he'd been glad of the company and the anonymity and stayed longer than he meant to. Outside, the fog was eerily silent and thick, smothering sound so even his own footsteps sounded strangely distant and faint. The night seemed full of unseen things he tried to tell himself were the results of an overworked imagination and the half bottle of whiskey he'd consumed, but cold memory told him it might be otherwise and he had been glad of both the dim sodium-yellow glow of the frequent streetlamps in this part of town. Raker had hugged one pool of radiance then another on his way back to where he'd parked a discreet distance away from the speakeasy, and never saw nor heard a living soul during the brief walk through the streets. The relief when he reached his motor car was more palpable than he'd have cared to admit to anyone.

His fingers had closed around the fog-slicked and cold metal of the door handle when the throaty rumble of two powerful automobiles traveling at dangerous speeds seemed to cut through the fog like a blade. Raker dropped low behind his own car on reflex, knowing that he had no time even to open the door and slide inside before they would be on him, and he was right. The twin sets of headlamps blazed across the street and swept the car, blasting its shadow across the bare brick wall behind him, and Raker dropped lower yet so that his knees hit the wet pavement and the two cars bolted past, growling like wolves in the night.

He watched them go, his breath caught in his throat with recognition; they had been identical black limousines with glossy sable paint jobs and white-walled tires, brand new and reeking of casual wealth, just like the one he had been bundled into outside the Asylum a few nights before. In fact, he would have laid good money on one of them being that very car. *Shawcross,* he thought, *no, not the man himself, but his muscle, it has to be.*

The twin limousines disappeared into the fog like phantoms, and he was still trying to get his mind around what it meant when the dim, ruddy smear of light over the rooftops to the north caught his eye. Like a false dawn it ate into the foggy night and stained it deep red, and it put immediately to his mind childhood memories of stubble-burning fields and vibrant dawns like the world had been set aflame, seen as he had finally walked home shakily from some dive or other after a night at the tables or at a bar. But this was no illusion of flame, he knew, this was the real thing, and no rural land clearance either, but a blaze roaring somewhere in the heart of Arkham.

A moment later, as if to confirm his thoughts, he heard the trill of the ambulance bell in the distance, panicked and mournful all at once, and he was walking. The manila file of newspaper clippings and notes left on the roof of his Ford where he had dropped it when he had first heard the speeding limousines, forgotten, just like the car itself. Drawn on, tugged inexorably as if he was a fish on a line and it was time for him to be reeled in, Raker walked through the fog, his pace quickening, his fears behind him. He walked toward the fire.

He was two-thirds of the way up to the summit of French Hill when his toe caught an uneven paving stone and he stumbled, and that small jolt was enough to bring him back to his senses. He did a double-take to find himself where he was, and was suddenly aware of others around him, a loose crowd of onlookers in the ruddy fog, while before him all was chaos and destruction.

At the crest of the hill, the Gothic mansion which housed the Silver Twilight Lodge burned, the shadows of its brick-buttressed walls standing out like bones surrounded by a translucent flesh of fire, acrid black smoke billowing from the empty-socket eyes of its broken upper windows, and jetting up into the air. The lodge house was clearly too far gone to save, and already the front porch had caved in on itself, bricks hanging loosely like broken teeth in a rotten mouth. Arkham's woefully inadequate fire truck and water wagon were instead leveling its hand-pumped hose at the roofs of nearby townhouses and manses, no doubt in fear that they too would catch light from the furnace-roaring conflagration. Around them, a dozen policemen milled, caught between staring in fascination at the fire and trying to keep back the growing crowd of onlookers, while two men whose features Raker could not see seemed to cower fearfully beside the ambulance parked a distance away.

He had never been inside the Lodge, but he had heard of it, of course, since he had first come to Arkham, since the nightmare at Stonegroves had pushed him into a hidden and sinister world of otherworldly rumor and dark suspicions, and in that world the Silver Twilight Lodge's reputation had preceded it. Raker had built up the place in his mind as something dangerous, a threshold he would not willingly cross unless forced to, and yet here it was going up in flames like some Viking funeral, proved mortal and cast down. It seemed wrong somehow, fearfully wrong.

The flames leapt higher and Raker felt more than heard a shudder pass through the onlooking crowd, something not of fear but pleasure, queasy and unwholesome. He was keenly aware of feeling "other," an outsider, not part of the crowd, as it began to draw in closer to the ring of police and firemen that circled all-but-helplessly beyond the low black-iron surmounted wall that surrounded the burning mansion. Raker looked around the faces that he could half-see in the fire-reddened fog, and they were like figures from Hell, the damned, lusting for the fires that consumed them, their mouths moving, forming words he could not understand. Raker felt a genuine, deep fear coursing like ice in his gut and began to slowly back away. A strange sound caught his ear and his head snapped around involuntarily, trying to find its source. It was a trill of music, a half-heard piping, cutting soft but razor-thin through the air, slicing the muffling fog and the crackling of the fire both, there and then gone again.

The roof of the burning mansion caved in with a deep, bass rumble like an angry sea, and the crowd roared exultantly, drowning the strange music. Raker saw fists raised in salute, faces contorted as if cheering on the destruction.

One of the firemen fell as if poleaxed, and the pump hose went wild, out of control. Raker saw something heavy go skittering away from the fallen man. *A cobblestone!* he realized with shock. *Somebody threw a cobblestone at him!* The other firemen rallied around and brought the hose under control, and something like an angry jeer went up from some within the crowd.

"Let it burn!" a woman's voice shouted, then a man's, "Let it all burn!"

At that cry, about a dozen figures from the crowd surged haphazardly forward, some toward the fire wagon and others just toward the fire, but to what exact end Raker could not guess and he doubted even they really knew. There was an ugly, panicked sensation sweeping over him like a tide, and Raker knew he had to get out, get away.

There were shouts and there were screams, police billy clubs were swinging, stones being hurled, Raker saw a knife blade flash crimson in the firelight, and beside him an old man collapsed to his knees, howling inarticulately and clawing at his chest. It was like the near-riot that he'd witnessed at the diner but somehow a hundred times worse, and behind it all, like a shriek too high-pitched to properly hear, was that insane, twisted piping. Raker fled, ducking past onlookers at the rear of the crowd too lost-looking to stop him, even if they had noticed him weaving through them. At the edge of the crowd, he looked back over his shoulder and saw a burly plainclothes policeman fire two shots into the air with his revolver as if in warning. It was a warning one man did not heed, rushing headlong at the policeman, hands raised above his head balled into fists as if he meant to simply pummel the lawman to the ground. Instead, the lawman simply shot him dead. That broke the spell somehow, and the main part of the crowd began to scatter and run pell-mell away from the fire; some simply collapsed sobbing though a few fought on and were quickly brought down by billy clubs swung with angry abandon.

As soon as he could, Raker dodged out of sight down a side street, away from the fleeing crowd. He felt as if he were being watched, being toyed with; as if at any moment a policeman's bullet would find his back...that or something worse would latch onto him and drag him down. Past backyards and through alleyways he tumbled, unsure where he was going, plunging into the thickening fog, simply happy to be beyond the crowd, beyond the light of the fire, but that strange music was still there, like an echo caught in his head he couldn't shake free.

Sudden shouts spilled out ahead of him and a dark shape loomed from the fog, blocking his path. There was a sharp, percussive *crack* and a jolt ran up Raker's arm. He looked down in shock to see the smoking automatic in his hand.

The figure slumped and fell, and in a moment of painful clarity Raker looked down in horrified fascination at a balding middle-aged man in a nightshirt and unbuttoned trousers. Blood was welling from the side of his thigh, black as ink in the darkness. The panicked shouting came through to him as if on a long-distance line; it was a woman's voice, calling on God and for him to stop, to "Please don't shoot my Jimmy!"

"What am I doing?" Raker whispered, still looking at the pistol in his hand, his mind trying to recollect drawing it, let alone shooting the man. Bile rose in his throat and he wanted to hurl the gun away suddenly, as if he were grasping a venomous snake, but his instincts for self-preservation came back full force, and instead he slowly, carefully, lowered the pistol to his side, his finger pulled well clear of the trigger. He'd hurt men before, killed when he'd needed to and only then, but always there had been a reason, and intent. This was different, like something had invaded him and worked him like a puppet; he felt sickened and violated at the empty helplessness of it.

He looked down at the man, and now the woman who was on her knees beside him, curlers in her hair, a housecoat flapping around her. From what he could see of her, she looked terrified, hysterical, but the man he had shot looked...vacant, blank almost, like a sleepwalker, not a man in pain, nor fear.

"I'm not going to shoot anybody!" Raker shouted hoarsely. "He just, just came at me." And then after a sharp intake of breath, "I'm with the Arkham police," he lied.

He did not know what reaction that untruth would illicit, but the woman sobbed in relief and began to apologize over and over in a rasping, childlike tone, her voice hitching between sobs.

Raker knelt down before the man and took a small flashlight from his pocket and shone it on his victim, his concern as much selfish as anything else. *Don't be dead, don't be dead,* he repeated over and over in his mind. To Raker's immense relief, the .32 had done nothing more than put a gouge in the meat of the man's thigh, having not struck solidly, and while it was bloody, the wound didn't look remotely life-threatening. Later, Raker would remember the sawn-off shotgun stashed under the passenger seat of his car, and replay the incident again as it would have come out if he'd carried it with him that night, and called himself lucky not to have murdered a stranger while feeling hollow and sick to his stomach.

"He kept saying he heard music, but I couldn't hear none," the woman whispered brokenly as they carried the wounded man between them back into his house. "He kept saying the music meant that he was coming, and Jimmy had to go and see."

Raker took a swig from an offered bottle of homemade brandy and looked into the bright and terrified eyes of the family's two small children peering from the kitchen doorway, as their father coughed and moaned and their mother bound the wound Raker had put in him. The man seemed to be coming round, very slowly, but coming round, and Raker was truly grateful.

"Who?" Raker asked, his own voice sounding dead and distant to him.

The woman shook her head uncomprehendingly.

"Who did he saw was coming?"

The woman looked down at the linoleum floor, not meeting Raker's eyes, her hands wringing restlessly together.

"The traveler," she said. "He says it in his dreams, keeps saying it, 'the night man's coming' over and over."

Raker looked at the man and the woman, at the children's terrified eyes, and felt cold. Cold and alone.

"Get out," he said slowly. "Get out of Arkham. Leave your husband if he won't go, but get them out, right out," he said, pointing jerkily at the children. "Go."

"Yes, sir," the woman answered.

Raker nodded and slipped out of the back door into the night. He took the bottle with him.

Chapter Seventeen

Arkham & The Woods

December 11, 1929

The day was hardly worth the name, having never cleared more than a bitter twilight, and the further they had got from town, the worse the weather had gotten.

Cold fog ran its fingers over Dr. Fields's face as he stepped from the metal-grate running board on the back of the truck onto the sodden dirt of the road. He turned his head, eyes finding only the impressions of bare tree branches, and the road fading into the whitish murk in either direction.

Around him the Hand of Solace formed a loose pack. All wore grey, the rough-spun fabric of their hooded robes, half concealed by shapeless coats and jackets, making them seem like figures congealed from the fog itself. The robes gave them a unity of purpose and role, a uniform almost, like soldiers, and besides, the time for subtly and secrecy was almost over. A gang of robed men was hardly the strangest thing abroad in Arkham right now, even if the fog had not been there to conceal them. Only Fields himself wore no such identifying robe, his mourner's black and charcoal grey suit making him a dark silhouette cut into the fog.

"Doctor?" asked a voice from behind him. He recognized Red's voice; the faithful but dull note to the man's words was as familiar to him as his own. He did not reply, but continued to look around him, listening, eyes trying to pierce the fog. Under his shirt his skin prickled. The fog had come up as they had approached Dunwich, seeping from the dank forests in thickening folds, gathering into such solid banks that they had almost lost sight of the road entirely, their headlamps futile, and they had had to stop the trucks. Now he was outside, the fog tugging across the skin of his face, he was sure that something was subtly wrong.

"Doctor?" came Red's voice again.

"We proceed on foot," he said with more certainty that he felt and looked around him at his followers. Faces nodded beneath grey hoods in reply. The fourteen he had chosen to accompany him in the stolen freight trucks were the strongest and most unimaginative of his followers in their loyalty, and they were all well-armed with guns and knives, even a few sticks of dynamite; that fact was another distasteful necessity he had grudgingly embraced. He was not sure what resistance they would face after the bloody debacle in the Miskatonic University library, but given the near state of anarchy that brooded over Arkham and the possibility that worse might be waiting for them, prudence was the order of the day. If the fragments the Walker woman had once possessed were in Dunwich, they would be ready to take them by force, and he would have his Hand shed as much blood as he needed to obtain them. The clock was ticking, he was sure of it; the time would be soon.

He pointed at two of his grey servants with the tip of his cane. "Red, Luther, get the lamps from the trucks." The two nodded and moved to obey.

Fields turned to look at the point where the road vanished

into the fog; it was a shame they had not brought flashlights as well, but their need had not been anticipated. It was mid-morning, the time chosen to avoid the chance of encountering certain forms of less than human opposition which he suspected now haunted the backwoods and byroads of the Miskatonic Valley, if the rumors were true. That was one of the reasons he had waited till now, that and a hoped-for clearing of the fog, but that had not come, and the pricking along his spine told him they had very little time left.

Still, their first destination would not be far now, and they could follow the road until they reached the turn to the farmhouse the rumors spoke of, the Gardener place; this would be their first port of call, and if that yielded no fruit, then on to Dunwich proper they would go.

Necessity, he thought firmly, *it is necessity that has brought me to this.* He had been too cautious before, too circumspect in his dealings with that puffed-up old lecturer and the university; he should have simply taken what he had wanted when he had the chance. He should have had his Hand take the old man that very night and forced the fragments out of him; instead he had watched and vacillated too long, and that chance had eluded him.

Other forces had intervened and he had lost his finest servant, Marrow, and what a loss the ghoul had been to his cause—a stolen child, a monster that dreamed of hearth and home dimly remembered. But rather than Marrow, it had been instead Landers, the young stevedore, who had survived. It was faith and dreams which bound him and the rest to Fields, and kept him alive when he should have died. Landers, who had found the Hand of Solace in a Boston gutter and whose fondest wish was to be reunited with a dead lover blinded and poisoned by raw gin spirits. That dream had been enough fuel to make it alive to the getaway car with smashed ribs and a belly filling with blood. He had not survived the journey back to Fields's side, but his dying words had. "Dunwich," he had said, "Whateley," and over and over again, "Woman."

He nodded once to himself and began to walk. The more he had thought on it the more sense it had made—all of it. Fields dimly remembered hearing of Dunwich as a distasteful rumor long ago in his career as a doctor as a byword for rural New England decay; a place of dilapidation, congenital disease, and rumored inbreeding. But that had been before, before Lemaitre, before Stonegroves, before he had become... *what? A sorcerer?* Yes, the epithet was a correct one, even though it still sounded ludicrous to that part of his mind that had clung to stolid normalcy for so many years. Clung to that blissful ignorance to which with the culmination of his quest he wished to return. For now, however, he knew better than to dismiss the benighted village of Dunwich as some mere decaying backwater. The dark wisdom he had learned since the massacre at Stonegroves whispered that Dunwich was far worse than haunted Arkham or dreaming Kingsport; Dunwich was a wound on the face of the world. A festering rent in the fabric of what mankind perceived to be real whose malignity poisoned the ground around it, and twisted those that dwelled there—and the Whateley clan had dwelled there since time out of mind. The stories went that the old man and his malformed child-progeny of a son had died and in doing so unleashed some horror years before. There was only one of the line left now, a woman named Hannah, of whom Arkham gossips spoke in hushed whispers as a witch.

A witch from a line of witches and half-breed monsters, drawn on just as Lemaitre had been, just as the madmen of the rapture cult had been by the Lord of Nightmare's promise. Yes, it all made sense—and here he had been worrying and scheming over the reappearance of that other survivor of Stonegroves, the one called Raker and the whereabouts of some chit of a librarian who no doubt had hidden the fragments in Arkham and simply fled in terror. The Whateley woman clearly had power, but so did he, and he would not be so easily dealt with as Marrow and the others. More, he had his Hand of Solace, and would spend every one of their lives if he needed to in order to get what he wanted. *There is no more time.* Panic and fear were everywhere in Arkham now—violence and the echo of madness haunted shuttered rooms and street corners alike; the moment would be soon, hours perhaps, days, no more than that. Fields could almost smell it, just as an animal could sense an impending storm. The Lord of Nightmares would walk very soon now—the riots and the murders were his sign—and Fields was determined to be there to greet the herald of the Ancient Ones when it appeared and bend it to his will. But for that he needed the fragments, he needed the precise time and place of transference so he might use the Obsidian Key upon the thing and have what he desired come to pass.

I will have all I have achieved, all I have sacrificed undone by some backwoods inbreed. Briefly the image of his daughter's pale face floated before his eyes and anguish stabbed through him. He forced the sudden feeling of helplessness and loss aside.

"Follow," he said, and behind him the Hand of Solace moved forward, the beams of their lamps stabbing against the encircling fog.

* * *

Grace Zabriski jerked suddenly awake and she cried out. Fighting for breath, she clung to the wooden posts of her bed like a shipwrecked mariner at sea clutching to a broken spar until she was sure she was awake.

"Dreaming, dreaming again. That's all it is. You're in your own bed, your own apartment," she croaked through parched lips as she fumbled almost blindly on the nightstand for her glass of water and drained it dry. "Safe," she whispered, and knew it for the lie it was.

The headache, the sense of panic was fading. She massaged her temples slowly as the pain receded, but the fragmented images in her mind did not. Just as every time before they had remained with her, every time she slept the dreams came, waiting for her behind her own eyes, inescapable. Her only comfort was that at least, unlike the first time, the dreams had not been accompanied by the unexplained and inexplicable in the real world; no more bloodstains on the walls, no more pain, *stigmata?* What else was there to call it but that strange word, itself a relic of an age of un-reason. *An age of un-reason*, wasn't that where she found herself now? Wasn't that where all Arkham had been consigned?

She had walked up to the edge of the abyss, but at the last she had faltered, she had refused to look in, to jump headlong into it, to walk the path she had discovered. She had found her proof in Lemaitre's office, but instead of acting on it, she had baulked, the fact rather than the theory had been too much for her to take, and she had retreated from it. The dreams—she couldn't help but feel they were punishing her for her delay, her vacillation. And they were getting worse. She'd spent increasingly little time with the psychiatric patients at the asylum in the last several days. She'd simply gone with what was left of the faculty's decision to sedate where needed and let the rest sleep on, even though that idea had filled her with its own private horror now. Instead she had used the excuse of her own hospital medicine experience to consume what she could of her waking hours to tending to the injured and the physically sick, and there had been a rising tide of casualties over the last few days. Dutifully she'd helped patch them up and sent the worse cases by ambulance to Boston, to

Kingsport, to anywhere that would take them. And when the nurses and the handful of other doctors whispered their fears about what was happening in Arkham, she'd turned away and been stony in her silence. She'd shut down to anything but the work, fixing the body, dealing with the machinery of flesh and blood, the solid and the explicable, pulling double shifts and hoping the exhaustion would bury the dreams, but it had not.

Finally, her hands reduced to palsied shaking by tiredness as she'd tried to suture a knife wound dealt by son to father, she had been sent home to rest, and told not to return for forty-eight hours at least. She had gone meekly, like a prisoner resigned to the gallows, and the dreams had been waiting for her again.

It had been of the journey to Dr. Lemaitre's office she had dreamed this time, a memory twisted as through a mirror darkly. In her dreams, corridors of the shut up ward had been more than deserted, they had been abandoned utterly, their shadows tenanted by spiders and the echoes of long-dead screams. Between the leaves and jungle canopy of the mural painted around the ascending stairwell, the painted tiger had stalked, flickering at the corner of the eye, burning bright, but it would not follow her down into the darkness. There, older and more terrible predators held sway, and into that place mere beasts would not trespass.

In her memory, the dim corridor that led to the mysterious doctor's door had been dusty and empty, scoured clean and left to sit in silence and be forgotten, but in her dream it was a place of restless motion and unseen spirits, where a chill hand like the dead autumn wind strayed across her face and tugged at her white coat, and bestirred a hundred forlorn newspaper clippings and torn-out diary pages that lay strewn across her path. She knew without having to look each would have its own pale face staring out, its own bleak story of the dead and the lost, the condemned and the damned.

The door with its faded painted lettering of *Dr. Joseph Lemaitre* waited for her mutely and opened as she approached. Without seeming to move, she was within, but what awaited her was not the bland office she had found but the wide ballroom of an opulent country house, the checkerboard tiles of the floor incongruous and vivid, as if they were made alternately of fresh fallen snow and the darkness between the stars. All around her in a widening spiral stood statue-still revelers, elegant men and women dressed for a masquerade, runnels of blood pouring steadily from the empty eye sockets of their masks. The howling wind she heard carried the screams of the dying, the distant rattle of machine gun fire, whispered prayers, and inhuman gibbering to the wild discord of pipes, but the air was as still as stone.

Inexorably she passed through the revelers, and each head turned to watch her pass: the fallen prince and the torn preacher, the broken thief and the doomed warrior, the forgotten teacher and the false prophet, all born to die, all damned to the dance.

Behind her, the nightmare child came, and Grace did not have to turn her head to know she was there—the terror of her coming pricked her skin like needles, the whisper at her back like a dying breath. Spiraling inward her pursuer came, obliterating blackness washing out from her like spilled blood un-making everything around her. Grace tried to walk faster, feeling the air turn to ice in her lungs, but she knew escape was impossible, she could only go on, stepping from white square to white square.

The light faded and in the nothingness vast and terrible things stirred. At the center of the chamber was a simple desk, green shaded lamp, and blue-black blotter on which a single manila file waited, just as it had waited for her before. She was at the desk now and nothing surrounded her but limitless gulfs of darkness and howling chaos. She reached out and a hand clasped over hers. It was a child's hand, a little girl's, and it was so cold, so very cold. Beneath those porcelain-white fingers her skin curled and blistered like newspaper hurled onto hot coals, her flesh cracking and splitting under the killing chill of contact. Agony like nothing she had ever experienced exploded across her body, unraveling her mind and blotting out everything but the sight of her hand breaking apart into shards of frozen meat.

Shuddering from the memory, Grace fought to control her breathing, clinging to the solidity of her bedpost, to the real. She slowly opened her eyes and looked into the pale face of the nightmare child.

"Run," the child said, in a voice as old and vile as sin, "it's no fun if you don't run."

Grace shrieked and fled, tumbling backward off the bed, her shift's hem ripping as the nightmare child's fingernails caught it like talons.

Grace slammed into her apartment door with bruising force, her breath ragged as she pawed at turning the key in the lock. Panic blurred her mind into confusion, but it seemed as if her body was acting of its own volition to save her as the door came open and she fell into the hallway, and half ran, half crawled away, bruising her knees on the hard boards and spilling a vase of flowers from a small table set by the banister. She screamed for help; there had to be somebody, anybody? She saw the apartment door beside her was ajar, and she thumbed on it with her hand, screaming inarticulately. The door swung open and her cries were answered by the murmurous buzzing of flies. The scream caught in her throat and her hands flew to her mouth. In the spill of light from the hall she could see the four fresh scratches in the varnished floorboards within the room, the broken fingernail splintered in the gouged wood.

A sound, caught somewhere between the flapping of a raven's wing and the whisper of a lover's breath, brushed her ear. She snapped her head round to look behind her, loose hair flaying wildly, just as a small white hand, its fingers flexing, crawled like a spider around the door frame. Fingers wrapped around her hand; the cold, the pain of it ate her world.

Her knees hit cold flagstones. She cried out again, not in pain but in anguish and despair as the world spun around her, her grasp on what was real spinning away with it. She felt herself sway drunkenly, heard her traveling case thump down beside her. The air was chill and damp, the world white shadows and spinning, drifting lights. She was falling slowly; she could feel it, like a clock winding down. Small hands clasped her arm, preventing her from falling. Blind terror gripped her; she couldn't escape—the nightmare girl had followed her again, out of dream, out of memory.

"Are you okay, lady?" a quavering voice asked close by.

Grace pulled herself back from the brink of hysteria. The voice wasn't the nightmare girl's, *but who?*

The figure resolved itself out of the white shadows. *Fog*, she realized. *I'm outside, but where?* It was a boy, he could not have been more than twelve years old, and not big for his age, in an oversized windbreaker and a cloth cap, a pair of Sunday shoes hung by bootlaces around his neck. She saw the battled-looking little suitcase behind him and everything snapped into place; she was at Northside Station, on the railroad platform. *But how did I get here?*

"Yes," she heard herself saying, "I'm okay. I just slipped, that's all, had a bad turn."

The boy nodded solemnly and let go of her arm. "Okay."

Grace steadied herself with her own traveling case which she found beside her, finding with some alarm that the fingers of her right hand were numb inside her glove and wouldn't work properly.

"Where's your folks?" she asked the boy, trying to stave off a gnawing sense that this too was unreal, and she might wake again at any moment to find herself somewhere else. Or that the nightmare girl would come walking from the fog, a specter of death all too real, and something she feared that if she faced again, she really would go mad.

The boy looked serious and sad, and suddenly very, very young as he replied, “Pops says I have to go stay with Aunt May Bell. But he can’t come, he has to look after mama—she’s sick.”

Grace steadied herself and dusted herself off. “Where is everybody?” she asked, looking up and down the platform, and seeing what she thought might be the shrouded figure of a conductor in a railroad company cap off on the edge of sight, a darker shadow picked out by the sodium glare of the station lamps.

“There’s only us,” the boy said almost apologetically, his voice garbling his words as they came out in a stream. “I thought there was just me and the railroad man, but then I saw you, but I didn’t see you before; I must have missed you in the fog.”

Grace glanced down at her watch. It was ten past twelve, and blearily she wondered whether that was night or day, so absolute was the fog and so dim the light. She was about to ask the boy where he was headed when out of the fog like a bellowing cyclopean monster, the locomotive roared, fixing them both with its blazing eye.

Reflexively she pushed her good hand down into her coat pocket and fastened her fingers around a ticket, which she pulled out and looked at disbelievingly as the iron behemoth bellowing smoke, ground to a halt beside her and the boy.

Kingsport, the ticket read. *Return.*

* * *

“Hold? What, I can barely hear you! I need… Yes, I’ll hold!” Meeks shouted angrily into the telephone receiver.

He was breathing heavily, his anger rolling up inside of him, making his headache worse. It throbbed behind his eyes and made him feel like something inside his brain was trying to cut its way out.

After what seemed an hour of waiting, the line clicked into life, but gave him nothing more than a rasping whine cut with pauses that may have been the breaks in speech.

"What? What was that? The line—"

With a harsh crack the line gave out and suddenly the telephone was as dead as stone. After a few moments frantically working the receiver for the operator and getting nothing, Meeks gave an inarticulate roar and backhanded the telephone across the office to shatter like smashing crockery against the wall.

He looked down at his hands and saw they were still trembling, balled them into fists and fought to control his breathing. Arkham had gone to hell; nothing made any sense anymore. Even the small victory of arresting Morgan thanks to Ryan Dean's tip-off had turned to ashes in his hands when he received orders to simply keep the prisoner at the Arkham police station and await further instructions. Since then, his every attempt to contact the Department had failed; first he'd just been rebuffed, but then the long-distance telephone lines had gone down, and no matter how many telegrams he sent, or where, he received no reply. Traveling into the fog on the country roads was all but suicide, and he'd even resorted to sending a man by the trains that still mercifully seemed to be running, but he'd still heard nothing.

Morgan's refusal to answer questions had soon become the least of his problems, as he, his deputies, and the remaining prohibition agents become quickly roped in by what was left of the Arkham police into trying to hold a lid on the rising tide of murders, assaults, and suicides that gripped the town. The fracas during the fire on French Hill had been the worst of it, and Meeks had been forced into shooting down two men to help quell a full-scale riot from erupting. That had been the worst, until he'd been called to the Simonds' house on the edge of town this morning. The side wall of the place facing the woods had been ripped open like a sardine can, actually ripped open from the outside. The inside of the house looked like a tornado had struck it, and the only sign of the family of four that lived there was a woman's shoe, the heel torn off and the sole smeared with blood. *What could have done that?* His mind skirted away from a poisonous memory, running from something that threatened to well up inside him, something he just couldn't take.

Meeks couldn't help but sneer when the local cops, their faces yellow-pale in the overspill from their flashlights, had looked to him like frightened children for answers, to be told what to do. They'd treated him like a pariah after the Sheldon Gang raid had gone south, but now he was the closest thing any of them had to a leader. It was a joke, even if Engle had lost it completely.

I have no damn answers, no answers at all; I'm just as sick and scared as the rest of them.

He'd focused on the practicalities. The fog had rendered all hope of a search as useless, and regardless, looking up into the shrouded woodland beyond Arkham's boundaries, he knew that nothing on Earth could have made him want to cross between that line of trees, and he knew the other men had felt the same.

Big man, U.S. Marshal, man-hunter, and he was terrified and he knew it and hated how it felt, and if any of them had said it to his face, he'd have pounded them bloody. But none of them had said a word as he had ordered them back to town; they hadn't even looked at each other, hadn't even looked ashamed.

The weight of it all had struck him driving at a snail's pace back into the town, past the blurred outlines of houses and businesses. In many, lights could be seen, but many others were as dark as tombstones, more than there should have been. There was no way of knowing whatever else was going on in the fog—had gone on—either in backstreets or behind locked doors. They'd only found out about the Simonds by chance, thanks to somebody trying to brave the road out of town; the sight of what was left of the house in their headlights had turned them back fast enough.

Meeks knew that the truth now was that policing Arkham had become some kind of tragic farce, a grim joke. The only thing that was keeping a lid on the town and the people inside their houses was raw fear. But that fear was already teetering on the edge of panic and worse; it was only a matter of time before the town tore itself to pieces. *If something else doesn't tear it apart first, literally,* he thought, remembering the splintered brick and boards of the gutted house that morning.

They needed help and needed it badly; not just more cops, they needed the damn army to come in and lock the place down in martial law, burn away the fog somehow, evacuate the town maybe. He felt so utterly helpless and out of his depths. He wanted to smash something, pound it into a bloody pulp, but where was the enemy? Like the fog, it melted away in his hands, and in his heart he knew he was afraid to find out what the fog was truly hiding.

The garbled line he'd just had cut out on him had been a last futile attempt to reach no further than the police department in Aylesbury less than twenty miles away, and beg some kind of assistance, that they pass on a cry for help if they could. It had been the last straw. They were on their own.

There was a train due to leave for Kingsport in about an hour. After that, the old stationmaster had said he couldn't guarantee any further service of Northside Station if the fog kept getting worse. Maybe the evening train, but after that? The company just wasn't going to risk the rolling stock. When that Kingsport train left, Meeks meant to be on it.

To fetch help, he told himself. *I'm not running away. I'm not.*

He got unsteadily to his feet, checked his revolver was fully loaded, and reached for his coat and hat.

No sense in hanging around and risking getting caught up in the fog. The words sounded empty even in the privacy of his own thoughts. He also knew that unless challenged, he wasn't going to say a word to anybody about leaving.

Dropping down a flight of stairs, Meeks looked left and right but saw no one, and felt a sudden spike of anger when his eyes fell on the half-glazed door of the sheriff's office.

Engle had shut himself up in his office filing paperwork like nothing untoward was happening for the last few days—worse—he'd refused to call in more help when that had still been possible. He'd taken to asking insanely trivial questions about town ordinances when confronted with evidence of mass-murder and mayhem in his own backyard. Soon it had been like he couldn't even see the words on the paper or understand what was being said. Today, he hadn't even come in, and there was no answer on his home telephone. But there in his office, the light was on.

He was marching toward the sheriff's door before he even knew he was doing it, the anger flaring up inside him like bile burning in his gut. Here at least was a reachable, tangible, human target for his wrath; if Engle hadn't been such an incompetent, maybe none of this would ever have gotten this far. If he hadn't allowed his town to rot like cancerous fruit, he'd never have been sent here.

Meeks's weight slammed into the door as he turned the handle, almost knocking it off its hinges, bitter words on his lips. Those words choked on shock for a moment at who he saw lounging behind the sheriff's desk, but an instant later his rage exploded with twofold force in him, wrenching out of him in a single snarled word. "Sykes!"

Sykes was sitting with his shiny-shoed feet propped up on the side of the sheriff's wide oak desk, thrown half into shadow by the lamp, cleaning his fingernails casually with the point of the sheriff's letter opener. "Marshal, how good it is to see you," he said conversationally.

Meeks's usually stony countenance twisted in uncontrolled fury, his eyes blazing. "You coward! Where have you been?"

"Oh, around. Did you miss me, Marshal?" he smirked.

"I'll bury you, Sykes, bury you! Dereliction of duty, I'll—"

Sykes guffawed, dropping the letter opener and holding up his hands in mock surrender. "Ya gots me, os-if-er!" he replied mockingly, feigning a movie-style Chicago drawl. "You delicious talking ape," he laughed, sounding utterly unlike anything human, then again in the faux-mobster voice, as the color drained from Meeks's face, "Whats'a madder, all of ya little friends dead? No more suspects to beat on for clues, aw!"

Something snapped inside Meeks, the thinning web of self-control that had been fraying ever since the night of the horror of the bootlegger raid in the woods unraveled at last, leaving nothing more than animal panic and rage in its wake. Instincts that would have normally warned him of danger, that something was very wrong here, were all blown away in the hot flood of anger that engulfed him.

Meeks crashed into the heavy desk, his long arms reaching across and grabbing Sykes by the lapels. An instant later he was trying to recoil in horror as his hands just sank into the hot morass of gluey tissue they found there, Sykes's jacket, shirt, and the flesh beneath it dissolving into grey-crimson sludge.

"You're right, you know, of course!" The thing that had murdered Sykes and stolen his face bantered cruelly as Meeks struggled. "He was a coward, petty and corrupt, surprisingly cheaply bought as well; happy to turn a blind eye as Mother went around her business. But after the unpleasantness in the woods, he had second thoughts, so I ate him. You can't imagine how busy I've been, being him and others, making sure the stage is set, the players in motion, and soon, I'll be you as well."

Meeks began to bawl helplessly like a child as no matter how he tugged and thrashed, he could not withdraw his hands from the Sykes-thing's torso. The monster laughed cruelly, its mouth opening wider and wider until it split its head apart like it had been guillotined at the mouth.

* * *

"When will we reach the farmhouse? We have been walking too long."

Dr. Fields turned to look at which of his followers had spoken. His eyes met Red's. The big ex-train brakeman had pulled his robe close around him, and his teeth were bared and chattering in a pale face. Behind Red, the rest of his followers were a loose huddle in the fog, their fog-soaked robes hanging from hunched shoulders; they looked broken, exhausted.

This is wrong, he thought. They had only just set out from the trucks, and the start of their path had to be no more than twenty yards back down the road. *Look at them, though,* a voice said at the back of his thoughts. *They look as if they have been walking for hours.* It was then that he felt the heat spreading across the skin of his chest. He scrabbled at his neck and pulled the amulet out from beneath his shirt. It was a simple thing, a circle of green stone, the marks carved into its surface almost lost from wear. He stared at it, his mind racing, thinking of all the sorceries and impossibilities this amulet had let him walk through, of its warmth against his skin as whatever power it held did its work. Now the green stone was glowing, lines of light flowing through it like veins of fire. He could feel the heat radiating from it as if it were a coal pulled from the fire.

"Look there," called a voice from behind him, an edge of panic rising in it. "What is that?"

He turned his head slowly. The wetness of the fog felt clammy on his skin, as though it was the rank exhalation of a dying creature.

A shape had formed in the fog, growing larger, its size and shape swelling and shrinking as they looked at it. A murmur of panic rolled through the Hand of Solace, growing louder as they edged back. Dr. Fields heard the metallic clatters and clicks of guns being primed for firing sweep through them.

No, he thought. *No, no, no.*

"Don't fire!" he shouted.

The first shot rang out, the dull retort of a heavy revolver, and for a heartbeat, a flat silence seemed to envelop them. The shape in the fog swayed but did not fall.

Then the rest fired in disordered volley, booming shotgun blasts and the rapid thunder of automatics blanketing the whitening world with deafening sound, and Dr. Fields screamed against the roar of gunfire, his eyes blinking closed.

Silence.

He opened his eyes.

The fog pressed against him in a thick white layer. He could see nothing. Against his chest the amulet felt as if it was about to blister his skin.

"Red?" he shouted. "Luther?"

Nothing, just the heavy roar of blood behind his eyes. "Red, Harmon, Bates, Goulding!" He dragged the names from his memory with sudden desperation.

The moan was low, like a nervous chuckle of pain. He whirled around, but the sound faded.

This is a trap, he thought. *I am a fool. We should never have come here. The information was a lie, worse, a lure and now I sit in some other's palm.* He thought of all the things he had learned since he had run from the mountain of dead gods, of the secrets that most would believe insanity, of the knowledge that once believed would burn sanity away.

"*Ul'sh'kau'thuk*," the word came to his lips with a wash of bile, and the taste of his own blood. His vision swam with oily light, and he felt as if he was going to fall.

The fog parted in front of him like a curtain pulling back from a hidden corridor. Roots crawled across the ground, and the shapes of twisted trees lined the path like half-hidden mourners, nodding with movement almost too slow to be perceived. He took a step forward. Black ooze welled up from around his foot, and the stink of rot and stagnant water filled his nose. The suck and squelch of his steps was the only sound to break the still air. He had a sudden, half-childish and incongruous fear that he would lose his boots to the mud, but the burning at his chest told him that would be by far the least of his problems if he lingered.

There was something in front of him, something huge and dark that cast a shadow into the fog from an unseen fire. He kept moving forward.

The tree formed as he edged forward, its branches reaching out of the fog like burnt hands from ash. He stopped, but the tree continued to grow before him. Its branches were dead and blackened. He reached out with a wavering hand and snapped a reaching twig off, and watched as it dissolved to slime in his fingers. He stepped closer. The tree's trunk appeared, seeming to grow downward from the crown of branches to the ground rather than up from it. Only then did he see the bodies. They hung from the branches like huge fruit; their hands and feet limp by their sides, drops of treacle-thick blood hanging from their broken fingers and blackened toes like red dew.

For a second he just stared, feeling his hands and face go cold as the blood drained to his racing heart. Then he stepped close to one of the hanging figures and raised his hand to touch its leg with horrified fascination. It turned with a slow creak of its rope, turning a flayed face to look down at him. It was then that he noticed the remains of the robe which hung from the corpse in tatters. It was grey, the grey of the robes of the Hand of Solace, of the dozen he had walked with into the fog.

He looked around, eyes moving between the corpse-hung branches. All wore grey.

They were alive, he thought. *They were with me just a moment ago, but they are bloated, rotten, like they have been here for days.* Vomit rose from his gut.

"Rapture…" the voice croaked gutturally from beside him, and Dr. Fields whirled to face the wall of fog as it flowed back. A man sat in the bowl of the tree, his head in his hands. Black mud caked the figure, which seemed otherwise naked, making the man seem as if he had just emerged from the ground.

"I saw it…," moaned the man, and Dr. Fields took a step forward. The amulet was still crackling with heat as he took it in his hand.

"I saw it," said the man again. Dr. Fields felt a cold breath of mist on the back of his neck, and glanced behind him to see that the path in the fog had closed. He looked back quickly at the man, suddenly afraid that he'd have vanished, but he still sat there. Under the wet mud he could see patches of wrinkled, raw skin taut on malnourished bones. The man seemed to be kneeling, his legs folded under him in the mud. Dr. Fields's eyes went lower. Dark liquid pooled in the folds of the churned ground.

"I saw it. Rapture. Just like the reverend said."

The liquid was red. The stink of offal and iron was suddenly thick in his nose, rolling down his throat and lungs; it was the stench of autopsied cadavers, laid open on the coroner's slab. The man shifted again and Fields saw then that the man was not kneeling, but had no legs left beneath the knee.

"Rapture, brother," said the man, and dropped his hands from his face. Where his eyes should have been were two burned holes. Dr. Fields turned to run. The mud-coated arm looped around his neck and yanked him back. As he fell, he saw a face of rolling eyes and snarling teeth and the glint of a serrated edge.

"Now you will see," said the man with no eyes.

Dr. Fields hit the ground, and felt the air rush from his lungs. There was darkness.

The darkness faded into the amorphous grey-white of the fog. The eyeless man was gone but he was not alone. Above him a figure straightened, limbs juddering as if driven by cogs. Blood spattered the grey robe it wore, the stains a mix of clotted brown and fresh arterial red. Dr. Fields could see teeth bared in a face that was a mask of streaked gore. The eyes were rolled back behind the eyelids. Breath panted between the half-rotten teeth. Slowly the figure reached down toward his face. Recognition came in a cold surge of terror.

"Red!" shouted Dr. Fields as the figure's hand grabbed his hair. "Red, it's me," he shouted as Red pulled his head and shoulders out of the black sludge. The ground seemed to shake around him; the reek of blood and rot was gone. He could smell the scent of flowers, thick, cloying, like burnt honey and soured milk. *This is it*, he thought. *My mind has come apart. Now, just as the end comes. After all the things I have done, I will never set it right.* He thought of his daughter, of Amelia, of the terrible things he had seen, and the worse things he had done, that were all for nothing.

Somewhere beyond sight the guttural voice of the eyeless cripple laughed. It sounded as if he was weeping at the same time, praying and begging. Fields saw the knife come toward him in the hand of one who had once looked to him as a savior, dry blood coating its twitching blade. "Red!" he screamed. "No!"

Red vanished with a sound like bursting fruit. Fragments of wet meat pattered to the ground around where Red had stood and bounced from his shoulders. Dr. Fields blinked in shock and started screaming. Bloated shadows swayed above him, reaching into a twilight that was suddenly clear and filled with strange stars that turned in smeared arcs across an alien sky.

Something vast stood above him, roaring into the thinning fog, turning where it stood on three legs, its thrashing crown of thick reptilian tentacles like bloated snakes ripping the dead from the corpse tree behind him. A hooting roar rose higher and higher and the smell of spoiled flowers and burnt honey was so thick he could not breathe. He saw a leg like the twisted trunk of a cancerous tree come down in a spray of mud and blood beside him, and pieces of flesh and bone showered the ground. The creature roared again, and he felt his bones twist inside his muscle. He could not move; he could only lie and watch as a doom more final than any knife came for him.

"Rapture!" shouted the blinded man at the base of the tree. "Rapture! Rapture!" The creature reached down, tentacles whipping around the man's body and tightening. The creature roared again and the man's shout became a wet shriek of tearing flesh.

The creature turned, its three legs moving with a broken rhythm, its immense body and crown of limbs swaying and waving like seaweed in a deep tide. A tentacle as thick as his leg whipped down to the ground, and swam through the mud like a viper. He felt the tip of one brush his face, wet with the blood of those he had led into this nightmare.

No, he thought. *No*. He clamped his eyes shut and gathered a breath to say a word he had glimpsed once writ in sorrow on a page old before mankind was born, but never dared to speak before.

"*Nag—*"

The syllable screeched and elongated without ending as darkness and stars spiraled in front of his closed eyes.

Dr. Fields gasped and his eyes opened to blackness. He retched, rolling from the narrow bed to the warehouse's bare floor. Shivers ran through his body, shaking him in tearless sobs. The image of the towering creature rose in his mind, pressing into his thoughts, its cry echoing inside his skull. He vomited, black liquid mud and blood splattering onto the floor between his hands. The image began to fade and he was breathing hard. Pain began to throb in his chest, clicking with every breath he took.

He shook, trying to wrap his mind around what had just happened: how he could have been out near Dunwich, then some other hellish realm, then here, shaking on the floor of his room in the abandoned meat packing plant with the images of what felt like a dream lingering on his thoughts like a bruise. Like the echo-pain of an amputated limb he felt the hole in his brain where the word had been, torn away and never to be spoken again.

He pushed himself up and sat on the floor. His clothes were damp and smelled of forest rot and spilled blood. The amulet was around his neck. He put his hand to it and felt the heat still clinging to it.

It was not a dream, he thought. *Or is there a difference anymore?* He closed his eyes and shook his head. Pain was beginning to flow through him, reminding him that age still had authority even when the will ruled otherwise. He had to think, to try and piece together a path through the pandemonium. What he had just experienced had been real, he was sure of it, just as he was sure that Red, Luther, and the dozen others would be missing when he gathered his followers again. Some force had devoured them, sucked them down into nightmare like a hungering mouth. And something moved behind that force, something that had set its will against them, and understood how to lure them in.

His mind went to the memory of a beautiful face, crowned with blond hair, and split by a cruel smile. But no; Lemaitre was gone, dead on a mountain of dead gods under a fading sun. So who? The Silver Twilight Lodge? *No, no, the Lodge burned*, he remembered suddenly, but not our doing, who? *Dunwich*, the word hammered into place in memory with the finality of a cell door slamming shut, *Whateley*.

"Doctor?" the voice and the creak of the door ended the chase of his thoughts. He looked around and saw a thin female face looking at him through the open door. Lank hair framed her, and whatever beauty she had once had had drained away leaving just its tired marks on her tired face. She looked like they all did, all of them that he had found, all he had offered hope to. Those that were left.

I look like that, he realized. It was the mark of those left broken by the embrace of a callous universe. He took a slow breath and summoned a tired smile.

"It is all right, Miriam."

Her eyes were wide with concern. He realized that he must look half dead.

"I didn't realize you were here. When the others didn't come back…"

"Hush, my girl," he said as kindly as he could as he forced himself to stand. "It's going to be all right."

She nodded and then shook her head. "You should know…," she said, and there was an edge of fear and excitement on her voice.

"What?" he said carefully. "What has happened?"

"Someone phoned…the telephone. The one you said only a few people had the number for. They asked for you. Knew your name. They left a message…"

For a second Dr. Fields did not speak. His mouth and tongue were dry, the taste of blood and bile forgotten along with the pain.

"What did they say?" he asked slowly. Miriam was hardly the brightest, and was wont to panic easily and become confused.

"The man said, *'Raker knows where it is. Follow him to find it, and let that be the end between us.'* Yes, that was it."

Fields tried to focus, think straight. "The man didn't leave a name?"

Miriam shook her head forcefully and bit her lip.

"That's all right, that's fine. What did he sound like?"

The pale woman looked glassily for a moment, as if deciding what to say. "He sounded, he sounded like a gentleman, like a real gentleman."

Sanford, Fields thought, adding it all together. *The Lodge may have burned, but that old devil didn't burn with it, and he's afraid either I'm after him or afraid of whatever is after us both, and fear makes for strange bedfellows.*

"Thank you, Miriam," he replied in a strained voice, "and bring…bring me some strong coffee." Then as a sudden afterthought, "What…what of Slaney, has he checked in?"

"Yes, Doctor, about an hour ago. The man you have them watching is still laying low. They should call again later this afternoon, if you want to speak to them."

Raker, he thought, *Raker*.

Chapter Eighteen

Arkham

December 12, 1929

"Morgan," the gruff voice called from the open door to the cell block. "You've got a visitor."

Tony Morgan lifted his head from his half-doze, sat propped up between the bunk and the cement sidewall of his end cell. He'd been halfway between sleep and memory, killing time within himself, putting his mind far away from this place and its problems, thinking of the places he'd seen in his youth, family, friends, and wonders, avoiding the brittle edges of those recollections, of losses, disappointments, and the pain of leaving things behind. It was a trick he had mastered long ago, like taking out mementos from a locked box when he wished, and leaving others to sleep unwanted.

"Who is it?" he asked with some surprise. He'd been a guest of the Arkham Police Department for seven days and aside from the shifting cast of prisoners—some sullen and some enraged—who passed through the other caged cells, the big marshal with the face like a slab of rough-cut oak who came in to posture and ask fool questions Morgan couldn't be bothered to answer with anything except silence, and the blue-shirt who brought him his meals, he'd spoken to no one and seen no one. No phone call, no lawyer either asked for or offered, but that hadn't surprised him.

The cop at the doorway just shrugged helplessly, his baggy eyes and disheveled hair making it seem as if he hadn't slept for days, which might well have been true. He'd heard the other prisoners passing and muttering sleepless, and those that did sleep cry out or babble in nightmare for each night he'd been here, but Morgan had slept like a babe. For him there were no dreams, bad or otherwise.

"I don't suppose I have a choice?" Morgan asked tiredly, but again the cop only shrugged and stood aside for a young man who came in leading with a briefcase. He was well-made, but thin, and wearing a good suit that didn't quite fit him and a silk tie that didn't quite match. The clean shave that he'd taken this morning couldn't conceal that he hadn't eaten or slept properly in days either, but looked like he'd drunk plenty. But it was the haunted, hunted look in his eyes which took the edge off a face that many would have called handsome in that glib kind of way that appealed to women that ought to have known better, and girls that didn't. Morgan raised an eyebrow as the young man protested to the cop that he should be allowed to speak alone and privately with "the prisoner," but got nothing but a blank dead-eyed stare in return until the warder finally shuffled off without a word.

Morgan had been expecting someone, but whoever this kid was, he hadn't been it.

"Good morning, Mr. Morgan. I take it that you are Anthony Morgan—"

"Shawcross must be getting desperate, sending some cheap hood in a borrowed monkey suit to see me; I imagine times just aren't what they used to be, are they? What's the matter? Can't get the staff? I didn't think I'd killed enough of his people to make a manpower shortage."

There was a slight twitch at the eye, but that was all the reaction he got out of the young man, who drew in a breath and carried on almost calmly. "You are Anthony Morgan, aren't you?"

Morgan simply stared back and smiled.

The young man tried a different tack. "My name is Raker, Charles Raker."

Now who's trying to find out who's heard of who? "Any reason I should care?"

The young man looked almost relived for a second, then carried on, "Not particularly. But you're right, I'm not going to lie to you, I'm here because Shawcross has sent me to find you."

"Oh yes," Morgan replied, relishing the game. "That much I know, and you can let that thin-blooded reptile…," Morgan watched for a reaction to that one and didn't see anything, "… that you've found me all right, large as life and just as ugly. Here awaiting his pleasure, so why has he kept me waiting?"

Raker stared at Morgan, as if unsure what to say next, as if this interview was not going as he had thought it would at all. When he spoke again, he'd clearly decided to cut away the bull and get down to brass tacks. "He wants the fragments, Morgan, that's all; you and the girl, the librarian, you don't matter, that was his message. He wants what was stolen from him, that's all."

Morgan closed his eyes and leaned back against the wall. He smiled and that smile became a chuckle, and that chuckle became a laugh.

"What?" Raker asked. "What's so funny?"

"You don't have a damn clue, do you, Raker? Not a damn clue!" Morgan said, and smiled wryly.

"What's your answer, Morgan?" Raker asked coldly, and Morgan could see there was a bleak anger in the younger man's eyes, not directed at him but at the situation perhaps, or even his role in it.

"What?" Morgan asked conversationally. "No threats, no more carrots and sticks, this it?"

"This is the whole pitch, Morgan. Give him the fragments, and you and him are done."

"Well, this must be a worse mess than I thought," Morgan replied, then after a moment considering Raker through the bars, he asked, "What's he got on you anyway, Raker? You don't seem like the kind of sap that's been dragged into this mess without some idea of what's really going on?"

"What do you mean?" Raker asked defensively.

"Oh, you know what I mean, I can smell it on you, see it in your eyes. Just as I can see it in the eyes of that blowhard marshal, and half of the cops in this damn station house. Do you know your Coleridge, Raker?"

Raker shook his head slowly and Morgan continued, "You're all alike and none of you will admit it. *'One who once having looked round walks on, and turns no more his head, because behind him he knows a frightful field, doth close behind him tread...'* Ring any bells? Shame Daisy isn't here; she'd have appreciated that one, I think."

Raker looked at him, his expression unreadable. If he thought Morgan was taunting him, he didn't rise to the bait. "You say I know nothing about what's really going on, well maybe I don't, and truth be told I don't care about you or the librarian or any living soul in this damned town. I just want something that was very precious to me returned, that's all, and if that means making a deal with the devil to get it, so be it, Morgan. This is nothing personal. So what's your answer?"

"My answer, Raker, is that I don't have them. Even if I was willing to give them up, even if I was fool enough to trust to

Shawcross's benevolence or as blind to what he really is as you seem to be," Morgan smiled cruelly, "or even willing to give him the satisfaction, I couldn't anyway. I don't have them, and short of them being maybe somewhere in Arkham and tied up in all this carnage and chaos that's going on, I can't say where you'll find them either."

Raker reached out and put his hands on the bars and sagged visibly for a moment.

"I'm sorry, Mr. Raker, it looks like your heart's desire is going to have to wait awhile yet; my blood alone, I'm guessing, won't suffice."

Raker let go of the bars and drew himself up again, and gave Morgan a hard look in reply. "Well at least I'm on the outside of the cage, Morgan, which is more than can be said for you."

Morgan made a tip of an imaginary hat in a gesture conceding the point, but said, "Are you so sure, Raker? Are you sure that's what's going on here?"

Raker turned to knock on the door to the outside world, but turned as Morgan called after him.

"Why do you think I'm still on ice here, Raker? Why isn't your boss here himself? I'll tell you, because he's terrified, Raker, terrified of this place and what's happening here. Why hasn't Shawcross, with all his money and connections, not to mention power, just spirited me right out of here? Eh? Why's he relying on cannon-fodder and skulking bagmen like you? I'll tell you: because he can't risk anything else."

The door opened and Raker pushed by the exhausted policeman, Morgan's shouted words ringing in his ears. "You may have made a deal with a devil, Raker, but it looks like you picked the wrong one!"

Chapter Nineteen

Kingsport

December 13, 1929

Raker watched Dr. Zabriski step from the ornamented stairs up from the street and onto the Kingsport station platform.

She looks ill, he thought. Her cheeks were hollow and dark moons of exhaustion hung beneath her eyes. She seemed strangely bled of color since last he saw her, not just her complexion but even the shade of her hair, as if it had begun to visibly grey in the days since he last saw her. She looked slowly around once, but did not see him. He was not too surprised, he had acquired a habit of not being seen, and besides which she didn't exactly seem herself.

He had been watching for a little more than an hour, clinging to the margins of the platform, leaning in a convenient nook and watching the world go by, and he would have freely admitted savoring a taste of a world not entirely shrouded in fog. Ironic, as he understood that Kingsport had a reputation for sea mists and the like, but today the skies were clear, if autumnal, and after Arkham, the bracing sea air was like balm from paradise.

Kingsport station was not overly large, but built with ornate style that belied its parochial location. The station house was a mock-classical confection of marble-fronted red brick which rose to a tiled gable, and was surrounded by an iron-filigreed canopy which extended from either side of it and sheltered the wide platform. Steam hissed from the midday Boston train as it got ready to roll out, billowing out from its breaks and smokestack and dissolving into the chill air. The fog had been thick over the land all the way from Arkham, and seemed to only be getting thicker when he'd caught the train out that morning—and he'd been lucky to get a train at all according to the feverish-looking stationmaster in Arkham. That had been the case almost to the very edge of the harbor itself, when the train had broken out of the fog and the daylight that had flooded the carriage had almost blinded him. A woman further along in the loco's single, sparsely peopled carriage had actually broken down and cried, and part of him didn't blame her. But that relief had been short-lived; the darkness Raker carried was inside him; it was his own fate, and fog or sunlight, that hadn't changed.

As soon as he'd stepped off the train he'd bought a local paper, then a Boston paper, then even a two-day-old copy of the *New York Times*; there was no mention of Arkham in any of them, nothing about the riots, the fire, even the fog, not even lies, nothing. He'd asked about a copy of the *Arkham Advertiser* from the seller and had been told they hadn't received one by delivery for weeks, and then forgot the question he'd been asked when pressed. There had been something so deeply sinister about that sudden forgetfulness that Raker had just walked away, and talked to no one else. Feeling like he was a stranger from another world in the dreamlike, half-deserted seaport, the tourists long gone, the further he walked away from the station, the more unsure and lost he had felt, until he simply retraced his steps and waited for the woman he was to meet to arrive.

He was running out of options and out of time. Morgan had refused him, and the resultant phone conversation across the crackling line with Shawcross had been brief and threatening in response. It had been a call he'd made from the shut-up general store where he'd been hiding ever since after the night of the fire. He'd woken up the morning after exhausted and hungover to find the boarding house deserted and the back door hanging off its hinges. He had no idea what had happened or when, but he had not waited to find out and so relocated to hide out at the store.

Shawcross had none of the composure or the arrogant power of when they had first spoke, but his final words were clear enough: "Find the fragments, that is all that matters now; do this for me and I will see you rewarded, otherwise I have no desire to speak with you again. Morgan is bait I will not take! Do you hear? I will not share Arkham's fate!" The line had gone dead and Raker had been left in no uncertain terms that he had been hung out to dry. Zabriski was his only hope now, and she was a thin one at best.

He watched her cross the platform and open the door to the little, well-appointed waiting room which doubled as a cafeteria and go inside; her steps seemed curiously hesitant and precise, almost as if she was unsteady on her feet. Only a handful of other people were on the platform: a youngish couple holding hands on a bench, a muttering baggage boy struggling with a trunk as the guard told him to hurry, and an old man dismounting carefully from a second-class carriage as if he'd changed his mind. He glanced at them all briefly, then unfolded from his place and walked to the waiting room and pushed the door open.

She sat alone on a wooden bench at a table, her back to the door, the only person in the room apart from the burly aproned woman behind the serving hatch who soon disappeared after he shook his head at her, declining service.

Zabriski hadn't turned at his entrance, made no sign she knew he was here at all. *She has had no need to learn paranoia*, he realized, *that or she's completely out of it.* She did not look up until he sat across from her at the little white table.

"Hello," he said, and smiled. "So what have you got for me?"

She looked right through him, then suddenly shock spilled across her tired face, and it took a second longer for her mouth to successfully form words. Her eyes were wide, startlingly so now he was up close, the irises and pupils like wide black holes in bloodshot whites as if she had been staring into the sun. He noticed that her skin seemed papery as well, almost translucent, and her hands were trembling where she clutched something rolled in newspaper. The glitter was gone from her eyes, the sharpness and the spark he had encountered and liked when he had first met her had been snuffed out. *She's not just tired*, he realized, *something has broken inside her.*

"What…wer…Mister…Mr. Raker isn't it? You came to see one of my patients. What are you doing here?" she stammered, and her hands shook afresh, the fingers gripping the folded newspaper more tightly.

"You called me," said Raker carefully, keeping his tone light and pleasant even though a strange, nameless panic was starting to rise in his chest. He kept his eyes steady as hers flickered and jerked from him to move quickly across the room and back.

"No…no…," she stammered, shaking her head. She touched her head to push back a lock of her hair in an oddly girlish gesture, before saying dazedly, "I'm sure I would have remembered…that…I'm sorry…I don't…" Her voiced trailed away.

Damn, she's not faking this; it's like she's in shock or drugged. "Then why are you here?" he said gently. "Why am I here, at

Kingsport station, now at midday on the day you picked." He showed her the face of his watch and tried to smile reassuringly. "Just like you said."

She shook her head again slowly, but he could see the fear and doubt in her face. Something took him back, some feeling, a resonance in her. He thought of what he had seen when Stonegroves had vanished, of the sound of reality tearing like paper, of the screams of another world meeting his own. There were things that would break your mind if you knew them; things that could happen that would put out your soul like a snuffed candle. He remembered her bright smile again, the life in her, the intelligence, and suddenly felt sorrow pull at his thoughts.

"I…," she began. "I called…"

"Yes," he nodded. "There was something you needed to tell me, something that you did not want to talk about in Arkham."

She frowned and made to get up, but he laid a hand gently on her arm and she sat back down again, blinking.

"It's okay," he said, as if he were trying to talk a gun from a madman's hand, when things were most assuredly not okay. "It's okay, just tell me why you came here."

"I don't know," she said, and bit her lip. "I really don't know. I can't sleep. God, I wish could sleep, but if I do it happens again." Her voice was trembling between laugher and panic. "I thought it might stop if I came, but it hasn't, it hasn't, it was what it wanted, but it hasn't stopped."

"What was?"

"Mr. Raker," she asked softly, fixing him with dead, lifeless eyes, "where am I?"

"Kingsport, we're in Kingsport, Dr. Zabriski. You came here, came here for something."

"Lemaitre," she whispered.

Raker's knuckles whitened against the edges of the table, but he managed to keep his voice level and calm; he knew anything else was likely just to panic her further, that or shut her down. "What about him?"

"Case notes," she said absently, "locked in his office, the first patient, the first one, you see? Origin. Singular catatonic response. I wanted to help, to know, so much. So very much. I thought if I understood, I could make sense…help…"

"The case notes, what did they say?" he asked, trying to steer her on track.

"Something had happened before, here, Kingsport…a storm, massacre…cult, ritual. I didn't understand, didn't believe. He came to Arkham because of it, Dr. Joseph Lemaitre, to the asylum, tried to study it, recreate…control…followers, feeding on false hope, Stonegroves, his version…his secret…the old man told him what he didn't already know, from the tragedy…"

Raker felt the air go out of him; she had said it, said the word, *Stonegroves*; she had been the first, the only one, the only one but him to acknowledge the place had ever existed, *and look what it's cost her.*

"The old man, here, address on Water Street," she continued as if talking to herself now, thinking aloud. "I had hoped to find his family, ask questions…found…found…oh, oh, no…the music, I don't want to hear it, the girl, please I don't want to, really, I'm sorry…"

Raker had never seen anyone look so pitiable and frightened as she did right then. The guilt stabbed at him as he took her by the shoulders and demanded answers.

"Who? What girl? Who was the old man?"

"Retired sea captain of all things, like something from a story… First patient, symptomatic, admitted to Arkham Asylum by his niece, Daisy Hannah Walker… He knew, from the old days, so old, wicked man… Lemaitre had forced it out of him, his secrets, he'd seen…terrible…the Lord of Nightmares, seen it before, knew what Lemaitre had forgotten." Zabriski's expression changed suddenly, became angry; her voice dropped low, became almost a growl. "He's wrong, wrong! Don't you understand, he can't control it, none of them can, it wants them to try, it feeds off them… I didn't want it… I don't know why I took it. Out of all the things in the old house… It's not as if it looks like much… I just wanted to understand… It wanted to be found, in dreams, don't you see?" She took a ragged breath and put her face in her hands. The bundle of newspaper in her hand dropped with a thud on the table between them.

"What did you take?" he asked levelly. She did not reply but simply sat there, unnervingly still and silent, her hands covering her face.

Slowly, cautiously he unfolded the newspaper. On it, resting on the grainy print, was a shard of black stone. Pictograms and symbols covered its surface which was polished to oil-slick sheen. Raker stared at it in amazement, not believing what it was, what it must be. The room around him faded at the edge of his eyes. It was as if the glassy-stone fragment was more real than anything else in the room. He blinked and swallowed, the sensation draining from him, but leaving a tremor in his hand as he wiped a hand across his forehead; a sheen of cold sweat had formed on his skin.

"You see, don't you?" Zabriski's voice seem to whisper in his ear, even though she was still sitting across from him, her hands covering her face. "I keep on wanting to throw it away, but every time I take it out, I just stare at it. I feel like I've stared at it for days and days."

Raker said nothing. His mind was spinning. This was it, a piece of the fragments that Shawcross had asked him to track down, the price for everything Shawcross had promised…and here it was, sitting on a sheet of creased newsprint, close enough for him to reach out and touch its surface. He could still win the game, one last throw of the dice. He let out a careful breath.

"I see," he said carefully. "I can help, though, I know someone who wants this and will take it away."

She said and did nothing, but in his mind that seemed as good as a refusal and a splinter of panic that he could somehow lose the fragment entered into his mind like a glass knife. "No," he said gently. "No, you don't understand—I can take it away, and once it's gone you won't have to see it anymore, won't have to think about it, won't have to dream. It will be gone, and then you don't have to worry. You will be able to sleep then." The lies slipped from his lips without him knowing where they came from.

Outside, the train's whistle blew and the table shook slightly and the locomotive pulled away from the station.

He waited but she said nothing. After a long moment, he reached out and took the fragment, wrapping the paper over it, and pushed it into his inside pocket. It felt heavy, heavy as the whole world.

"There," he said, and slowly got up. Still the woman didn't move, but remained like a strange statue made of flesh. *See no evil,* the thought came to him from nowhere as he backed away. Raker felt something pull at the back of his mind, a pang of warning that whispered of his callousness. He cut the thought away.

The damage is done already, he thought, *and she will be better off without this piece of rock; I might even have saved her life.* He tried to hold onto the thought, but it faded. He turned to walk slowly to the glass-paned waiting room door, his mind already working out what he'd say to Shawcross, how he'd make the deal, keep himself protected. He pushed the door open, and the fog slipped in on a breath of cold air. He paused. *Fog? There was no fog… It's finally reached here then; that was quick.*

"I didn't call you," she said in a flat voice from behind him. He opened his mouth, unsure what to say, but pushed on outside and the door was swinging shut on the grey murk behind him.

He had another three hours till the Arkham train—*No, why go back? Why not cut the deal from here? So much safer, surely?* The smile spread slowly across his face, and then he felt the laughter coming from his mouth. Impulsively, he took the fragment from his coat, unwrapped it in his hand and looked at it again. He had done it; he had won at a game he did not even realize had an end other than death. It was almost over. He would return the fragment to Shawcross, and then everything would be right. For the first time in his life he would not need to run anymore, or to live with the scars of lost chances.

Still smiling to himself, he set off briskly through the gathering mist toward the stairs down to the town. A man stood in his way, fog coiling around his dark suit, his head tilted to one side as he looked from Raker's eyes to the fragment in his hands. White-grey hair framed the face that looked both kind and weary, and as hard and unforgiving as a scalpel's edge. The image of the old man stepping from the train as Raker moved past him flashed across his mind, just as Dr. Zabriski puzzling words again filled his ears: *"I didn't call you."*

Move! screamed a voice in Raker's head, but he had not taken a step away before the man stepped forward and spoke. "Hello, Mr. Raker," said the old man.

Raker reached for the gun inside his coat, his free hand a blur. The rough-sawn wood of the stock met his palm, and froze.

He could not move; every muscle felt as if it had turned to cold stone. He stared at the old man, who had raised a hand and marked the air with a flowing line which burnt with a hot coal light. He tried to speak, but his tongue was numb against his teeth. The old man shook his head sorrowfully. Raker noticed with paralyzed fascination that a bead of blood had formed at the corner of the old man's mouth, which he reached up and dabbed away carefully with a pocket handkerchief before he spoke again.

"We have never met," the old man said, "but I think we know one another. My name is Fields, and I think you have something that I need."

Sweat beaded Raker's skin. His eyes clouded with hot tears. Numbness was soaking deeper into his flesh, shutting down sensation throughout his body. He could not blink or turn his eyes from the symbol glowing in the air at Fields's fingertips. It seemed to throb in time with his racing heart. It held him still, swallowing all his will to move, to pull his gun and fire at Fields as he stepped slowly forward.

"I am sorry," Fields was saying. "I truly am. I believe you are a good man, or at least were one once, and perhaps were things different we could have worked to the same end."

Raker tried to take a breath and felt the air trickle into his lungs as his chest began to go cold. *I am going to choke*, he thought. *I am going to drown here, standing in a station full of air I cannot breathe.*

"But now I fear that we could not come to an understanding," Fields continued, "so I can only say that I will put this right. When the time comes, this will never have happened."

Panic flooded Raker. His last breath was burning in his lungs. He had to move, he had to look away from the sign that now glowed like a rip through the wall of a furnace to the flames beneath. He poured strength into closing his eyes, to breaking the sign's hold on him.

"For now, though, I beg your forgiveness," said Dr. Fields as he extended a hand toward the fragment.

Raker blinked. Air rushed into his lungs as the sign flared bright beyond his closed eyelids. He could feel the rough grain of the sawn-off shotgun stock in his hand as he dove to his right, the cold metal of the trigger guard. A sound like tearing paper filled his ears. The sign flared and grew, uncoiling like a snake. The light failed. Paint on the station walls began to peel, charring to flakes that spun upward to vanish in a spreading pall of shadow. Dr. Fields was yelling with pain and panic as cords of fire whipped up his arm. The smell of burnt flesh filled the air. Raker hit the ground, rolled, and came up behind an iron and wood bench.

The sign was still a red bruise on his sight, and his head spun with nausea. He pulled back one hammer and fired, half-blind, then fired again; the shotgun bucked wildly in his hand, roaring across the still air. Windows shattered, and splinters of wood leapt up from the row of benches.

Raker ducked back behind the bench, breathing hard and coughing on the smoke that was rolling up the walls. He still had the fragment clutched in his hand. Sweat was pouring from his skin, and he felt as if he was about to be sick. He glanced at it, jammed it into a pocket, broke open the shotgun, and scrambled two fresh cartridges into the breach before snapping it shut. A moan came from somewhere across the platform.

Raker rose slowly, the sawn-off shotgun steady in both his hands.

He edged forward. Dr. Fields lay on his side, half behind a bench, curled around his burnt arm. Raker could not tell if one of his blasts had hit the old man or something else entirely had laid him low. Fields eyes flicked up to Raker, pupils contracted to pinpricks of pain.

"My daughter," croaked Dr. Fields. "Please. All I wanted was to make things right."

Raker thought of the promises Shawcross had made him, of having his lost life back; of his life being something other than violence and pain, and empty coldness. He thought of what the Hand of Solace had done, of the lies it had used to turn people into monsters for the promises of hope. He leveled the shotgun at Dr. Fields, and watched the old man try to shake his head. Around them fire leapt up the station house walls and smoke began to clog the air, whirling into vortexes with the fog.

We are the same, thought Raker, as he looked down the barrel at Dr. Fields. *I am now like them, a monster made from the lies of solace.* His finger tightened on the trigger.

"No!" called Dr. Fields.

Raker dropped his aim slowly. Fields was still looking up at him; he had not looked away. *Brave,* thought Raker, and turned away.

Pain lashed through him, spiraling through his body like a barbed cord dragged through his veins. Raker felt himself fall, the floor meeting him with bone-breaking force. His body was white heat and jagged pain. Muscles spasmed, snapping their bones with a sound like wood exploding in a fire. Screaming filled his world, pouring from his throat to fill his ears, ringing through the smoke. Above it all he heard the words, a string of jagged syllables that exploded through him like the cracks of a whip.

Dr. Fields rose unsteadily above him, holding his burnt arm, blood bright on pale lips as he chanted. Raker did not feel it happen as the old man pulled the fragment from his pocket. For Raker, pain was all there was, a red-bladed prison to hold his thoughts. Fields looked down at him, and Raker saw an echo of his own pain in the weeping eyes. Fields raised Raker's shotgun, still chanting with heaving breaths. The gaping mouths of the twin barrels trembled in his good hand.

Raker tried to deny him, to shout at him to stop, but only the pain came from his mouth while behind the scarecrow-thin figure the flames grew, staining the fog to dull orange and ember red.

Dr. Fields shook his head, and then pulled the trigger.

Chapter Twenty

Arkham

December 13, 1929

Harvey Walters sat behind the wheel of the little yellow two-seater touring car he'd "borrowed" from an absent colleague from the science department and fretted nervously, his fingertips tapping nervously as his thoughts raced.

"What are you doing here, Harvey old boy? Just what do you think you are doing?" He sighed heavily. "And now you're talking to yourself out loud in the third person as well, making a habit of it in fact. You're coming apart at the seams, old fellow. Better just drive along to the asylum now and check yourself in…well, perhaps not the one in Arkham at any rate."

He fetched out his pocket watch and checked the time; it was a quarter past one in the afternoon, which meant he'd been parked here on French Hill for nearly twenty minutes, and it was almost an hour ago that he had been rebuffed from visiting Morgan in the police station for the second time in two days. Though this time he had waited till he had seen that awful bullying marshal, Meeks—and never in his mind had a man been so inaptly named— drive off first. The first time he had tried to see Morgan, the man had taken him to one side and given him a grilling, and when Meeks's questions had not elected the answers he wanted, he had seemed on the edge of violence. Harvey was convinced it would not have stopped at threats, had Sheriff Engle not intervened and let him go.

He had been unwise in the extreme to go back and try and see Morgan for a second time, but he didn't know what else to do; he felt more lost at sea now than he had in his near seventy years of life. Whispers about the town ever since the bloody affair at the library had spoken of other suicides and assaults, and a dozen souls gone missing, and there was talk of a hushed-up murder-house found on Independence Square besides. Then one of the town's oldest and finest colonial mansions, the one that had in recent years held the philanthropic society of the Silver Twilight Lodge, had burned down to its foundations, and more than a dozen bodies had been pulled from its blackened timbers. Several nearby houses had also caught light and there had been rumors of a near-riot, even several fatalities.

To top it all off, the damn fog still had not lifted in the four days since, only waxed and waned as if the whole town was tapped somewhere south of Hades. Phone and telegraph connections to the outside world had become erratic at best, the railroad service had been disrupted, and you were taking your own life in your hands trying the roads over any distance. The university had finally begun to shut its doors that morning, closing the semester early with all the air of a barn door being slammed long after the horse had bolted.

The dean's hastily concocted open letter to the faculty and students with its vague talk of "unhealthy and highly unusual climatic conditions" and "possible influenza" in the town was as transparently spurious as it was oddly unnecessary. What had surprised Harvey had been how few of the remaining students and staff seemed inclined to flee, or at least, disinclined to go immediately, now given the "official" open option to do so. He had heard talk of going, of course, from almost all of them he'd met; plans being made between students in the common rooms and staff members behind closed office doors, but they amounted to the same thing: "I'll go soon…but not yet…I'm waiting for the fog to lift" or "I'll need to put things in order first" or "I'm waiting for my father to wire me the money for the train." All of it rang hollow.

The truth, Harvey feared, was all together more insidious and more sinister; Harvey had begun to feel that they were trapped somehow. Trapped in Arkham like flies caught in amber, and it was too late to flee. Harvey felt that strange pull to stay as well, but unlike the rest of them for whom it was a nameless oppression that had settled over them and cut them off more surely than the fog had shrouded the town, Harvey Walters knew the truth; he guessed at the true horror of what was coming and that whatever it was wanted an audience for its arrival; that and something else—it wanted blood.

He also knew that he had it in him to start the little yellow motor car, get on the road for Boston and drive, drive out of the fog, out of Arkham and leave every horror that had been and every horror that was yet to be born behind him. Unlike the rest, he had the will to escape if he wished; he knew this and had considered why, whether because of his foreknowledge or his experiences, or even maybe because of the little corroded amulet on his watch fob, whatever power held Arkham's people in place, had no hold on him. And yet he did not leave, could not, no matter the painful ache that still throbbed in his shoulder to remind him of his brush with death at the library, despite his years that weighed on him like never before thanks to days of stress, fear and near exhaustion. Despite even the acute spiritual terror he felt when he remembered the thing of darkness and black frost he had confronted and the utter alien depths of it, despite even the hopelessness of Morgan being dragged away in handcuffs. Despite these things he could not do what his mind and all rational sense screamed at him to do and just leave. *Afterward. This one last try to do something, fight it, and then go. I'll go then.*

He chuckled sadly. "It's because of that bloody girl, you old fool, and because you said you'd stay and help. Because it's the right thing to do, and it's going to get you killed and serve you right."

Harvey struggled out of the car, his aching joints protesting after being settled in one place for too long. He buttoned up his overcoat against the chill mist, which mercifully was at its weakest this time of day, and slung his satchel, today containing a small selection of tools more suitable for a housebreaker than a college professor, over his shoulder.

Beyond the grey, dead-looking hedge that bounded the abandoned property, the squat, black bulk of a building even older than the now-burned colonial mansion not so far away loomed like an ogre's fortress out of the mists. It was a building with its own dark legends aplenty, and those legends were no small part of the greater tapestry of myth and superstition that made up Arkham's own. It was a building in which Daisy had shown particular interest, and he was sure it was a pin-mark—one of three—in a map he had seen affixed to a board in her impromptu study in the Administration building tower. It was a map he now suspected he had been meant to see. Of the two other points, complete with crimson thread connecting them to the center, one had been just outside of Dunwich and the other by the bay at Kingsport, while the center point connecting both had been here, in Arkham, at the Witch House.

"Oh, Mr. Morgan," Harvey breathed aloud, pulling his coat collar high, "I wish you were here."

The rotten wooden gate hung off its hinges and was no bar to his progress, and all the way up the pathway, covered as it was with brown weeds, fog-slicked and dead, Harvey felt as if he was being watched. The cold and damp made his arm ache and his joints stiff, but still he tottered on resolutely to the looming black portico door that fronted the cracked and crooked manse.

To his knowledge, the last time the place had been in use was as a dilapidated boarding house some twenty years ago, long before his time in Arkham, although memory of one of their students found dead there had lived long in the Miskatonic University's collected folklore. That fact, along with a score of other stories and dark legends that crowded round the place was no doubt why Daisy had shown such an interest in the infamous Witch House of Arkham during her researches. It was a dangerous place, a forlorn place, one avoided by the people of Arkham and one he felt sure Daisy had visited alone previously. Where better then to start in a search for her—that was what he had been about to tell Morgan at any rate, when the police had come crashing in at the roadhouse.

Under the sagging portico, the air was, if anything, damper and colder, with a foul, spoiled undercurrent to it, as if something had crawled in between the boards and rotted away. The front door was warped and pitted, blackened as if by fire in places, and the corroded lion's head knocker leered at him leprously as he stood indecisively before it.

"Come on, old man," he whispered under his breath, "what are you expecting, Marley's ghost?"

He took out his little iron jimmy and pushed cautiously at the door with it, for there was no handle he could see to turn, and was surprised when it swung soundlessly and swiftly open as if on a sprung counterweight. Somewhat taken aback, he looked inside to find the hallway just as decaying and mold-stained as he expected, but was somehow surprised to see the remains of furniture, fixtures, and fittings, stained and phenomenally rat-eaten as they might be, entirely present. It was as if the owners had simply shut the door a decade ago and left without looking back, and time and vermin had perhaps done the rest.

Walking in, Harvey thought about shutting the door behind him and decided against it; the few cold curls of mist snaking across the threshold were somehow more comforting than the thought of being shut in the Witch House alone. *Or not alone,* he added mentally and wished he hadn't. The light filtering through the greenish, mildew-caked windows was poor, but still enough to see by and Harvey, pushing past his nervousness and apprehension, forged on with his plan of attack. He would systematically search quickly but carefully each room in turn, starting on the ground floor and working upward. His plan was to disturb as little as possible unless he had to, and linger as little as possible while doing it.

He started with the entrance hall he was in and moved outward, moving in tight, fussy circles, opening drawers, prodding carefully at mold-eaten draperies. He touched as little as possible, opting to use the point or the hook of his jimmy whenever he could, and held a scarf over his mouth to avoid breathing in the swathes of choking detritus that occasionally erupted from his probing. He'd spent enough time in the company of archaeologists to understand that dust could be malignantly dangerous all on its own, given fungal spores and carrion decay, and this place looked like it had more than its fair share of both.

It took him about half an hour to search the ground floor, the actual size of the place and the arrangement of the rooms uncomfortably defying logic on several points, but found nothing but an increasing sense of some malignant presence watching him, and the cold in the air, if anything, growing worse. He wanted to dismiss the feeling of fear he felt as the product of exhaustion and past shocks, but given what he had seen in the university library, he could not. He wavered at the bottom of the stairs, undecided as to whether to go up and search what looked to be at least another three floors, or simply cut his losses and run. He was taking too long, and the fear he was feeling was corrosive; it was eating away at his gut and demanding he should go, go now before something terrible happened.

It was then the music started.

It drifted down from the spaces above with the strained, warbling quality of a gramophone record not quite turning at full speed. It was something plaintive in nature: a string piece he didn't recognize and would have seemed eerie anywhere, but here in the Witch House it seemed designed to instill dread.

Well, that's done it, Harvey thought.. *There's someone here all right.* He found himself reasoning that if they were playing a record, then at least they were a "person" so to speak, not a creature, but that didn't somehow fill him with the relief it ought to have done.

Harvey swallowed hard. "Hello!" he called out, somewhat weakly at first and then with more vigor, "Hello, hello is anybody there? My name is Professor Walters! I'm from the university! Hello?" He wasn't sure what else to say, and felt somewhere between idiocy and terror for shouting his name out loud in this fearful place. But his only answer was the music and nothing more.

Harvey listened intently for a few moments, but could hear only the strangely melancholy and yet subtly threatening sounds of the music. Beneath that was the settling creaking of the Witch House, and something else, a faint skittering, scratching sound. *Rats,* thought Harvey, *rats in the walls.*

"Bother it!" he exclaimed, and started to make his way up the stairs, pausing only on the first landing to look around and see the decay here was even worse—plaster cracked and crumbling, exposing blotched wooden lathes like diseased bones—before walking up again toward the source of the music.

The twin doors to what must have been a master bedroom back in the late sixteen hundreds when the house had first been built stood open at the end of a short corridor, and the music floated insidiously forth from within. Harvey called out again, and again received no reply. He stepped inside and found no one, but what he did find were signs of recent occupancy in abundance. Here the worst of the moldering plasterwork had been torn down, exposing the wooden slats beneath, onto which a host of diagrams, pictures, and newspaper pages had been pinned. On a cleared table was a spill of papers and open books beside which a battered cabinet gramophone plotted its dwindling course over a twelve-inch disk of glossy shellac whose sleeve proclaimed it to be the music of Eric Zahn. To Harvey Walters it all seemed shockingly familiar.

His fear momentarily forgotten, he rushed over to an old blackboard on an easel propped up by the window and the white-shrouded world beyond. On it was a map of Arkham and the surrounding area, the duplicate of one that he had seen in the high room in the university Administration building. "Daisy," Harvey breathed allowed.

For the briefest instant the light cut out, and everything was washed in a strange muted purple glow; the record skipped and Harvey turned to the window, but the white fog, dimmed green by the mildewed window had returned and the strange darkness had passed. A wave of sudden vertigo passed over him, but he shook his head to clear it, studying the map intently. It was just like the one she had in the university, the three connected cardinal points, one of which he was now standing in, but marked were a plethora of other pins all within the off-kilter triangle they formed, each painstaking numbered and annotated in a tiny, precise hand he recognized as Daisy's own.

He peered at the words, his lips working aloud as he made them out. "Stonegroves, Legion of Rapture, lost girl, Fête of Shadows, asylum deaths, murdered seer, Innsmouth inheritance found, Lemaitre's lair, Raker, beheaded serpents, point of transfer, mountain of dead gods, suicide of family, burning Lodge, street killing #3, broken heart, woodland raid… What is this?" he said with mounting horror, his eyes darting to where he knew the university should be, a sinking feeling in his gut at knowing what he would find there before he read the words. "Crossfire, fragments, M + W, survive." *"M + W"—"Morgan and Walters."* He breathed hard and put his fist to his forehead, his world spinning.

How? How could she know? How could she see it all, how? But Harvey Walters knew the answer already; he'd worked it out before, he'd suspected, and here was the proof, but he didn't even want to think it.

Behind him, the gramophone screamed and scratched into silence. Harvey startled and turned, and what he saw made him recoil as he struck his elbow, catching the blackboard map and sending it and him crashing down to the floor.

The rat-thing leered over the gramophone cabinet where it was perched with all too human bloodlust in its twisted mockery of a face. It was bloated, pox-scarred, and its grey-pink flesh hung about it in folds; its body was that of a pendulous rat's but as large as a hog's, complete with a lashing worm-tail, while its spindle-monkey-like limbs ended in sleek, glossy hooked claws as black as tar. It made a skittering, hissing noise, and the numbing horror that had seized Harvey was brought to a sharp focus by the sickening realization that the nightmarish thing was actually *laughing* at him.

Harvey hurled the jimmy he still held in his hand at it, but the rat-thing leapt away, landing deftly and running across the sheer surface chattering madly. Harvey scrambled away, but it leapt again, as fast as a striking hawk, and slammed into his side, crashing him again to the ground. He fought back frantically as his leather satchel was shredded like tissue paper and a second later, razor-sharp pain slashed bright lines across his back. Harvey screamed and rolled. The rat-thing leapt and found the desk, turning back to face him, whipcord-spry. Harvey crawled helpless across the floor away from it, his breath ragged and pained as if something had broken in his chest. His back burned and wet spread down the arms of his jacket as he struggled to escape. He saw with appalling clarity the blood dripping from his fingers to make ink blots in the dust of the floor. He half collapsed—it was useless, he knew he would never make it; *I'm too damn old and too damn hurt!* He turned painfully and looked at the rat-thing, his free hand groping in the pocket of his overcoat. The monstrous abomination was licking his blood from its claws with a long grey tongue, its bloodshot red eyes rolling ecstatically. It was toying with him, and when it wanted to, it would eat him alive.

Harvey's fingers found the pistol. The revolver had been the one the girl from the Hand of Solace had been carrying when she had tried to kill him in the library. Morgan had reloaded it for him and given it to him for protection, and it might be the only thing to save him now. But it was heavy, so very heavy in his hand. With a herculean effort he pulled it from his pocket and drew back the hammer, it wavered as he shakily aimed it at the looming horror. It chittered excitedly, and something hitched in fresh agony in Harvey's chest as everything went dim. "No!" he exclaimed in a voice barely above a whisper as the pistol began to slip from his blood-slick fingers and with nightmarish slowness tumble away and fall to the wooden floor with a thud.

Harvey's hope died then, and tears were running freely down his cheeks as he saw the eyes in the darkness, red and fever-bright, hundreds of them. Peering from the fogged window, from behind the slats of the walls, peering somehow through the solid matter of the room, a swarm come to the feast, their chattering insane, its volume increasing until it threatened to burst his skull. Harvey closed his eyes against the horror and knew that if he had the gun in his hand, he would at that moment turn it on himself, but nothing would spare him the agony of what was to happen next.

Silence as deafening as a thunderclap blasted away the chattering of the rat-things. The chattering erupted again, but this time it was different, shrieking, panicked. Harvey fought his fear and his pain and opened his eyes. The rat-thing that clung to the desk was cowering, its mangled face darting right and left, searching for an avenue of escape. The others were already vanishing, their fever-lights of their eyes snapping out; then came a sound as of a thousand clawed paws running, scrabbling away into forever. But for the rat-thing in the room with him, there was no escape; it was caught in the open and had nowhere to run. It leapt for the window, but was caught mid-air and snapped backward; screeching as if snared by an invisible lasso, it hurtled through the air above him. The rat-thing's frenzied screeching ended in a wet cracking sound that went on for long seconds while Harvey lay there, his mind reeling.

The corkscrew-twisted remains of the mangled rat-thing thudded onto the floorboards before Harvey's face, bloody-striped like a ghoulish barber's pole.

"Nasty, verminous things," a cultured voice said from behind him, "but effective as guard dogs nevertheless. But not, I think, meant for you."

A pair of immaculately polished black shoes appeared at the edge of Harvey's vision as a figure walked smartly round to face him. It was a youngish man he didn't recognize, dressed in a sharp, modern suit and with an expression of deep cruelty and amusement etched into his lean features.

"Why, Professor Walters, I confess you have surprised me. I wondered who would make it this far, and were I a betting man, I wouldn't have laid odds that it would be you."

Harvey tried to speak, but found he could only cough.

"What was that, Professor? Have we met? No, I think not, not like this anyway, but you never met the late, unlamented Agent Sykes of the Bureau of Prohibition, did you? What about this?"

There was no transition of sight, merely a sickening lurch in reality, and somebody else was standing over Harvey, a face he did recognize if dimly, a person he knew to avoid. "Sanford…," he croaked.

"Yes," the man who now wore Carl Sanford's face replied with a venomous smile. "One of my more demanding parts and with the most difficult audience. I would have enjoyed tasting your mind, though, Professor; such a dear old man, so trusted, so wise—think of all of the wonderful mischief I could have made in your skin. But Mother had other ideas."

"Enough Turncoat," a woman's voice spoke and the changeling's head bowed like a penitent schoolboy caught in misbehavior and he stepped away. "Fetch," she continued, addressing his hulking, fish-reeking companion abruptly, "get him a chair and sit him up—gently, loosen his collar, he's been hurt."

Harvey was skipping between light and darkness now; sounds were just unimportant echoes and even his pain had faded like an ebbing tide. He was half-aware of being lifted effortlessly and set up in a sitting position; of hands deftly moving over him, of a bitter liquid that burned like raw spirits forced spluttering down his throat, then came true darkness, fathomless and endless.

When he came to the room had been set to rights, the blackboard stood up, the now blood-stained papers reassembled on the desk. The woman in the dark green dress and the high, old-fashioned boots stood by the window with her back to him, raven hair spilling down her back, her hands clasped behind her in a darkly familiar posture, clasped around a small, battered notebook.

Harvey coughed involuntarily for about a minute, but found at the end of it he felt far better than he ought to. The pain in his back had been replaced with a tight warmth and his heart beat again steadily in his chest, and he could breathe without the horrid broken gasp he had been left with on the floor.

Harvey tried to think of something to say, but he couldn't form the words; it was too much, all too much to take in. He looked at the brownish bloodstains in the dust, already almost dried.

The woman looked over her shoulder at him. "Miss Walker holds you in high regard, Professor Walters; that's the only reason you're alive now and the only reason I choose to keep you so."

"You are…you are Hannah Whateley, aren't you? I don't believe we ever met?"

She nodded and smiled coldly. "A gentleman to the last. No, we did not. Of the un-decayed line, or so they say."

"Daisy? Miss Walker?"

"She's safe, Professor, as safe as anybody could be; pressing that matter further would not be healthy, understand?"

By the doorway, a dark figure loomed.

"I understand," Harvey replied slowly, "or at least, I don't understand, not really. The fragments, the *Valusian Book of Days,* tell her I lost...but you know that already, don't you?"

She said nothing.

"This, this thing you are doing...it's too late to stop it, isn't it? Far too late."

"You do understand," she said, her voice barely under a whisper.

Harvey staggered to his feet and surprised himself by being able to walk freely.

"Get out of here, Professor, get out of Arkham while you can, if you can. The pieces are moving across the board. There is very little time left now before the endgame, hours, minutes."

"What...what happens then?" he asked, but she did not answer.

Instead the figure by the door answered for her after a pause. The face and voice was another he didn't know, but the same urbane cruelty he recognized. "Why, Professor Walters, everyone dies."

"Go," she said simply, "and be careful which doors you choose on your way out—not all of them lead to where you might expect."

Harvey nodded warily. Beaten and spent, he pulled his tattered, blood-stained overcoat around him as if against the cold as he walked toward the landing. As he drew level with the cruel-voiced man, he turned again to Hannah Whateley and said in a broken voice, "I never wanted, never meant for Daisy to...for all this to happen...none of us did... I could have changed it all... you know that, don't you?"

She did not turn to face him, but replied, her voice faraway and cold, "She knows, Harvey, she knows. And if you should see Morgan, tell him this is the way things must be. The only way."

Harvey fled the Witch House, stumbling, sure that a child's laughter followed him like a distant echo.

Chapter Twenty-One

Kingsport

December 13, 1929

Dr. Fields winced as he staggered back down toward the platform. His right arm was crooked and bent at his side, the skin and flesh charred black to the bone beneath his ragged coat sleeve, and it had taken every ounce of his strength not to give into the pain over the three hours he'd waited in the shadows of the station, killing time. In the other hand, he clutched the fragment, his fingers a bloodless white against the black stone. Pain rose and fell through him with every breath and step, but he kept moving. There was no strength left in him for further sorcery; it had taken all he had left to help douse the fire and twist the minds of the few station staff that nothing was amiss. Now sand lay scattered across the blood-stained boards and miraculously no alarm had been raised; the fog, rolling inland from the direction of Arkham, had no doubt helped. Raker's body was gone, tipped into the black pit of the coal bunker. It made a poor hiding place, but it would only have to keep its secrets until he was away from Kingsport.

In front of him, the train thundered slowly in and steam hissed from its vents. Its whistle blew, but aside from him, nobody else waited to board and to return to Arkham. Shouts of activity rose around him, echoing without direction in the fog: the brakeman, the conductor busying themselves, shining colored lights in the fog as points were switched and tracks clanked. A few people passed him, stepping off the train, but he paid them no heed. No one looked back at him either, and even if they had, what would they care? He was a wreck, a broken old man limping along in ragged clothes, his face filled with fear.

What have I done? The memory of the shotgun's roar and the bloody fragments scattering across the floor flashed across his mind. *It was necessary. I had no choice. He would not have stopped.* Fields raised his wounded, poorly bandaged hand to his face. Blood mingled with the tears that ran from his eyes. He glanced behind him; there the fire was a growing blot of light in his eyes, branching through the fog as if alive—was it real or just an echo, a phantasm of the mind, a "what might have been"? Or something worse? In his head, Dr. Fields heard the glowing embers faintly scream with the voices of the dead, the voices of men and women that had trusted him, that had seen him as a savior. *What have I done?*

Fields felt the weight of the fragment in his good hand and thought of the day he had come to Arkham to talk to his daughter, to persuade her that the cult she had turned to could offer her no true hope. It seemed so long ago, a lifetime.

I was wrong, he thought, and gritted his teeth as a tide of pain and dizziness washed through him. He looked at the doors hanging open down the two passenger carriages, their contents spilled into the fog and gone. *I need to get away*, he thought, aware that he had passed into a state of shock, feverish and hollow.

He staggered to an open door, and pulled himself into an empty compartment with some difficulty. It was empty, the smell of tobacco smoke lingering from whoever had left the faded seats. He struggled and pulled the door shut. A guard ran past outside, shouting for the train to leave, waving his lantern.

The fire, we must hurry, can't you see the fire? Dr. Fields collapsed against a worn leather chair back and groaned in pain. His breath was wheezing and he could feel smoke scratching at the insides of his lungs.

Doors slammed, and a moment later the carriage juddered and bucked as the train pulled away, leaving Kingsport station to the flames only he could see.

Fields closed his eyes as shivers ran through his body. He felt cold, as if he had been dragged from a river flowing beneath a layer of winter ice. The edge of his sight was smeared with shadows, and he could feel the soft hands of unconsciousness trying to pull him down into oblivion. In his hand, the fragment felt heavy, as if it pressed into his palm with the weight of oceans. He heard footsteps moving down the passage beyond the compartment's sliding door. The steps were unhurried, falling with the rolling rhythm of the train.

A guard, just a guard, thought Dr. Fields, hugging his burnt arm to him and trying to hide it in a fold of his coat. His thoughts were flowing with the thickness of clotting blood. Beyond the glass, the fog streamed past as the train gathered speed. He closed his eyes and tried to hold onto the pain without it overwhelming him. He had to stay conscious, balancing on a precipice between black oblivion and red agony, giving in to neither. *I have to get back to Arkham. I have to—*

The compartment door slid open. Dr. Fields forced himself to open his eyes and looked up; for the briefest instant he saw a flash of green eyes before the hand struck the side of his head. He fell sideways, crumpling bonelessly into the broad bench seat. Splinters of color boiled across his eyes. Strong hands pulled at him. He struck out blindly, jarring his burnt arm and sending a fresh river of pain through him, making him cry out helplessly. Another blow slammed into his chest, and suddenly he was gasping for air as the world became a choking rush. The strong hands pulled his hands aside and he felt the cord holding the green stone amulet around his neck snap.

No, he tried to say, but it never got further than a strangled gasp. He turned, twisting his body around the hand that held the fragment.

If I lose it then it will all have been for nothing! Despair ravaged him, worse even than the pain. *I cannot fail now. Not now. Please…*

He saw Raker's face again in the moment before the shotgun blast had punched through his skull. Another blow landed, like a sledgehammer into the small of his back, and this time he could not stop the world falling from his grasp. His limbs went slack, and from the buzzing haze of half-consciousness he felt his arms being pulled open, then his fingers, then the weight of the fragment vanishing from his palm. Then his coat was rifled, the Obsidian Key ripped from its secret pocket stitched to the lining. He was being stripped of everything, he realized, everything of value, and he was impotent to stop it. He shook, trying to move, to rise, to fight back, but he was utterly spent.

Slowly his eyes cracked open, wet with tears. He looked up into a pretty young face sharpened by cruelty. The green eyes glittered, and the mouth was smiling. It was a face he had last seen screaming in a temple at the end of time. Her name was Jacqueline Fine, and he had thought that he had seen her die.

"No," he croaked. "You cannot be here. You—"

"Oh, but I am here, Doctor." The woman smiled and sat on the seat opposite him. She wore a pale fur coat, her hair hid beneath an ermine-trimmed hat. She smiled, and Dr. Fields felt a cold spark of familiarity at the expression. "The face is different, so I understand why you might be confused." The woman raised her hands, and Dr. Fields saw the fragment glint back at him.

He let out a slow breath, and dragged what little of his strength he could reach.

"*Ug'fl*—" he began, but the words seemed to suck from his mouth like a stolen breath.

The woman tilted back her head and laughed, and then she looked back at him, eyes glinting like flints. She held up a hand and he saw his amulet hanging between her fingers.

"Thank you," she said, and dropped her hand. "I am glad you tried. Your struggles have been of service. You found what I could not see, and brought it to me. I always knew you could be more than you were." She held up the fragment in her other hand. "And thank you for this."

Dr. Fields blinked; he could not tell if he was weeping or if sight was just slipping from him.

"Why, Jacqueline?" he croaked. His tongue and lips were caked with drying blood. The woman laughed, and the sound was like the cracking of ice beneath his feet. She shook her head.

"Even now you are blind, my friend," said the woman, her voice edged with an accent he had not noticed before, an edge of an older world. Dr. Fields felt cold spread across his skin. His limbs were shaking.

"No, no. It is not you. I saw you dying."

Lemaitre smiled with Jacqueline Fine's lips.

"By now you should have realized that most things that seem one way often are another way."

Dr. Fields pushed against the leather of the chair, trying to rise. The strength drained from his legs long before he could stand, and he crumpled back, slipping from the seat to the floor, gasping from the pain. Lemaitre's eyes had not wavered.

"It is over, Doctor. There is no way back for you now. It would have been best if you had stayed away, and let things take their course."

"My daughter..."

"Would have died like the rest, like the followers you led to Dunwich, like the fools you had blundering around Arkham like third-rate spies. They died just as Charles Raker died—at your hand. I have followed you, seen what you have done; there is blood enough on your account now, Fields. So tell me, do you still think me a monster, even after having walked part of my path?"

"I would have set it right," spat Dr. Fields. The effort sent worms of bright colors squirming across his vision. Lemaitre stared at him, and then nodded slowly.

"I made you well in my image, didn't I?"

Dr. Fields did not answer. He could not feel his limbs, and every breath had a thick, iron taste.

"It is over now, though, my would-be usurper, your part in this chain of murder is over," said Lemaitre, and Dr. Fields thought he heard an edge of relief in the words. "I have all that I need now, thanks to you. The time and the place, the exact hour down to the turning of the world and the light of the fated stars, where the black suns of beyond will shed their radiance on this place. Heralded by carnage and madness, the Lord of Nightmares will walk again and I and I alone shall be there to greet it. It is a matter of hours now; reality will rip open all over Arkham, but I shall be there at the right place, at the right moment." Lemaitre crowed, "The Hand of Solace will serve me well again, I am sure, in one final task. For that, I think, I should also thank you."

Dr. Fields eyes flickered open. "No," he managed. "No, please. They only wanted hope. That is all they wanted."

Lemaitre stood and wrapped the fur coat closer around Jacqueline Fine's thin frame.

"You should have learned the lesson, Doctor. There are many cruelties in this universe, many that we can see, and many more that most will mercifully never dream exist." Lemaitre paused and looked to the rushing wall of fog beyond the window. "Of those there is no poison stronger, or fire that burns deeper in the human hearts, than hope. And there is no worse fate than to be without it, to have it betrayed. I suspect to certain entities, it is like seasoning on well-prepared meat."

Lemaitre looked back at Dr. Fields. There was no anger in the green eyes, no cruel gloating, just blankness and weariness. Lemaitre nodded once, then pulled the compartment door open, stepped into the passage, and was gone. Dr. Fields stared after the fur-swathed figure, his eyes unfocused, the tears rolling down his cheeks in silence.

After a long minute, he closed his eyes, and took a deep breath. He stood, limbs shaking, eyes blinking at the pain. He pulled himself up slowly, broken, his lips peeling back from his teeth with the effort. Trembling, he tried to straighten his clothes with his un-burnt hand. Slowly he turned his head and looked at the fog streaming beyond the window glass, his pain distant, empty. For a second he saw himself as he had been before he had come to Arkham: an old man who had done his best all his life, and found it sometimes not enough. He nodded and stepped closer to the glass, and with a sharp breath extended his hand. The worn metal of the door handle was cold against his skin.

"I am sorry," he said, his voice strong and clear. He pressed the handle down and pushed the carriage door wide to the rushing air; somewhere beyond, the ground below sped past. "I am sorry for everything."

A second later, the wind caught the door, and clattered it shut on the empty compartment.

Chapter Twenty-Two

Arkham

December 13, 1929

Morgan looked at the clock mounted on the wall of the corridor through the bars of the cell. They were late bringing the six o'clock meal, nearly an hour late; they'd been tardy before but never this bad. Something was wrong.

He looked around the small cell block. Aside from a mid-morning arrival who had just mumbled all day after being hauled in for trying to steal a car and failing miserably, he had the block of cages all to himself. The rest, including the so-called rioters they'd brought in, had all been sent off in the police wagon to Boston or been relocated to the asylum, as had been appropriate, yesterday. From what he'd overheard, the wagon hadn't come back yet and was overdue. Morgan hazarded a guess they'd never made it as far as the Aylesbury turnpike, let alone Boston.

Morgan stood by the cage door of his cell and listened intently. There was something, some commotion, raised voices beyond the main door to the cell block. The man in the other cell kept muttering and making soft thumping noises, and Morgan glanced over to him, thinking of demanding quiet, but one look told him it would have been pointless: the soft thudding was the man's head against the brick wall and there was already blood there.

A muffled voice came through the door, agitated, getting closer. Then, "…I simply must insist, gravely urgent!"

Morgan heard the key turn in the cell block door; it shuddered as it opened, as if whoever pushed it didn't expect it to be quite so heavy.

Morgan, despite everything, found himself smiling. "Professor, nice of you to visit… Are you all right? What happened?" His tone changed when he saw the state of the older man. Harvey's face was grey, his eyes bloodshot, and his overcoat darkly stained and hanging almost in rags off his back.

On seeing Morgan, something between joy and utter exhaustion warred for control of the old professor's face and he half ran, half staggered to the bars of the cell and collapsed against them. Morgan quickly reached through and held the man up, he felt like a dead weight.

"Fools, Mr. Morgan," he said, and there were tears in his eyes. "We've all been played for fools."

"Professor! Stay with me, what's happened?" Morgan said desperately.

Harvey Walters's eyes flickered then found their focus again. "You see, not just us, cruelly used, the cults, whoever sent the creature to take the fragment at the library, Lord knows who else, all of us, used, dancing to her tune. The chaos, the fog, all of it, ceremony, it's beginning, it may already be too late… Have to get you…you out of here…stop it."

"Slow down, Professor. Stop what? Go where?"

"I saw her…"

"Daisy? Is she alive?"

Harvey Walters looked at him and his expression was unreadable. He gathered himself, composed himself again before answering. "Yes, Daisy's alive. A woman named Hannah Whateley has her; she has the fragments, the *Book of Days*, and she's bringing forth the Lord of Nightmares, like at Kingsport, just as the Legion of Rapture tried with Annabel Ryan, except that it will be worse this time, far, far worse."

There was something else, something the old professor wasn't telling him, something he was holding back; it was there in his eyes, a secret hidden in the pain.

Harvey Walters reached out a shaking hand and laid it on Morgan's shoulder. "We are going to have to try and kill her, seal the breach, I fear it is the only way, God help me. It may already be too late. I was there, and I saw her. I was wounded but I got away, but I passed out in the car, I don't know how long…how I'm alive…" Harvey's voice trailed away.

Morgan saw that whatever last reserves of energy that were keeping the old man going were fading. Already his lips were an unhealthy shade of blue and Morgan could clearly see the veins in his temple throbbing dangerously fast.

"Rest, Professor, breathe…"

"No time," the old man whispered, "no time. The Witch House, French Hill, you must get to the Witch House…"

Harvey Walters's legs gave way and Morgan slowly lowered him to the floor through the bars, and began to shout for help.

"Important…," Harvey managed, his eyes closed. "Must stop, worked before, lies all lies…trap…all I could think of…she said…no other way…sorry…un-decayed line…never knew… don't…rust…"

Morgan felt the old man's pulse at his neck; it was faint, but still there, at least for now.

Meeks walked in, head lowered; beneath the brim of his hat all that could be seen of his rough-hewn face was grim and expressionless.

"Get this man a doctor," Morgan demanded.

Meeks shook his head. Advancing toward the cell-cage door, he reached into his coat.

Morgan stood up, eyeing the advancing marshal coldly; if this was it, there was no point in trying to run, he had nowhere to go, but he was damned if he was going to turn away.

Meeks reached the cage door and pulled the bunch of keys out from his coat and unlocked the door with a clank. Meeks looked down at Professor Walters, saying, "We can make the old man comfortable upstairs. If we can get him a doctor later we will, but that's the best I can do. Before then, I need you."

Morgan looked at him closely, catching the ragged edge in the normally powerful voice. "Why?" he asked directly.

Meeks threw open the cell door and stepped back. "I need anybody sane, anybody that can handle a gun, and that's you."

"You're deputizing me now? And how are we on the same side all of a sudden, Marshal?"

Meeks looked right at him for the first time, and Morgan could see the fear in his eyes as he spoke, "Monsters, there are monsters in the streets of Arkham."

Chapter Twenty-Three

Arkham

The End Times

In Arkham, the final terror had begun. Around the campfires in the abandoned lot behind their deserted warehouse, the remnants of the Hand of Solace huddled together against the fog and the chill, against the fear, and waited for their savior to return. They were the weakest, the lost, old men, women, and children, their strongest already fallen, their faith was all that was left to them. As darkness fell, the woman that walked smiling out of the mist wore a young woman's stolen body wrapped around an ancient, night-black soul. In her hands she bore a solid black tablet of glassy stone, held reverently before her like a testament of God. What came next was unspeakable.

An hour after sundown, cold winds began to gust through the streets, bringing with them the copper reek of blood and the echo of distant piping, and beginning at last to blow away the cloying fog that had so enshrouded the town for days. Where that terrible music was heard, madness flowed in with it, a tide of murder and rage, lunacy and terror, gathering pace, redoubling and increasing. For every mind that succumbed to its insistent melody there were a dozen that did not, at least not at once; there's was to look on in horror, to suffer the blade and the fury of this tide of insanity, to hear the screams and the taunts, to bear witness to suicide and mutilation, to every horror made manifest. From houses and apartments once shut up against the fog and the fear, bodies spilled out into Arkham's streets, some in panic and terror, searching for help or fleeing friends and loved ones turned would-be murderers. Others, their red work just begun, came in search of fresh victims for their bloody revel.

And with each murder and each terrified scream, the barriers between worlds wore thinner, and thinner, stretching and contorting, deforming, snapping.

At the asylum, Nurse Heather screamed as she saw darkness flowing like ink from the mouths of the inmates along with their dying breaths, raveling together, forming reeling, dimensionless night-black figures, tattered and clawed. A pale child with eyes of nightmare appeared from their shadowed folds, and the only witness to her coming was struck dead, her heart stopped before her body crumbled to the floor.

In the old graveyard down by the Miskatonic River, unseen by any human being, the ground quaked and split, collapsing down to reveal a tangle of worm-bored tunnels, splintered coffins, and gnawed bones. From this charnel darkness, grey-limbed jackal-things crawled, their feral heads turned searching for a siren song that drew them on.

Two blocks away on Benefit Street, an elderly woman plunged a carving knife into the back of her husband of forty years, and began to write strange signs across the walls in his thin blood, which shone with crimson light so bright it tore into her flesh and what remained of her burning body was filled with hungry stars.

In the basement of Ma's Boarding House, lambent green light welled up from the walls like fluid flowing against the will of gravity, and sticky, iridescent masses of eyes and mouths dripped like ichor to flow together and form a far larger, abominable whole, and something vast and inhuman forced its way in to feast.

Something with thunderous wings of dust and shadow slammed into the side of a speeding baker's truck attempting to flee along the Southside road, and it jackknifed into the air, tumbling into a parked Ford whose owner was desperately trying to start it with a crank handle while his wife screamed at him, and both blossomed into fire and spinning metal.

At Hibb's Roadhouse, behind his wide office desk, Ryan Dean listened to the pandemonium of screams and gunfire down below, took a last stiff shot of the good stuff before putting the barrel of a pearl-handled revolver into his mouth and pulled the trigger.

From the vaults of the University Medical School building, the dead walked, and above the campus, strange colors rippled like aurora in the sky with brittle teeth like winter ice, and what few students that remained sane sought sanctuary behind locked doors and in old family prayers half-remembered.

On the outskirts of town, huge, dark things began to move closer, misshaped and lumbering, drawn on by the distant echoes of scream and riot, by the dim lights of fires burning, and the unhallowed piping that played a dance of destruction, calling them in.

The end of the world had come to Arkham.

* * *

Morgan raised the Thompson to his shoulder and sent a long burst of fire thundering into the oncoming car. He could see by the red spray on the inside of the windscreen that the driver had already had it, but whatever the greenish glowing mass in there with him was, that was Morgan's target. The heavy submachine gun spat a tongue of fire; brass shell casings danced around him furiously as the bullets ate their way across the Ford's hood, shattering headlamps and smashing the radiator grill. The car slew widely from side to side, ricocheted off a fire hydrant and swerved back toward him, but he stood his ground, still firing. The left tire burst against the curb and the Ford flipped and rolled, missing him by inches and causing the Arkham cop who stood behind him to scream and dive out of the way. The Ford, turned on its side, slew crazily across the payment as it flew by, metal bodywork screeching, sparks flying in gouts. Morgan turned with it, still firing, emptying the last of the Tommy gun's drum into the Ford's underside, hoping to find the fuel tank. His wish was granted and the wreck went up in a fireball, the concussion taking Morgan down to one knee as he turned away.

Morgan coughed against the smoke, the sound of gunfire and screams in his ears as he fumbled in his trench coat for a fresh magazine.

The Arkham cop that had been by his side staggered up, purple-faced; he looked like he was having a heart attack.

"Where's Meeks?" Morgan growled

"I...I haven't seen him, since, since the attack...," the cop replied, the revolver shaking in his hand as if it was palsied.

Morgan shook his head and spat a foul, ammoniac taste from his mouth. The blazing Ford was bellowing yellowish-black smoke, and whatever was burning in there wasn't just gasoline.

As soon as the sun had gone down, Arkham had gone to hell; whole streets were burning fanned by the storm winds that had risen up and shredded the fog. People were running in panic, screaming, fighting, and Meeks had been right, there were monsters, monsters everywhere. Some seemed half-human, ruined and twisted things like he had fought before on the cliffs of Kingsport—they at least fell when you put enough bullets in them, but there were other things abroad in Arkham that didn't.

Before it had all truly gone crazy, Morgan had argued with Meeks that they needed to head to French Hill, but it was only after a blood-spattered reporter from the *Advertiser* had staggered in and told them that a "procession of monsters" was making its way up the hill killing anything that stood in their way, with a "young woman" leading it, that Meeks had acquiesced. So their rag tag "army"—Morgan, Meeks, three Arkham lawmen, a deputy marshal, the reporter, and some half dozen other local men that seemed to have stayed sane and that Meeks and the police had managed to shanghai into joining them—had headed out in three cars to the hill. They'd been well armed at least—three Thompsons and a dozen rifles and shotguns between them—but in the end that hadn't mattered a damn.

They'd got no further than three blocks over the river when they ran straight into a riot, cars overturned, trash cans set blazing. One of the rioters had run up to the lead car and rammed a crowbar right through the chest of their lead driver. Meeks and the others had shot him down in a withering crossfire before they saw he had a nest of worms in place of a face.

An entire corner block had collapsed as if an invisible freight train had smashed into it and buried half the street in rubble, and an unearthly, undulating howl had drowned out even the sound of their guns. It had been bedlam; they'd been attacked from all sides, and soon escape any way they could had seemed the only survivable plan. Just as his car had screeched away, scattering a press of bodies that threatened to overwhelm it, Morgan had seen a vaporous black form sweep down from overhead and a slew of bodies come apart like they'd been passed through a threshing machine, the pavement beneath them bubbling like hot wax.

They'd managed to get clear and Morgan had lost count of the amount of attackers he'd shot and battered clear of their Packard before its radiator had finally blown and the motorcar had given up the ghost. There'd been four of them in the car when they'd taken off, and now there was just him and the purple-faced cop left, which brought him to his current mess.

"I have to get up there," Morgan said, pointing upward to French Hill, no more than a mile and yet a world of horror away. In the skies above it, a strange, roiling cascade of greenish-blue light was starting to form, as it was doing elsewhere over Arkham, the unclean aurora throwing the town into a final, false twilight.

The cop looked at him uncomprehendingly. "I can't stand it… the piping, make it stop…," he muttered, his lip quivering.

Morgan took one look at him and pulled the revolver from his shaking hand. *No point taking chances, and no help here.*

He looked around desperately; he knew he had no chance of making it on foot. Across the street stood a corner thrift store, its door slamming open and shut in the gusting wind, and in front of it, trembling on its kickstand in the gusts, was a motorcycle. Morgan took off and ran to it, not looking back as the Arkham cop pleaded for Morgan not to abandon him. He threw the Tommy gun over his shoulder on its sling and kick-started the motorcycle, letting out a thankful sigh when the battered-looking Indian caught with the first try.

Now, he thought, *all I have to do is make it up one, little hill.*

* * *

It was like a scene from a madman's painting of Hell—the end of the world, by any means. The Witch House, or what Morgan assumed to be it, had swollen, like a trick of the light, a false perspective, so that it loomed like a squat, black cathedral to unspeakable gods above which a hellish cascade of sickening darkness and color rippled and spun. Dark and tattered shapes whirled and turned above it like vultures above a kill, and around it were strewn broken and mutilated bodies, human and inhuman amid the debris and shattered ground.

Morgan let the motorcycle drop from beneath him beside the hulking body of a giant of a man with an unwholesome, half-ichthyic face, round which were a pile of smaller bodies, degenerate and mutated, some of which were still clutched in the giant's death grip. He looked down at those broken bodies and saw the tattered remnants of grey robes and on one upturned hand, a signet ring bearing the symbol of two clasped hands.

"Here lies the Hand of Solace," he whispered, "and I'm too damn late."

He looked around him, his mind struggling to take in the carnage and destruction, the stench of acid and rot co-mingled were overwhelming. He half-staggered toward the gaping entrance of the Witch House, looming before him like the gateway to a titan's temple, picking his way through fused, half-molten bodies, and fungoid heaps of flesh, still quivering loathsomely.

"Morgan…," a voice hissed from beside him and was choked off in a sibilant rattle that might have been a laugh.

He turned and saw Meeks, or perhaps what was left of him; half that craggy face and a single flailing arm amid a humanoid shape of scorched meat and blackened eel-like coils. The mass shuddered as if trying to rise and Morgan slammed back the bolt of his Tommy gun, readying it to fire.

"No…no need Morgan," it said in a grating voice that had nothing of Meeks in it. "Save your bullets, you might need them…" Again the rasping laugh. "Poor Turncoat is undone and dear Mr. Fetch dead along with him."

Meeks's hand reached out, vainly indicating the corpse of the hulking man surrounded by the cluster of mutated bodies, and as his did so, Meeks's remaining hand seemed to blur. It twisted; a cluster of gilded rings rose up from his fingers and sank again without trace as the flesh sloughed into a dripping, bloody morass.

"What are you?" Morgan asked through gritted teeth.

"A servant, nothing more. She said…she said you would be the last, and the dear professor did his job and led you here too, just as she said he would."

"It doesn't matter," Morgan said bitterly. "I've come too late."

The mound of eel-flesh shuddered again. "Oh no, ape, this isn't the end, this is only the prelude; your feeble brain cannot imagine what comes next."

A horrid vibration passed through the thing and Meeks's face dissolved away, coming apart into other faces, fragments of visages Morgan could not recognize. "Of them all," it said, the voice distant and fading, "you she was most unsure of. Clever, ruthless Morgan…the killer with nothing to lose. Mother saved you for the…last."

The creature came apart in a wash of muddy, boiling froth that ate into the ground around it, and Morgan recoiled, just in time as the broken paving at his feet dissolved away.

Turning away, Morgan raced up the steps, the dark bulk of the distorted Witch House looming over him like an eclipse, plunging him into chill shadow.

Morgan passed beyond the oblivion of the open doorway and fell into nothing.

For an eternity there was no sight and no sound, and then he was tripping, falling against rising ground, mud and stones slamming into him as he fell face first into wet earth.

Atop a blasted, bare hill, purple-black lightning arced across a storm-filled sky. A woman's voice cried out, the words making Morgan flinch with pain, and the sound was followed by a hard, percussive crack and the stench of ozone. Morgan, as if struck, rolled and fell down the slope, arresting his headlong fall on a gnarled tree root a few yards later. He looked around him; wherever he was, it certainly wasn't the Witch House.

He was on a low, blasted hill surrounded by endless dead and petrified forests, shrouded in heavy fog, the wind howling above, but below, the fog hung thick and still concealed the slow, coiling movements of vast, horrible forms in its depths. Morgan coughed and spat; for a moment he wanted to do no more than let himself tumble helplessly down the hill, into that nightmare wood, find death, and let it be over. But from whatever bitter core gave him strength, and the urge to surrender to dark fate was snuffed out with cold anger.

Morgan regained his feet and started to climb, recovering the fallen Tommy gun which had mercifully not fallen as far as him, and dragging himself up the slope.

He could see the top of the hill now; it was surmounted by a flat, thick table of rock, perhaps a dozen yards wide. On opposite sides of the rocky plate were two women, neither of whom Morgan knew. One was standing tall, her long black hair whipping round her head, her hands raised up, blood staining one side of her face. The other looked like an emaciated scarecrow in the shredded remnants of a fur coat; she was down on one knee, snarling and spitting, and with a jolt of recognition, he saw the glassy black tablet clutched to the woman's chest like a bible, *but which was Hannah Whateley? Which do I need to kill to stop this madness?*

Ruthless, that was what the monster had called him, and it had been right.

Morgan quickly began to circle round and upward; the air around the women was twisted, coruscating, and Morgan tore his eyes away, his brain fashioning the shapes of eyes and mouths, faces and stars within it.

He had them both in his firing line, the raven-haired woman with her back to him, the scarecrow further on. He crouched and braced the submachine gun against his shoulder and let it rip. The gun thundered and flashed; bullets sang across the distance and cut the two women down instantly: raven-hair toppled forward, blood spraying from her, while the scarecrow staggered backward and fell.

The tortured air screamed as Morgan struggled against it, rushing toward the fallen women; he had to make sure. He rushed toward the first fallen woman, looked down, and skidded, his feet sliding out from under him. It was Daisy.

Daisy Walker in the raven-haired woman's clothes; his mind couldn't take it in. There were a dozen oozing exit wounds in her chest and belly, but her eyes were open, her mouth struggling for air.

He couldn't take his eyes off her, the sight of her blotted out everything else. *I've killed her,* he thought; *I've killed her,* over and over again.

Behind him, Lemaitre struggled to his feet; one arm hung useless and blood-slick, smashed by bullets, the other clutched onto the *Valusian Book of Days* in a death grip. Foul words, older than human hate, boiled from Jacqueline's lips. Morgan started to turn, bringing up the Tommy gun to fire, but it was too late. Something grey and ravening smote the air between them. The submachine gun came apart first, unraveling in a cloud of rust and splinters. Morgan tumbled backward, his chest caving into dust. His head lolled back on the rock next to Daisy's, the echo of a smile on his dead lips.

Lemaitre began a long, half-hysterical laugh that broke into a howl of triumph at the sky. He raised the tablet above him and bellowed the words of the forbidden incantations in triumph; the victory was his, the moment was nigh.

Again and again Lemaitre screamed the words of commanding, of breaking forth, but was answered only with silence. Exhausted, bleeding, Jacqueline's body at the final ebb of its strength, Lemaitre collapsed to his knees. "Where is the Lord of Nightmares? Why does he not walk?" Lemaitre whispered brokenly, all that he had slipping away from him. He let the tablet drop to the stone before him and drew out the Obsidian Key, useless now, and let that tumble beside it, and laughed in horrified despair.

"I do not understand," he whimpered, and let his head roll back skyward. "The book…the *Book of Days*, the fragments…"

"Lied," came a soft, feminine voice, cold as night and soft as snow.

Lemaitre snapped his head round and almost toppled. Kneeling beside the body of the dead woman and cradling her head was a pale girl child. She was wreathed in darkness, her face serene and terrible, her eyes pits of blackness that went on endlessly.

"What…," Lemaitre gasped.

"Clever Daisy made it lie. She made a new fragment, and made it lie." The pale girl smiled like winter.

"No, this is not so!" Lemaitre said, staggering to his feet. "I am the master here, I have—"

"—been used, just like the rest."

"Who are you?" Lemaitre rasped.

"Annabel. I'm Daisy's friend, and she always thinks of such clever games for us to play." Her hand reached out and touched Morgan's blasted body. "Betrayal and tragedy, madness and dreams." She looked up at Lemaitre and smiled. "False pride and the death of hope."

"But the traveler, I must…the question… You don't understand… So long I planned, waited, fought my way back…for this!" Lemaitre despaired.

Annabel smiled cruelly. "Daisy's question was much better than yours; she asked, 'How do I put it back the way it was?' And the answer was quite unexpected."

Lemaitre's jaw dropped in horror. "Not even the Lord of Nightmares may… The summoning, the chaos, all of us… I thought it was my will, the rents in reality…"

Annabel laughed. "Yes, she really was a Whateley you know, by blood, but she found that out later. That's why she was so very good, why she knew, deep down, she always knew."

Above them the sky had darkened to a lightless black beyond depth or sight.

"What is this place?" Lemaitre whispered.

"Sentinel Hill, Dunwich, before time, tomorrow, elsewhere, it's all the same; you think so small, little sorcerer, pacing out your petty years and thinking them forever."

The winds changed; their chill was the cold of the void, their breath the faded dust of dead worlds.

Lemaitre collapsed once more to his knees, his good arm flung over his eyes. For the briefest moment he had glimpsed it, descending through the darkness, vast phantasmal spheres like nightmare suns, dark, writhing limbs large enough to crush stars in their coils.

"Who is this, who comes…?" The words were dragged out of him against his snapping will, blood flecking his lips.

Annabel's voice was no longer her own, it was that of the Lord of Nightmares, and the question would be answered.

The Key and the Gate of whom I am the herald, the answer and the question, the sunderer of worlds, the Hungering God—Yog-Sothoth!

Lemaitre's soul-stuff was harrowed from his stolen body and cast into the abyss, screaming forever.

Epilogue

I don't want you to come here, Father. The last message she had sent him rolled through Dr. Fields's thoughts as he watched the summer rain patter on the coffin lid. Droplets of water fell from the edge of the umbrella above him, and ran down the arm of his black mourning suit. The water had soaked through the fabric, and he could feel its clammy touch on his skin. He did not move; the cold was just another feeling he did not know where to place. At his feet, the open grave looked back at him, unyielding in its reality.

"Excuse me, sir," said a low voice from just behind him. He did not move. There was no reason to move, no reason to do anything anymore. "I am sorry, sir, but we will have to begin to fill it in."

He looked up. A man in clothes the colors of earth and hard work was looking at him, an apologetic expression on his face. The priest was long gone, of course, and no one else had come to the funeral. He was not certain how long he had been standing there; perhaps it had been minutes, perhaps hours. He looked away from the gravedigger, and back to the coffin. The wind rose and he felt the cold spray wet his face. He had persuaded the local doctor to record a fake cause of death, of course; suicides could not be buried here. The priest had known, of course. Dr. Fields had seen the look in the man's eye as he hurried his words over the grave.

"Sir?" asked the gravedigger. Dr. Fields nodded slowly, but did not look around. After a long minute, the first shovel of earth scattered across the wood of the coffin.

That is my only daughter, he thought. *Just there beneath the wood, about to be covered by earth.* It did not seem real, as though he had woken from the dream of another life to find the cold present waiting for him.

I should have come to Arkham sooner, he thought, and the words turned over and over in his mind as they had ever since he had received the news. It had been rat poison in the end, swallowed down with enough cheap booze to stop her throwing it up too soon.

I should have been able to make things right. After the death of her son and her husband, Amelia's life had crumpled, and she had spiraled into the cold corners of her own mind. He had been to the asylum where she had been treated that morning. His old friend had greeted him with a face of sorrow. "She had nothing left," Dr. Zulock had said. "When hope is gone, there can seem only one path."

The earth had covered the coffin, and the rain was coming down harder, spattering the rising bottom of the grave to mud.

I failed her. She was alone with everything she knew and loved gone. I should have been here. I should have found a way to make her better.

The gravedigger paused and straightened for a second, breathing a white cloud into the air. Dr. Fields watched as the man lifted a cross and saint's medal to his lips before tucking it back under his shirt. For the first time in his life, he wished that he could honestly believe in the words of priests.

Perhaps if she'd had hope, things would have been different; perhaps she would have found a way to live.

He waited until the grave was filled and the light was cooling to shadow, and then he turned and walked away. Behind him he heard the gravedigger mutter a prayer. Dr. Fields blinked, suddenly aware that tears had come to his eyes at last.

* * *

The silence of the cell was broken by the small watch-hatch being abruptly opened, waking Morgan instantly. The cell was still pitch dark, but for the square of light framing a pair of eyes.

"You checking to see I haven't run off? Don't worry, I would miss the service," he jibed at the face in the light.

"You got a smart mouth, Morgan; we'll see how smart it is when they strap you down in the chair."

The hatch slammed shut and Morgan was alone again in the darkness.

* * *

The coffee arrived half cold in a chipped mug. Raker looked up at the girl behind the counter and nodded thanks before she could ask him if he wanted anything else. The diner was quiet, just him and a fat man in a post office uniform looking at the sports page. Out beyond the diner's windows, the curved front of the Boston train station shone with light in the warm summer night. He glanced at his watch as he dumped sugar into the tepid brew.

How have I gotten here? It was a question he had been asking for years. It was not as if life was difficult; he had money, and he had survived in a line of work that had seen others broken in every sense. In a time when misery was the cheapest commodity, he was one of those who had managed to struggle to the surface of the stream of misery. He did not like what he did, he knew that, but he figured that was what had allowed him to rise in a world where mindless cruelty was like air. There was little in life that could trouble him, and what could was not worth thinking about at close to midnight. But other thoughts ran thought his mind as he watched the sugar dissolve into the swirling coffee

Could I have been something else? If things had been different, could I have been something better? The questions had been following him for over a year, sneaking into his thoughts when things were quiet. It was as if he had missed something, an opportunity that he had not even seen, but could feel now that it was gone. Time was the violence bothered him, but not so much anymore.

The door to the diner swung open behind him and the warm night air brushed his cheek. He did not look up.

"Deep thoughts, Raker?" said Schmidt close to his ear, and prodded him in the back. "Could have got the jump on you there—bad idea to sit with your back to the door." Raker turned to look at the slab-bodied enforcer.

"Yeah?" he said, and smiled. It was not a kind smile, and Schmidt took a step back.

"Just joking, pal, jeez." He pulled his bulk onto a stool and waved his hand at the girl. "Coffee," he said. The girl nodded, and began to move with all the hurriedness of a geological event.

"We don't have time," said Raker, gulping his own coffee down and making a face. "We have to be on the midnight train, and you're late."

"Just sorting out a little business," said Schmidt. Raker snorted, but said nothing more as he got down from the stool and flicked a handful of coins onto the counter. He turned for the door, making sure to smooth his grey suit over the bulge under his arm.

"Come on," he said. Behind him, Schmidt grunted into motion.

"So this guy we are after, who is he?"

Raker grinned.

"You don't normally want to know."

"We don't normally have to go outside Boston to collect a debt.'

Raker stepped onto the night-shrouded street. The clock on the station front showed five minutes to midnight; that was good, they had time.

"He's called Hugo Bradbury. He's from some big family with a big house out on the edge of a town called Arkham."

"Never heard of it," sneered Schmidt. "Thought he could run, eh?"

"They always do," said Raker softly.

* * *

There was pain, bright pain, and a stream of sensations flowing through her: fire leaping into a sky above a city, blood drizzling onto a stone floor, fire rolling across a mountainside covered in a forest of statues, blood spreading across white fabric as a dagger plunged deep into flesh, fire coiling on a dry wind like a molten iron serpent, blood on her tongue as she screamed...darkness, darkness so deep there was no word to encompass it.

"Are you quite all right?"

Jacqueline Fine looked up at the sound of the voice. The eyes looking at her were cold and set in a wrinkled face above worn black velvet. She blinked. Her head was swimming and a throbbing ache pulsed behind her eyes. She looked at her hand. It was grasping the frame of a door she had just stepped through. Her knuckles were bone white against the black painted wood. Behind her the dusty glass of a shop front looked out on a street soaking in sunlight.

Where am I? she thought, and closed her eyes as a fresh wave of dizziness filled her head. She tried to remember what had happened before the vision poured into her head, but every memory seemed blurred and slipped from her mind as she tried to grasp them. There was nothing solid, just sludge of congealed fever dreams. *No, not everything.* One image rose in her mind like a coin shining at the bottom of a muddied pool. A face. A clear face, made beautiful by cruelty, staring at her from the swirling colors of a crowd.

"Who are you?" The words surprised her as they came from her lips. She blinked and her eyes refocused in time to see the old man frown with puzzlement.

"I am the keeper of this shop of curiosities, madam." The old man titled his head to the side as if examining her from a different angle. "Can I help you?" She looked past him. Shapes waited in the cool shadows, some softened by dust, others dulled by age. Her eyes slid away from a painting daubed with thick color, to a polished skull which stared back at her from beneath a glass dome. She took a slow breath. The place was familiar but unsettling. A fact flitted across her mind, and she almost gasped with relief.

"My name," she began slowly, "is Jacqueline Fine."

The old man's lips twitched back from yellowed teeth.

"Of course, madam. You left a message with my assistant. Did you wish to take possession of the book you reserved?"

She looked at him, her heart beating into the lengthening moment. In her smeared memory the face smiled.

"No," she said after a moment, backing away from the gloom of the shop. "I'm sorry, no."

* * *

"Professor Walters, isn't it? It's good of you to come," Dr. Mintz said as they stepped into the clean, white room. It was one of the better-appointed, private rooms, and the view from the upper floors was actually quite pleasant. Harvey was glad of that.

"I understand you're acting on behalf of the university as her guardian, am I correct?"

"Yes, yes I am. It was the least I could do. She was...is, such a lovely girl. It breaks my heart to see her this way."

Dr. Mintz nodded sagely, his smile full of compassion that was not echoed in his eyes.

"There's still no firm contact with her extended family then?"

"Oh no, they're proving hard to track down, I'm afraid," Harvey replied.

A young, prim-looking woman in a white doctor's coat let herself into the room quietly and smiled at Harvey.

"Ah," Mintz said, "this is Dr. Zabriski. She's new with us, but very highly recommended; she's taken over Miss Walker's day-to-day needs. "

Harvey shook her hand, smiling and immediately liking her. *If I was thirty years younger,* he thought ruefully, *I probably still wouldn't have a chance.* "Has there been any improvement?" he asked.

Dr. Zabriski smiled. "Actually, yes, very minor. She's having periods of greater responsiveness; though she hasn't spoken yet, she is slowly becoming aware of her surroundings again. It's only a little progress, I'm afraid, but in a case like this, any progress at all is an excellent sign."

"Oh, Doctor, that's wonderful news, simply splendid," Harvey said, beaming and shaking her hand all over again.

"Don't get your hopes too high, Professor," she replied, smiling. "This is very liable to be a long road, if she recovers herself."

"Of course, of course, but where there's life, eh?" Suddenly he started to search his pockets. "Perhaps this will help; I found it in my things just this morning. Can't for the life of me work out how I forgot it before."

Harvey handed the doctor a small bound notebook.

"It was hers, very precious to her, I believe, sort of diary-cum-workbook, I think. I thought perhaps you could use it to jar some memories."

"That's an excellent idea," Dr. Zabriski replied, and took the notebook from him.

It was not until Harvey Walters was outside the brooding asylum building and crunching his way along the gravel path to his little car that he shuddered suddenly, and felt a brief spike of something very like fear, but it passed as quickly as it had come.

"Somebody walking over your grave, old man," he said to himself. "Still, can't be all bad, can it?" After all, he was sure he could hear children laughing somewhere nearby.

The End

About the Authors

Alan Bligh is a full-time writer and game designer from Nottingham, England. His credits have included radio scripts, various roleplaying games, such as *Dark Heresy*, *Rogue Trader*, and *Cthulhu Britannia*, and the *Imperial Armour* and *Horus Heresy* book series of sci-fi wargaming expansions for Forge World. *Dance of the Damned* was his first published full-length novel. It let him bring together his long-time loves of cosmic horror, noir, and dangerous old books. He has a fondness for tea and cats, at least one of these tendencies which he shares with H.P. Lovecraft.

John French is a writer and freelance game designer from Nottingham, England. His novels include *Ahriman: Exile* for Black Library and *The Lies of Solace* for Fantasy Flight Games. The rest of his work can be seen scattered through a number of other books, including the New York Times bestselling anthology *Age of Darkness*, and the *Dark Heresy*, *Rogue Trader*, and *Deathwatch* roleplaying games. When he is not thinking of ways that dark and corrupting beings could destroy realty and space, John enjoys talking about why it would be a good idea…that and drinking good wine.

A Game of Suspense and Supernatural Investigation

As mysterious and unnatural events plague the museum and the surrounding area, a handful of investigators suspect that its many powerful treasures, kept in close proximity, have begun to awaken unspeakable horrors.

Elder Sign is a fast-paced, cooperative dice game of supernatural intrigue for one to eight players. Players control investigators who must undertake explore the museum to gather the clues, items, and eldritch knowledge they need to seal the dimensional rifts. An insidious dice mechanic pits them against monsters and other mind-numbing threats to their health and sanity. Thwart the Ancient One's return...the desperate race to locate Elder Signs has begun!

WWW.FANTASYFLIGHTGAMES.COM

FANTASY FLIGHT GAMES